Comments about Steve Diggs' books, live presentations & broadcasts…

"Whether it's on the football field, or in real life, one of the keys to victory is good coaching. Steve Diggs has blessed people worldwide. Steve is a life skills coach who knows his subject and communicates it with authority. He gets to the point, he tells the truth, and he shows others how to enjoy abundant success. He has blessed my life. I know Steve will bless your life, too."
- *Gene Stallings, Legendary Football Coach*

"The message that Steve Diggs presents is one that needs to be told as often as possible. It is a message that is easy to understand and practical in today's society."
- *Dr. David B. Burks, President, Harding University*

"Steve Diggs is an amazing person! A friend of mine for years, I've watched him go from business success to true significance—and triumph! He's eminently qualified to help others develop the life-skills and God-skill that will help them go the distance."
- *Pat Boone, Entertainment icon*

"Steve Diggs is REAL, and he talks REAL. Steve presents real solutions…If Steve doesn't make you want to be a 'Brand New You', you aren't breathing in and out! He motivates people to achieve their potential and gives them real tools to do it."
- *Country Radio Broadcasters, Inc.*

"Steve Diggs helps us in our struggle between…the temporal and the eternal. We all need this kind of help.
- *Cal Thomas, FOX News & USA Today columnist*

"I have heard nothing but raves. Thanks for the good work you do!"
- *Dr. Cecil May Jr., Dean, Faulkner University*

"(Steve Diggs) is a public relations expert."
- *CNN News*

"Steve Diggs is our Resident Money and life-Skills Coach. Steve is wise about money. He knows all about it and he's looking out for your best interest."
- *FOX Television, Nashville*

"You are helping an incredible number of people!"
- *Bobby Ross, Managing Editor, The Christian Chronicle*

"Wow... As an Air Force chaplain I've walked a thousand flight lines from Europe to the Middle East. Your communication skills are second-to-none and command the attention of all ages. God has gifted you, my friend. Continue to use it for His glory."
   - *Colonel Michael Whittington, Command Chaplain of Pacific Air Forces (Retired)*

"By using humor, practicality, and authenticity Steve presents a Biblically based and informative model of good stewardship for all ages and life situations."
   - *Jerry and Lynn Jones, Marriage Matters Ministries*

"I could not have been more surprised at how fun and pleasant Steve's presentation was. Instead of beating people—like me—up, he gave us hope and a roadmap out of trouble. Steve brought hope and peace."
   - *Patrick Mead, Senior Minister, Rochester Hills Church of Christ, Detroit*

"When it comes to finances and life skills, Steve Diggs is the real deal. The modern world is changing faster than ever—Steve stays ahead of the curve and lights the way for the rest of us! You've got to see Steve!"
   - *Charlie Chase, Radio & TV Host of "Crook & Chase"*

"Audiences across America invite Steve back over and over again because he says what they need to hear in a way that stimulates, penetrates, and motivates. Don't miss Steve—he nails it every time! Your life will be blessed."
   - *Joe Beam, Chairman & Founder, LovePath International*

"Good easy to understand stuff...thanks for being a servant to the brotherhood!"
   - *Randy Becton, Hope for Life and Herald of Truth Ministries*

"What other (author) on successful Christian living will make you laugh out loud, move you to tears, and turn your previous notion of success totally on its head? No more name-it-claim-it nonsense about Christian success. (Steve Diggs) is confessional, convicting, and refreshingly biblical."
   - *F. LaGard Smith, Attorney, Author & Educator*

"Is it right for Christians to prosper, live well, and enjoy life? Or should achievers feel guilty? (Steve Diggs) calls for people to pursue excellence to God's glory...(and) will challenge the best and holiest within you."
   - *Dr. Rubel Shelly, Author and President of Rochester College*

"Just wanted to say 'Thanks' for a great seminar...The feedback has been very positive. I'm sure the seminar helped a great number of people."
   - *Bob Temple, Shepherd, First Colony Church of Christ*

"Only time will tell the benefit your presentations will provide to our church and community."
- *Dan Williams, Licensed Marriage & Family Therapist*

"Thank you so much for helping us and so many others understand God's principles...You are a gift!"
- *Tim Martin, Third Day member (First Day Ministries)*

"Thank you...Steve has a way of communicating God's principles (that is) a cut above...Steve communicates with ease and enthusiasm (making) it comfortable and enjoyable for his audience. I fully commend you."
- *David Ryal, College Professor, Morro Bay, California*

"Steve Diggs...was just what the Christ Church people needed...presented with clarity, humor, and good common sense...We had nothing but positive comments."
- *Pastor L. H. Hardwick, Jr., Founding Pastor (Joint comment), Christ Church, Nashville*

"All I hear are good things about the presentation—the professionalism and the awesome material. Steve you did a wonderful job."
- *Dr. David Henniger, M.S.; M.F.P; D.PC; Marriage Therapist*

"Scripturally sound, (Steve) provides no-nonsense, practical how'to's in living a balanced, successful life of integrity and faithfulness."
- *Dr. Steve Brown, KEY Life Network*

"Steve joined my real estate firm upon graduation from college. He was an instant hit at age 22—By age 25 he was in the top of all Realtors in the U.S.! If you want to learn how to sell—see Steve—he knows how to put a jet pack on your sales force!"
- *Dave Floyd, Principle Broker, Silverpointe Properties*

"I wanted to reiterate my gratitude for the work you are doing. (Your) lessons will carry over into the advice that I give all my clients...I feel that next to the Bible, your book is the best financial success manual I have ever read."
- *Ryan K. Scott, President, Complete Wealth Management, LLC*

"Steve Diggs knows all about the trappings of success. He is the founder and owner of the award winning advertising agency. Yet through it all, he has discovered the keys to enjoying Godly success."
- *Christ Community Church, Franklin, Tennessee*

"I wanted to...express how meaningful the time you spent with us was. Your sincere spirit and personality enhanced everything you said...Our men were both encouraged and blessed by the experience."
- *Pastor Ken Polk, Northside Baptist Church*

Stop Running
On Empty!

ALSO BY STEVE DIGGS

Putting Your Best Foot Forward
Free To Succeed
No Debt No Sweat!
How to Speak Like a Super Hero
No Debt No Sweat! Money Boot Camp
Moms & Jobs
Life's Too Short to Miss the Big Picture

Stop Running On Empty!

8 Powerful Strategies
That Will Change Your Life
For the Better—Forever

Steve Diggs

BOYD &
FRANKLIN
PUBLISHERS

Brentwood, Tennessee

PRINTED IN THE UNITED STATES OF AMERICA

IMPORTANT NOTE TO READERS

This publication is designed to provide accurate and authoritative information with regard to the subject matter covered. It is sold/provided with the understanding that the author and publisher are neither one engaged in rendering financial, accounting, legal, life-skill, counseling, or other professional advice. If such advice or professional help is required, you should seek the services of competent professional(s). Remember that author/presenter/publisher hold a Christian worldview and that all material herein is based upon author's understanding of the Bible and may, or may not, always coincide with what is most prudent in strict financial, psychological, business, life-skill, or other terms. This material is presented broadly and may not apply to your situation. Material herein is believed to be accurate, but mistakes can be made. Always confirm for yourself before acting upon anything herein. Author/publisher specifically disclaim any risk, loss, or liability that may be incurred by application/usage of any material herein. Material herein is presented simply for your consideration. Subject matter is general in nature and not intended to be exhaustive—simply part of your broader study program. Other materials may be helpful in giving you a broader, timelier, more accurate, and/or balanced understanding. In some instances names and details have been modified to protect identities.

Scriptures marked NASB taken from the NEW AMERICAN STANDARD BIBLE®, Copyright © 1960,1962,1963,1968,1971,1972,1973,1975,1977,1995 by The Lockman Foundation. Used by permission. All rights reserved. Scriptures marked GNT taken from GOOD NEWS TRANSLATION, Second Edition. Copyright 1992 by the American Bible Society, used with permission. All rights reserved. Scriptures marked MSG taken from THE MESSAGE. Copyright © 1993, 1994, 1995, 1996, 2000, 2001, 2002. Used with permission of the NavPress Publishing Group. Scriptures marked NIV are taken from the NEW INTER-NATIONAL VERSION. Copyright © 1973, 1978, 1984 by International Bible Society. Used by permission of Zondervan Publishing House. The "NIV" and "New International Version" trademarks are registered in the United States Patent and Trademark Office by Biblica. Where indicated Scriptures are taken from the NEW LIVING TRANSLATION Copyright © 1996. Used by permission Tyndale Publishers, Inc., Wheaton, IL. All rights reserved. NKJV taken from New King James Version. Copyright © 1982 by Thomas Nelson, Inc. Used by permission. All rights reserved.

ISBN: 978-0-9624293-7-8

Editing by Emily McMackin. Cover Design & Photo by Inhaus Creative, Nashville, Tennessee (www.inhauscreative.com). Interior text by Ben Stewart.

Visit Steve Diggs at www.RetooledandRefueled.com or www.SteveDiggs.com

To Bonnie, my "Best Buddy."

I told you on our first date, February 10, 1972, that
I was going to marry you. For better and worse,
you've always been there.

Thanks for picking up my option.

Contents

Foreword
By Pat Boone

"Wisdom is good with an inheritance,
And profitable to those who see the sun.
For wisdom is a defense as money is a defense,
But the excellence of knowledge is that wisdom
Gives life to those who have it." (Ecclesiastes 7:11-12, NKJV)

Steve Diggs has gained wisdom the way most of us do, through life experience. He has had the unquenchable desire, as well, to share what he has learned and to let others profit by his experience.

And many thousands have.

He has crisscrossed the country for years, speaking to larger and larger groups, business executives, professional people, and "just plain folks."

A couple of things really qualify him as a capable—and wise—teacher. One is his absolute lack of shame in confessing his own faults and letting others learn, as he has, from mistakes he's made. Not many are willing to be that transparent, but most of us appreciate knowing a man who has learned not just by his success but also by his mistakes.

Secondly, and perhaps most important, Steve is a devoutly believing son of God, and he shares much of what he has gleaned from his study of God's word—as it applies to all the practical situations, problems, and obstacles in life. He laces his examples and advice with pearls of wisdom from God's own "Book of Advice, His Manufacturer's Handbook."

Steve has done what so few men do today; he's actually taken countless hours to read the "Divine Instruction Book," and learn what the "Manufacturer" instructs about His creation, and how it all works successfully. This has enabled him to bring great insights to people high and low about how to get out of debt, how to be prosperous, how to give lots of sound advice about relationships, emotional stability, and deep and long spiritual health. All his books are valuable and have helped many.

Steve has always been, and still is, in his way, a preacher, as was extremely wise King Solomon, author of the book of *Ecclesiastes*. Because Solomon asked God for wisdom, not power or wealth, God gave him all three in unequaled abundance. And from that storehouse he wrote:

Words of the wise, spoken quietly, should be heard
Rather than the shout of a ruler of fools
And moreover, because the Preacher was wise, he still taught the people knowledge;
yes, he pondered and sought out and set in order many proverbs.

The preacher sought to find acceptable words;
and what was written was upright—words of truth.

The words of the wise are like goads, and the words of scholars are like
well driven nails, given by one Shepherd.

And further, my son, be admonished by these. Of making many books there is
no end, and much study is wearisome to the flesh.

Let us hear the conclusion of the whole matter:
Fear God and keep His commandments
For this is the whole duty of man.
For God will bring every work into judgment,
Including every secret thing, whether good or evil.
(Ecclesiastes 9:17 and 12:9-14, NKJV)

Steve Diggs is an amazing person! A friend of mine for years, I've watched him go from business success to true significance—and triumph! He's eminently qualified to help others develop the life skills and God skills that will help them go the distance.

God bless you!

Pat Boone

Introduction

Recently I was with a friend who has done it all—a true Renaissance man. He has written best-selling books, starred in blockbuster movies, sold millions of records, and owned a host of successful businesses. Referring to how fast his life has passed, he said, "Steve, I feel like I've spent my life on one of those Japanese bullet trains!"

The more I pondered that comment, the more I liked it.

As you and I get acquainted in the pages of this book, you'll soon see that I put a high premium on living out loud. My goal is to encourage you to grab the apple of your life and eat it in big, bold bites. Life is too short and too precious to waste it sitting on the sidelines.

There is a tendency to "live" life without ever really experiencing it. There's nothing wrong with most folks that a good taxidermist couldn't fix. Many of us could be replaced with a mannequin—and no one would be the wiser.

I don't know how or when I will leave this earth. It may be tonight in my sleep. It may not be for another forty years. Possibly it will come in the form of a heart attack while running from one plane to another on a tight connection. Or maybe, just maybe, I will be blessed to stand hand in hand with Bonnie as Jesus comes back to get us. All I know for sure is that, in this period between the flood and the fire, the minutes count. God wants us to redeem the time he has given us to be as productive as possible.

That's what this book is about: making the most of each moment. In the following nine chapters, we will explore ways to live with passion and finish strong.

In our first chapter, we will rethink success. As I redefine the word, I will challenge you to stop listening to the noise of the world and really understand how God's plan for you is as unique as your fingerprints. This means allowing God to reign supreme in your life. In other words, if God is your copilot, it's time to trade seats.

Then, in each of the other chapters, I will take you by the hand and share a life skill that is essential for a full, balanced, godly life. I won't waste your time with scholastic jargon and arcane theory. This book will move fast. You will end each chapter with a clear understanding of the particular life skill I want to teach you—and how to apply it. You will learn new techniques that will improve your people skills. Each chapter will hold specific takeaways that will enhance your relationships—starting right now.

1

It's Time to Get Retooled & Refueled

There once was a beautiful young woman whose father owned a cobbler shop. Due to hard times and bad decisions, her father had borrowed heavily from a greedy moneylender. When the debt came due, the creditor arrived at the old man's shop to collect his money. Discovering that the cobbler was unable to pay, the moneylender dragged him into the town square to publicly humiliate him. As a crowd gathered, the lender ranted and raved about the cobbler's failure both as a businessman and a person. Hearing the noise, the cobbler's virginal daughter ran to the scene and stepped between her father and the bill collector. "What can we do to appease you?" she demanded.

> "You may be disappointed if you fail, but you are doomed if you don't try."
> – BEVERLY SILLS

> "Don't be afraid your life will end; be afraid that it will never begin."
> – GRACE HANSEN

"I'll tell you what you can do," the greedy lender began. "I will pick up two stones from the street and put them in my cloth money bag. One will be brown, and one will be white. You, my dear, have three choices. If you do nothing, your father will owe me his debt, and I will take his shop. Or, if you prefer, reach into the bag and pull out a single stone. If you retrieve the

1

white stone, I will cancel your father's debt, and he will owe me nothing. But if you pull out the brown stone, your father will still owe me the money, plus you will agree to marry me."

As the young girl weighed her options, the lender reached to the ground to pick up the stones. She noticed that instead of a white and a brown stone, he slipped two brown stones into his money bag. As he stood up, the girl said, "I will accept your offer to pull out a stone."

Quickly she reached into the bag and retrieved one of the two brown stones, but before anyone could see it, she "accidentally" let it drop to the ground, where it immediately mingled with all the other brown and white stones. Then she looked the shocked lender in the eye and said, "Whoops! It appears that I dropped my stone. But that's no problem. Simply look into the bag and see what color the remaining stone is. That will certainly tell everyone which stone I pulled from your bag."

Too embarrassed to admit what he had done, the lender walked away with no debt to collect—and no wife.

Our Destination

Simply put, my goal in this book is to equip you with effective ways to get out of the box and apply creative strategies that will change your life for the better, forever!

Just as it was for the young girl in our parable, these creative solutions are often much closer than we realize. I hope to open your mind's eye and help you see them more clearly. Because, as a wiser person than I once noted: a mind once stretched will never return to its original position.

Entire books have been written about most of these eight life-skill strategies. (Actually, I've written some of those books myself.) But, if you're like me, there have been times when you were 200 pages into a 300-page book, and you asked yourself, "Do I really want to know this much about this topic?" In most of those cases, my answer was "No!" Usually all I needed were the tips that would get me from where I was to where I needed to go. That's what this will be: a scorched earth, take-no-prisoners book—filled with helpful strategies and takeaways.

Think of This as the P.S.

Have you ever sent someone an e-mail or a letter and wondered if they even read it? I have.

Let me share a little strategy to help you with that dilemma. The next time you complete a letter, do something just before you hit the send button. Reread it. Decide what your most salient point is. Then move that all-important line to the very bottom and put a "P.S." in front of it. In fact, many people who don't read the body of a letter will read a P.S. if one is attached.

In a similar way, that's what I'm doing now. This is the P.S. of this book. It's the section that would usually be called the preface. But, if you're like me, you frequently skip a book's preface trying to get to the good part. So, since this portion of the book is going to determine how much benefit you will derive from the rest of it, I'm calling this "Chapter 1." Whatever you prefer to call it is fine, but read this chapter first!

Think of this first chapter as the instruction manual on how to use this book. With some twenty years of experience in the publishing business as a writer, marketer, and publishing company owner, I've learned some important things about how and why people buy books.

For instance, many people initially pick a book up for four reasons: the title, the promise (otherwise known as the subtitle), the cover design, and the author's name. Then, it's typical to scan the back cover for more "promises" to learn what the book will do for the reader. The next step is likely a quick glance at the contents page to review the chapter topics. Finally, assuming everything up to that point passes muster, the first chapter gets a brief perusal. That's when the consumer either buys the book or returns it to the shelf with sixty thousand other books.

Different people use books differently. There are people with type B personalities who want to savor every nuance and appreciate the anecdotal and emotive aspects of a book. Then there are the type A's whose idea of romance is "kill and eat!" As a world-class type A (my wife would say, "type A++++"), I understand the desire to cut out the extra words, and get to the point!

In writing this book, I've tried to keep both groups in mind. You type A's probably won't spend time reading every word. For you, this book will be a handy, utilitarian resource—something to be grabbed and gulped down in a moment of perceived need. That's fine. For you, I've taken what I call the *USA Today* approach. Just like in the popular newspaper, you'll find lots of:

- Bullet points
- Quick-start action lists
- Thought sparklers, brain teasers, and takeaways
- Things you can do *now* to make immediate improvements

As for you type B's, you will probably prefer to read this book from cover to cover to capture the full scope of its material. You will relish this book like a fine meal. After all, you would never go into a candlelit restaurant with live music and tell the server to rush your order. For you, this will be a holistic experience, allowing each chapter to open the door to another vista and build on the preceding chapter.

But whether you're a type A or a type B, I believe you will find an abundance of strategies, suggestions, methodologies, and life skills that will challenge your thinking and improve your ability to deal with others.

So, type A's: Enjoy your twenty-minute lunch break; and, type B's, I believe the maître d' has your table ready.

Increasing Your Odds of Success

To succeed at the life skills I will be sharing, it will be important to clearly understand what success is—and what it isn't. As you get into the upcoming chapters, I will be sharing eight vital life skills. You may already be well along the road to developing some of these skills. In those cases, I hope to reinforce what you're already doing and challenge you to go further.

For other readers, these will be fresh, exciting new concepts. I hope you'll open your eyes to what others have called "possibility thinking." I want to help you catch the vision of what can be.

We all desire to live significant lives. After all, biographies aren't written about mediocre people. One of my goals in this book is to convince you that you really can achieve extraordinary life changes, provided you're willing to do a few extraordinary things. Near the top of that list is learning to approach the eight life skills in this book from a different perspective.

By applying a few basic strategies, you can do exactly that. None of these strategies are beyond your reach. But they are ideas the average person either doesn't know how to do or is simply unwilling to execute. The good news is these life skills are egalitarian by nature. Your success will not be dependent on your gender, family connections, bank account, or even your formal education.

On that last point, let me zero in on a concept with which some of you will disagree. Indulge me for a moment as I step onto my soapbox—okay?

Some of the most successful people I've known are not the most academically brilliant people on the planet. Maybe this explains why many great leaders and achievers weren't particularly good students. As a matter of fact, less than an hour ago, I finished having lunch with a dear friend who has been extremely successful in the business world. He has owned successful businesses in several states. His family lives in one of Nashville's finest golfing neighborhoods.

Since he is a devout Christian, he is also a generous giver of his time and money. But I'll let you in on a little secret; my friend wasn't the brightest crayon in the box in college. As we compared notes at lunch, he admitted his college GPA was a two-something.

This is all to illustrate that maybe the popularly accepted linkage between higher education and real-world success isn't as rock solid as we have been led to believe. Now, if you're the product (or a deliverer) of higher education—don't break out in hives. I'm all for college and sheepskins hanging on the wall. As a matter of fact, I've taught college, and today I sit on advisory boards at two universities.

But let's admit the truth: A college education doesn't always live up to its billing. It's not a guaranteed ticket into the fast lane of life. Universities are not always the great philanthropic institutions they claim to be. The hard fact is colleges are in a competitive business. And that business, stripped down to its basest level, is to sell semester hours.

While I believe most people do better in life with a college degree, it's safe to say that a degree does not ensure that the recipient has enough common sense to refold a road map. I regularly counsel college grads who have huge student loan debt but can't seem to secure a good job. Often these graduates have never learned how to read a contract, do a budget, or even balance their checkbook.

> **Think about it.** Some of the most influential people in today's society never wore a mortarboard. Do you know what Microsoft founder Bill Gates; America's undisputed king of talk radio Rush Limbaugh; and the late Peter Jennings, ABC News chief and anchorman, all have in common? None of them graduated from college.

In my experience, successful people are usually extremely hard workers who use their heads, learn from their mistakes, develop street smarts, and get up just one more time than they are knocked down. While success for you may not look the same as it does for me, your spouse, or a coworker—there are certain constants among virtually all people who succeed. Granted, I can't force a person to change, but I'll be glad to loosen the cap so you can pop the top. The following nine "Success Truth Keys" will serve you well as you begin reading the eight upcoming life-skill chapters.

Success Truth #1
Not Everyone Is Going to Like You—Get Over It!

Most of us are pleasers. We want other people to like us. Granted, up to a point, this is fine and commendable. But, like any other virtue, it can become a vice when taken to the extreme. There were days when Jesus enjoyed great adulation and popularity. But there were plenty of times when he had to look hard to find a friend. Isaiah, the Old Testament prophet, foretold Jesus' destiny:

"He was despised and forsaken of men, a man of sorrows and acquainted with grief ...." (53:3a, NASB)

Daniel had a similar experience. After six decades in the Babylonian world, his faithfulness to God had made him an important government official. Under King Darius, he had become one of the most loved, respected leaders in the Babylonian empire. Quite a feat for a Jewish fellow! But not everyone shared this sentiment. Daniel's success bred its share of resentment and jealousy. In the book of Daniel, we read about a group of 120 kingdom flunkies who weren't happy seeing Daniel get so many attaboy's from King Darius. So, naturally, they hatched a plan to bring him down a few notches.

The only problem was *"they could find no ground of accusation or evidence of corruption, inasmuch as he was faithful, and no negligence or corruption was to be found in him."* (Daniel 6:4b, NASB)

So like any self-respecting pack of politicians, they conspired to use Daniel's devotion to God against him. Through some chicanery (and kingly flattery), they got Darius to rewrite the laws proclaiming

7

the dear old king as the only "god" to be prayed to. True to form, Daniel ignored the edict and continued his daily prayers to Jehovah from his public balcony.

Of course, most of you know the rest of the story about how this resulted in Daniel spending a night in a den filled with unusually passive lions. The next morning, much to Darius' relief, Daniel was fine. Immediately upon his exit from the lions' den, Daniel's tormenters became breakfast for the felines who were, by then, ravenous.

The lesson here is clear: If you do the right thing, you will often not be liked.

But, let's get real. Unlike Jesus and Daniel, our detractors can point to actual mistakes and sins in our lives. This is where it gets a bit knottier. When there's an element of truth in our critic's complaint, it's much more difficult to stay the course.

As Christians, this is when we must put our trust in God. By realizing that God forgives and forgets even the worst behavior, we will be more capable of forgiving ourselves when we repent. The Bible tells us that the devil is the accuser of the saints. His stock-in-trade is to constantly revisit old failures and remind us of our sins. But when we have repented and asked for forgiveness, we can lay the old things away.

Most of your detractors are acting out of jealousy or a sense of failure in their own lives. Remember, there are only two ways to own the tallest skyscraper in the city: build it or tear down all the other skyscrapers. Your critics will try to turn the kernel of your failure into a giant bag of popped corn. Don't allow it!

The key is to maintain a soft heart that is sensitive to God's prodding—and a thick hide that doesn't let your critics destroy you.

Success Truth #2

Successful People Are the Biggest Failures

That's sort of an odd comment, isn't it? But it's true. I am convinced that most of us would not fear failure so much if we understood its benefits. In fact, many of today's most successful people are the same folks who have suffered some of the greatest failures.

How did they accomplish this? I'm glad you asked.

Used correctly, failure can catapult us to success because it forces us to develop the skills, strategies, and disciplines we probably would never learn under better circumstances. And when these skills, strategies, and disciplines have been effectively used to drag us out of our failure pits, we can then use them to get ahead of the curve and do extraordinary things that most of our friends will never achieve.

The key is not to wait for the right mood, the perfect opportunity, or the most desirable circumstance. The key is to start doing the right thing right now.

Don't do the right thing because you get praised, get the raise, or get it reported on the news. Do the right thing because it's the right thing.

Here in Nashville, hit songs are rarely written by people who occasionally "get in the mood to write a song." Instead, hits are written by hardworking people who may come into an office with a guitar five days a week and work eight hours each day. The fact is most of their songs are junk—failures. But by consistently applying the skills, strategies, and disciplines they have honed over the years out come those occasional, rare golden nuggets the rest of us call "hit records" that become the soundtracks of our lives.

9

Success Truth #3
Successful People Approach Problems Differently

Let me explain. Suppose I asked you to select a number between one and a hundred. Then suppose I told you emphatically that I can predict which number you have selected in seven guesses or fewer, provided you tell me whether my guesses are too high or too low. You might be skeptical, right?

After all, mathematically speaking, seven is only 14 percent of a hundred. So doesn't it follow that with only seven guesses, I would have only a 14 percent chance of picking the correct number? Maybe so, but maybe not.

What if I knew a strategy (or principle) that would increase my odds of selecting your number from only 14 percent to 100 percent? That would be a pretty helpful strategy, right? But to accomplish this feat I can't do what most people would do—make random guesses. I'll have to step back and approach the problem in a different way.

Here's how it might work. You secretly pick a number, say eighty-four. Okay, now I make my first guess. But instead of picking just any number, I guess fifty—exactly halfway between one and a hundred. You say, "No, it's too low." Then I split the remaining difference and choose seventy-five. Again, you say, "No, still too low." Again, I split the remaining numbers in half and pick eighty-eight. This time you say, "Nope, too high." So I split the difference between seventy-five and eighty-eight and pick the number eighty-three. This time you say, "Too low." So, again, I split the difference between eighty-three and eighty-eight, and ask if it's eighty-six. This time you tell me the number is too high.

So, after only five guesses, there are two options left: eighty-four or eighty-five. Even if I incorrectly select eighty-five on my sixth try, I'll pick eighty-four on the seventh guess.

In the same way, we can dramatically increase our odds of success in any venture—by stepping back and looking at the problem in an unconventional way. Avoid "herd-think." Look at any task from your vantage and develop your own attack strategy. And, as in the case above, the cool thing about such a success strategy is it's simpler than you would expect. When you learn the strategy (life skill), the overwhelming suddenly becomes very manageable and doable. This illustration isn't new with me. Knowing stuff like this might be helpful if you're thinking about applying for work with a highly creative company. It's reported that Microsoft CEO Steve Ballmer uses a similar test with high-level job interviews. He apparently puts great stock in an individual's ability to deconstruct and reconstruct a problem in a fresh, innovative, different-from-the-norm way.

Success Truth #4
People Who Excel Focus On Their Strengths

This sounds like a no-brainer. But most people do not follow this fundamental principle. Studies show that more than 85 percent of people believe the key to success is found in fixing their weaknesses. In truth, feeding and growing your strengths is far more productive. While fixing problems has its place, no person, church, family, or business will excel until it first maximizes its strengths. This isn't news for most major corporations. Corporate types have understood and applied this principle for years.

> Jack Welch, retired General Electric CEO, says, **"If you don't have a competitive advantage, don't compete."**

However, on a more pedestrian level, most individuals, families, small businesses, and religious communities don't seem to understand this principle, although this concept goes back to the earliest days of the church. It was an undergirding belief of Paul's as he spoke to his friends and protégés at the church in Philippi about his personal journey.

Remember, more than most people, Paul had a lot of baggage. After all, before his conversion to Christ, Paul had persecuted the church, jailed her members, and murdered her leaders. But he understood the fact that living in the past was of little use, as he points out in this scripture:

"Not that I have already obtained it or have already become perfect, but I press on so that I may lay hold of that for which also I was laid hold of by Christ Jesus. Brethren, I do not regard myself as having laid hold of it yet; but one thing I do: forgetting what lies behind and reaching forward to what lies ahead, I press on toward the goal for the prize of the upward call of God in Christ Jesus." (Philippians 3:12-14; NASB)

Once we've dealt with the past (our weaknesses), our greatest good is accomplished by focusing on the future (our strengths). The key is to play to your abilities. Figure out what you're good at and do it more productively.

Success Truth #5

There's Always One Best Way to Do Anything

There may be five, ten, or even fifty different ways to accomplish a task. But there is always only one best way to do anything. Successful people are those who find the best way to do something, then repeat that process over and over and over again.

In the business world, this truth is widely accepted. The wealthiest people out there are usually those who have found their strengths, developed them, and reused them a million times over. On the other hand, most people who spend their lives hunting for a "quick score" and jumping from one thing to another never perfect any particular skill. Those are the people who end up in pine boxes with a stack of unpaid bills in their apartment.

The same thing happens in the investing arena. Having taught investing strategies to thousands of people, I can tell you that the ones who commit to a broadly diversified plan and set aside regular contributions almost always outperform the ones who are incessantly searching for the next hot stock that's sure to make them rich. The old adage "buy low and sell high" is fine and good—until it doesn't work. Then what do you do? You can't go back and not buy.

It is your job to find the single best and most efficient way to achieve your goal. Then ignore the "noise" that surrounds you. There will always be those (sometimes the very people who are closest to you) who will laugh and give you a hundred reasons why your plan won't work. When you are certain of your goal and direction, maintain a laser-beam focus. Don't let anything knock you off track.

Success Truth #6
Successful People Are Mentally Ambidextrous

"Great, so, what does that mean?" You ask.

Do you remember that kid in your class in grade school who could write equally well with either his right or left hand? The word for this ability is ambidextrous. In a similar way, most successful people learn to work from both their right and left brains. We've all been told that the world is divided into two groups: right-brained thinkers (those who are primarily artistic, sensitive, and creative) and left-brained thinkers (those who are dispassionate, analytical, and rational).

As I ran my advertising agency over the decades, I realized I didn't have the luxury of working from just one side of my brain. I gradually saw the need to work from both sides. That's when I coined the phrase "mentally ambidextrous." I recognized that if I was going to succeed, becoming mentally ambidextrous was critical.

More than in most businesses, ad agencies are a microcosm of the broader culture. There are the clients, account managers, and number crunchers (left-brained thinkers) who approach everything from an analytical, concrete worldview. Then there are the creative types (writers, photographers, artists, and the like) who are right-brained thinkers. For them, it's all about the art. Frequently,

I had to translate what a client (left-brainer) wanted to an artist or photographer (right-brainer.)

The left-brainers were always worried about the budget and whether the ad spelled their name right, while the right-brainers were always striving for something edgier and more artsy than what our competitors would provide. The two sides approached the challenge from their individual vantages, but they both shared the same goal: to sell the client's product. My job was to help both sides communicate with one another and draw out the best from each other.

No matter what the task, people who are mentally ambidextrous accomplish more. By making full use of your logical, analytical side and then adorning it with an aesthetic, artistic presentation, you will accomplish far more.

I feel more and more encouraged because today more thinkers, writers, and educators on all levels are finally awakening to this reality. In fact, to fully succeed in today's world, one *must* be mentally ambidextrous. Daniel Pink, author of *A Whole New Mind: Why Right-Brainers Will Rule the Future* says, "What's troubling is that our system is obsessed with standardization at the very time when the future of our economy depends on the opposite."

The old, dependable, staid jobs many of the past generation depended on (bean counting, repeated chores, and the like) are being increasingly outsourced and sent overseas. Perceptive companies are awakening to this reality.

USA Today reports Lazlo Bock, a vice president at Google, as saying, "We're convinced that true innovation comes at the intersection of different fields. New employees are assessed on their "Googliness"— meaning their capability to resolve issues in out-of-the-box ways while thriving in a loosely constrained working structure."

Again, I call this being mentally ambidextrous. On the next page is a chart illustrating some of the attributes, downsides, hobby

Left-Brainers

Work Preferences:
- Accountants, Mathematicians, Researchers, Analysts, Real Estate Lawyers

Hobbies:
- Solo video games, crossword puzzles

Attitudes:
- Willing to take "no" for an answer.
- Dip their toes in the pool first.
- Could be a stand-in for Dr. Spock on "Star Trek."
- Slow to decide, want to "Think about it first."

Worldview:
- Literal

Planning Approach:
- Probably includes calculators, spreadsheets, and lots of data

Right-Brainers

Work Preferences:
- Sales, Communication, Acting, Artists, Trial Lawyers, Entrepreneurial

Hobbies:
- Social networking, bungee jumping

Attitudes:
- "No" means figure out another way.
- Dive off the board without checking to see if there's water in the pool.
- Really dig reruns of "McGyver"
- Ready and rash, "Let's rock 'n' roll!"

Worldview:
- Subjective

Planning Approach:
- Dreamers

interests, and job preferences that tend to distinguish left- and right-brained people.

Success Truth #7
Successful People Practice A Lot

It's human nature to desire success without effort. We'd all like to live in million-dollar homes and drive BMW's without having to get out of our pj's and go to work. But unless you have a big inheritance (or a mask and a gun), that probably won't happen. The Bible puts a high premium on diligence:

"The sluggard craves and gets nothing, but the desires of the diligent are fully satisfied." (Proverbs 13:4, NIV)

The most successful people get that way by putting out the most effort. While the old saying "practice makes perfect" may not be literally accurate, practice certainly will get you closer to perfection. The more I do anything, the better I get at it. To this day, I still practice before I dare step in front of an audience. When I write a television segment, I practice it several times before we go on air. Why? Because I don't want to look stupid! I still make lots of notes and memorize them. I practice in front of a mirror. Usually the easier something looks, the harder it was to prepare.

Successful performers know this. That's why they're so good at what they do. Often, an act will rent a rehearsal hall and methodically plan every nuance of their performance for weeks before they take it on the road. Once the touring begins, every night's show is another practice session. The great acts never stop critiquing themselves and asking how to do it just a little better. They realize there are thousands of other groups waiting in the wings—and they must keep their edge. Practice involves more than just going through the motions. It means being gut honest. It requires continually rethinking, "What makes this thing work?"

I remember a conversation I had with Al Jardine of the Beach

Boys. By this time, the Beach Boys had been in the entertainment business for decades. The group had produced scores of hit records and sold-out concerts. If any group in America had the right to rest on its laurels, it would be this one. Yet, I recall how introspectively Al answered my question, "What is it about the Beach Boys that has made you so successful?"

He answered, "We don't just sing songs. We build moods." An insightful answer from a practiced pro.

Success Truth #8

Avoid the "Plan A or Nothing" Mentality

Perfectionism is the great killer of the good. Successful people learn to roll with the punches. People who insist on things going their way in every case (Plan A) will be frustrated and feel like failures. If Plan A equals happiness, you will be unhappy about 90 percent of the time—and frightened of becoming unhappy the other 10 percent of the time. Learning to embrace change is one of the most freeing, invigorating skills we can develop.

I still remember the advice that Porter Stark, a dear friend and business associate, gave me at a crossroads moment in my life. I was thinking about selling a company I had owned for a number of years. Frankly, too much of my self-identity and ego was tied up in owning that company.

"Besides," I wondered, "what will I do without the company?"

Porter's simple comment was, "Steve, there comes a time when every plant needs to be repotted in new soil."

When you boil it all down, most of us resist change for three reasons:

1. Fear of the unknown

It amazes me how people will sometimes live endlessly in a painful situation simply because they're afraid of trying something new. Let me be clear here. I'm not suggesting that the solution is to necessarily run away from a problem. Sometimes the "unknown" involves remaining involved and engaged as you search for new solutions.

2. Laziness

A lot of good change never happens because we're simply too lazy to do some tough stuff! I'm not immune to this myself. Thus far, I've been too lazy to learn how to fully use my BlackBerry, so I pay the price. I sit on airplanes wasting time because I don't understand how some of the apps work. Often, the best thing one can do is get busy. I'll discuss this more in a later chapter, but for now, think of ways to fill the cracks and crevices of your day with learning and teaching. Read user manuals, watch how-to videos, peruse a thought-stimulating assessment of a political issue, go to the gym, tackle a chore, and, by all means, spend time with your Bible.

3. In the words of singer-songwriter Neil Sedaka, "Breaking up is hard to do"

Change breaks rank with "group think." When we change, we will leave behind the status quo and those who bow before its altar. That's hard to do. There will always be the timid, fearful, and frightened people who don't want to test the waters. Sometimes it's best to look over that next mountain with, or without, the gang. There's a special type of dignity that comes when an individual leaves the group behind.

How do we overcome Plan B avoidance?

Think about starting out slowly and gaining speed gradually. For instance, depending on where you are on the spectrum, you might start with some very simple, non-threatening changes, such as:

• Go to a different restaurant for lunch—with, or without, the regular gang.

- If you only read nonfiction, find a good novel.
- Wear a bow tie.
- Order a 7-Up instead of a Coke.
- Wear boxers instead of briefs.

As you accomplish these small changes, you will graduate to bigger changes, such as:

- Instead of the same vacation resort, drop your finger on the map and go there this year.
- Write a letter to someone you've admired from a distance for years. Ask if you may call and schedule a lunch visit.
- Leave a $100 tip for the server at the restaurant. Then sit in your car and watch her find it.

Stepping out of our comfort zones is frightening but invigorating. It frees us from the fear of the unknown. It rewards our extra efforts. It helps us break away from the pack of same-thinking people who will be eating the same tuna fish sandwiches and telling the same college war stories when they retire.

Truly successful people refuse to be trapped in Plan A thinking. They learn to accept, embrace, and even look forward to the Plan B's and C's and D's.

Success Truth #9

Successful People Realize True Success Is Not Outcome Based

This truth is not one you will find in most success manuals. It runs counterintuitive to what the world says about success. But I believe it is the most important of the success truths I've shared with you in this chapter. In fact, grasping this particular truth, more than any of the others, will help you understand and apply the rest of this book. To make sense of this, let me repeat: True success is not outcome based.

> **True success** is the determination to do the right thing—no matter what the cost.

This means that we haven't necessarily failed simply because things didn't work out as we would have hoped. Some of the most successful people are the ones who, by all outward appearances, have failed. Of course, it is very possible to do all the "right things" and still not achieve the desired results. Think of the farmer who prepares, plants, and does everything right, but the rain never comes.

If we are playing by the rules just to get what we want, our focus is wrong. But if you are playing by the rules because you value those rules—then you are a successful person. It might be fairly asked, "So who determines the value of a rule if the immediate result of following that rule isn't the measuring stick?"

I believe the short answer is God. Ultimately, success happens only when we have a relationship with God—on his terms. He has promised, *"For I know the plans that I have for you … plans for welfare and not for calamity to give you a future and a hope."* (Jeremiah 29:11, NASB)

With this as your worldview, things change. No matter what the short-term outcome is, you are a successful person. Success happens when a person does the right thing because it is the right thing to do. Granted, short-term outcome can be indicative of success—but not always.

As I said, it is possible to do everything right as a marriage partner and still end up in divorce court. It is possible to be a loving, involved, attentive parent and still raise messed-up kids. It is possible to be the most proficient person in the company and still get laid off. Some of the world's most successful people didn't feel very successful in their day. Consider these examples:

› Although widely held as one of our greatest presidents, Abraham Lincoln was skewered by the newspapers of his day.

› Noah was the laughingstock of the neighborhood as he built the ark in the middle of dry land. But when the rains came, he was the only guy in the neighborhood with a boat that would float in the worldwide moat!

› The prophet Daniel went against strong political headwinds when he disobeyed the royal order not to pray to Jehovah and found himself camping out with a bunch of hungry lions.

Hebrews 11 is widely regarded as the Bible's "Hall of Fame of the Faithfully Successful." It tells of one person after another who saw the big picture and became a legendary success story. Yet in their day, they were mocked, ridiculed, imprisoned, and murdered.

"There were those who, under torture, refused to give in and go free, preferring something better: resurrection. Others braved abuse and whips, and, yes, chains and dungeons. We have stories of those who were stoned, sawed in two, murdered in cold blood; stories of vagrants wandering the earth in animal skins, homeless, friendless, powerless—the world didn't deserve them!—making their way as best they could on the cruel edges of the world." (Hebrews 11:32, The Message)

Successful people look beyond the instant gratification of the moment and go for the gold: long-term gratification. So what happens to people of this sort? The answer comes immediately in the first verse of the next chapter. These people are referred to as the "great cloud of witnesses" whom we should emulate.

"Therefore, since we are surrounded by such a great cloud of witnesses, let us throw off everything that hinders and the sin that so easily entangles, and let us run with perseverance the race marked out for us." (Hebrews 12:1; NIV)

It is generally understood that this "great cloud of witnesses" are Christians who endured abuse and punishment in their earthly lives and are now in heaven watching and rooting for us! What a tremendous example of delayed gratification.

> **Takeway:** Pleasure isn't always a good thing, and pain isn't always a bad thing.

Again, for me to teach this with a degree of intellectual honesty, I must make a final disclaimer. Don't think for a minute that just because I write about this concept of success, I have achieved it. I still find myself worrying too much about the present. I do a lot of good things for the wrong reasons. My talk is much better than my walk. But, despite it all, there is hope even for me—and for you. Remember, the great saints of scripture were very human humans. Thankfully, God elected not to gloss over their flaws.

Think about Moses, the great leader of the Israelite nation. Wasn't he the same guy who committed murder? Didn't he run to avoid the penalty of his sin? Didn't he do everything he could think of to avoid God's call to lead the Israelites out of Egypt? Yet there he is, in the middle of Hebrews 11, "God's Hall of Fame of the Faithfully Successful!" Nor did God omit the sins of King David, Samuel, or Peter.

I believe this most important success principle is the one none of us will live long enough to fully attain or see. But, fortunately, God is much more interested in our direction than in our position. We may not totally accomplish this trait, but we can still shout with Paul:

"I'm not saying that I have this all together, that I have it made. But I am well on my way, reaching out for Christ, who has so wondrously reached out for me. Friends, don't get me wrong: By no means do I count myself an expert in all of this, but I've got my eye on the goal, where God is beckoning us onward—to Jesus. I'm off and running and I'm not turning back." (Philippians 3:12-14, The Message)

So, If You're Tired of Running On Empty...

In this chapter, I've attempted to set the stage for the book you are holding in your hands. In the coming chapters, I want to share with you eight concrete life skills that will help you retool and refuel—and stop running on empty. Unlike Solomon, wisdom has not always been my closest friend. In my case, what wisdom I have developed has taken a lot of time and mistakes—and patience from God. That patience is available to you, too.

As I said at the beginning of this chapter, my goal here is to give you a handy, grab-and-go handbook with a "just the facts, ma'am" approach. Some of you will think I'm too preachy. I don't mean to be. But anyone who knows me will tell you I'm passionate about what I believe. As you've no doubt already noticed, I hold a Christian worldview. So it makes sense that some of my references will come from the Bible. But be clear: This is not a Christian life-skills book. It is a book of universally essential life skills written by a Christian. I write books and speak to audiences about this stuff for a living. In this case, I use the phrase "a living" in two senses:

1. Yes, I earn income from my books and speaking.

2. But more importantly, I do this *to* live. Frankly, this is more than a job for me—it's a calling.

It doesn't matter much to me whether my message is being shared through a book, via an Internet article, on television, or to a live audience at a business, a charity, a marriage retreat, a church, a college, a conference, or a convention. My goal is to help you do more than stay alive. I want to help you thrive in this world and the one to come.

Ultimately, all I can do is stand on the sidelines and point you toward the goal. I can't force you to do anything. But if you'll treat this as your playbook, I'll bet you'll cross the goal line with fewer bruises. Okay? So let's get suited up and ready for the big game.

2

Bat In the Majors

How to Grow Success from Your Life Experiences

One of the best ways to assure defeat, pessimism, and depression is to approach life with an all-or-nothing attitude. That is, if you don't get the whole cake you won't enjoy the party. Sure, I believe in striving for excellence, but there's a difference between excellence and perfection. Perfectionists are some of the most miserable people on the planet. For a perfectionist, everything has to be perfect before he or she enjoys anything. That's a recipe for disaster.

Our challenge is to enjoy life with the realization that there are going to be a fistful of heartbreaks. As I write this, memories flood my mind—pictures of some imperfect people who are enjoying extraordinary lives.

> "You don't have to hit a home run to be a winner. The truth is it's an exhilarating experience just getting up to bat in the majors. Approached correctly, life is a beautiful path of stepping-stones— each experience can be linked to the next—much like stepping-stones across a stream."
> – STEVE DIGGS

I think of Mark Steele, who was an honored police officer before he threw it all away with a drug addiction that cost him almost two years in prison. Yet, today, he has rebuilt his life. He and his wife,

Lisa, are deeply in love. His children adore him, and he's one of the most respected men in his church.

I think of Mike Cope, who is one of the most effective preachers in Texas. Yet his life hasn't been perfect either. He and his wife suffered one of the most painful things any parent can face when their daughter, Megan, died.

> "The world is round, and the place that may seem like the end may also be the beginning."
> – IVY BAKER PRIEST

I think of my dear friend, Alton Howard, who was one of the most successful businessmen in the history of American retailing. He experienced some brutally painful times, however. In the early 1980s, Alton suffered grueling financial setbacks that threatened to cost him his business.

I can think of a number of people who love life and always seem to be filled with joy, yet they are battling life-threatening illnesses. I'll bet you're just like me. In five minutes, you could make a list of winners you know who have faced plenty of losses and defeats. Maybe you're one of them.

What's my point? Simply this: I want to show you how to get up to bat in the major leagues of life. Maybe you'll hit a home run. But you probably won't. That's okay. The fact is most people live their entire lives sitting in the stands, wishing they were on the field. Always dreaming—but never doing. Why? Usually it's because they're afraid of failure. The great lie is that they believe that the definition of failure is anything short of a home run.

That sort of thinking has never worked for me. I would much rather get a chance to step up to the plate and give it my best shot than to spend all my life watching from the stands. Who knows, maybe I will hit a home run. But even if I don't, that's okay. I might hit a single, a double, or even a triple. Or I might strike out. But at least I've given it my best! I'm no longer destined to a life of wondering, "What if…"

The Stepping-Stone Effect

As I mentioned earlier, each life experience, when approached correctly, can be linked to the next, like a path of beautiful stepping-stones. That's why I encourage people to step up to the plate. Sure you may strike out, but what an experience you will have had! And who knows? That experience might lead to another, and another, and another. Eventually, enough of these experiences linked together (like stepping-stones) become a life.

Here's the best part: As you follow your passion (and lose some of your life-crushing, suffocating inhibitions), you may "accidentally" stumble across your dream.

My Story

Let me try to make sense of this. And, since I'm the person I know best, please excuse the personal nature of this story. As a young boy, I wasn't very popular. I wasn't good at sports. I hated it when my classmates chose sides—usually I was at the very end of the line with the girls! The guys ragged me mercilessly. In school, the kids would touch me, then run and touch someone else, and say, "Steve Diggs' contamination—no gives!" The girls thought I was a klutz; my teachers knew I was. Life wasn't much fun.

Stepping-Stone ❶

The Loser Becomes a Salesman

So, I spent a lot of time reading comics. I kept noticing ads in comic books that showed the prizes and money to be made by selling greeting cards and flower seeds. Since I didn't have many friends to hang with, I decided to become a salesman. In the early 1960s, I ordered my first case of all-occasion cards. If I remember correctly, they sold for about $1.50 a box—and I got to keep a whole 50 cents! In those years, 50 cents was a lot of money. Minimum wage was less than a $1.30 per hour, and a dad could support a family on $4,000 per year.

And guess what? It worked! I started to make money and gain confidence. Finally, I was doing something I was good at! As a teenager, I started going door-to-door selling a cleaning product named Swipe. As my sales skills kept improving, so did my income—and my confidence.

I was learning something important: To succeed in life, it meant I had to be able to ignore the "noise" all around me. It meant ignoring the pack mentality. It meant doing stuff my classmates were too cool to do. It meant I had to break the rules and not necessarily accept the traditional "wisdom" of group think.

Stepping-Stone ❷

The Salesman Goes Into Show Business

This income led to the next stepping-stone. Since my real goal was to get into show business, one of the first awards I selected from my greeting cards sales was a guitar. Despite a profound lack of talent, I was determined to be the next great thing in entertainment.

In high school, I had tried to write songs and sing a little bit. I even built a shabby recording studio in our basement. (I thought it was cool!) I started appearing on local early morning television shows in Knoxville. Because of my interest in radio, I began hanging out at local stations. To this day, I can still remember when WYSH in Clinton, Tennessee allowed me to read the weather. It wasn't a paying gig but who cared? I was on the radio!

Before long, I met a wonderful man named Bud Carrigan. Bud had worked with a large radio station before starting WECO—his own 1,000-watt, day-timer in a small, rural east Tennessee town named Wartburg (yeah, you read it right). The station was located next to a cow pasture, and the station's tower resembled a flagpole.

But Bud liked me, and I liked him. Bud needed someone to sell advertising, and I wanted my own radio show. It was time for me to use the stepping-stone of salesmanship that I had already begun to develop to get the radio job I wanted. So we made a deal: I'd sell advertising, and Bud would allow me to do a daily radio program. I was ready to start signing autographs!

Stepping-Stone ❸
Gaining the Courage to Speak Up

When high school graduation approached in the spring of 1970, I did something else that was out of character. Due in part to the confidence I was gaining with my sales and broadcast work, I summoned the courage to audition to speak at my high school graduation. What were the chances a nerd like me would be permitted to speak to thousands of kids and their families at commencement? But my self-confidence paid off. The committee asked me to speak at commencement! It came with all the trimmings: a newspaper article, lots of attention, and a beautiful date! My stepping-stones were starting to work.

Stepping-Stone ❹
Selling in the Big Time

It was the summer of 1970. My plan was to leave for college in Nashville in the fall. At this point in the story, it would be appropriate to explain why going to Nashville was so important to me.

In his various business and professional involvements, my father traveled quite often, but he was the quintessential family man. Dad loved bringing the whole family on his trips. Since Nashville was a frequent destination for him, we had made a lot of family trips to the Music City throughout the 1960s. For me, that was heaven on earth! As soon as we got into Nashville, I would head straight for Music Row and spend hours visiting recording companies and studios.

Nashville represented everything I loved. The idea of going to college there thrilled me. Of course, it all had precious little to do with the small, Christian college I was scheduled to attend. It had everything to do with the fact that it would put me within close proximity to the radio and recording businesses I'd dreamed of being a part of for years. I couldn't wait for college to begin!

My plan for the summer of 1970 was to continue adding to my stepping-stones. I had agreed to sell books door-to-door for the Southwestern Company. But there were some tense days in the late spring when we thought my summer plans were going to vaporize, and I'd be heading off for duty in a rice paddy. (Remember, we were at the height of the Vietnam War, and the draft was on.) Thankfully, that never happened. But little did I know I was headed into another type of war—this one would be with myself.

Until now my sales experience was very limited and sheltered. I had enjoyed all the upsides with none of the downsides. If sales were good, I had extra spending money. If I didn't sell enough Swipe or greeting cards—no problem. I still had a warm bed and supper at home. But that was before I ran headlong into the real world in June 1970.

The famous Nashville-based Southwestern Company I was working for had, for decades, sent thousands of young people all over the country with a mission: sell books. Some of America's greatest sales and business leaders are Southwestern alumni. I soon learned why a successful Southwestern salesman was a respected guy. As the summer began, we attended a week of grueling sales training. Sales school was when the first batch of kids washed out. The prospect of memorizing sales talks and working eighty-hour weeks chilled a lot of early summer bravado. We didn't even know where they were going to send us. At the end of the week, the company told us where we would go. Then, with a road map in hand, and hopefully a friend's car or a cheap bus ticket, we headed out.

I ended up in rural southern Georgia—not America's home to the rich and the famous in 1970! This was in the day when mobile homes were still called trailers. Boy, did I see my share of them! Some of the "real" houses were wobbly-looking, board-frame structures—many about a quarter of a mile apart. I remember visiting one house that had a dirt floor! Midday temperatures often surpassed a hundred degrees. Off to the side of the road was a swamp that came alive with bobcats and snakes at night.

And, here's the clincher, the only income I would earn that summer would be based on what I sold. There I was, a seventeen-year-old kid on a bicycle with my sample case!

My field sales leader wasn't much help either. He was supposed to be my advisor and mentor. Instead, he gradually became so depressed he didn't get out of bed some mornings. When he did, he was likely to go to the nearby theme park.

But that summer was a major stepping-stone. I learned a lot about sales and persuasion—things that continue to help me to this day. I learned how to stare adversity down. I learned that it's best to eat your problems for breakfast. And, since I was working on straight commission, I learned that each day I could expect to be paid exactly what I was worth—not a penny more or a penny less. I began to understand that most people believe a deadly lie. Most Americans believe job security means getting a paycheck from someone else. They have been conditioned to believe that working for someone means there will always be a job and benefits.

Face it: If you work for someone else and the business gets into trouble, who loses their job first: you or the boss? Many people think they are secure in their jobs for the wrong reason. They suppose they're safe because someone signs their paycheck. Nothing could be further from the truth. In that situation, an individual is relying on the sales efforts of others. And make no mistake: Virtually all businesses exist because someone else is able to generate income through their ability to sell. So, if you're concerned about job security, it's fair to ask: What if the other person stops selling?

During the summer of 1970, I realized that true security (humanly speaking) comes only when an individual develops a skill set that is marketable in any economic climate. Today, I still believe that the single most adaptable, recession-proof skill is learning to sell. When one learns to sell (a first cousin to becoming an entrepreneur), he or she is always able to find work.

At summer's end, I was one of the top salesmen in the country—complete with a great paycheck and a number of awards for my efforts. But, even more importantly, I left the "book fields" of south Georgia with a calm assurance that, no matter what happened in the future or how bad my grades were in college, I could always make a living because I had learned the art of selling. By the way, that awareness (along with the check I received from Southwestern at the summer's end) became another important stepping-stone.

Stepping-Stone ⑤
The Move to Music City

That fall, I finally got to move to Nashville—and my parents paid for it! The only catch was, I had to agree to go to college. It wasn't that I had a problem with that. It was just that I was too busy getting a "real world" education to be bothered with classes! But I'll give you more perspective on that as I continue my stepping-stone analogy.

Once in Nashville, I had two goals: I wanted to get a radio show and a record deal. Thanks to the stepping-stone of my high-school radio experience, I had enough of a resume to start knocking on station doors in Nashville. And, thanks to my bookselling stepping-stone, I had the money to begin a recording project.

Before long, I persuaded a Nashville radio station to give me my own show. The deal included my agreement to sell advertising. Thanks to the stepping-stone I'd developed by learning salesman-ship, I was good enough at it to land an on-air shift. Suddenly, I was doing the afternoon drive shift in Music City!

Stepping-Stone ⑥

Recording Contract With a Major Label

The next task was to get busy on that record deal. Now, that was quite a different matter. The cards were pretty well stacked against me. Why? Because I can't sing. That's right. I can't sing a single note. No, this isn't false modesty. As anyone who has ever heard me try to sing will tell you, I'm terrible. When I start singing, they start collecting money for the cure! Seriously, when our daughter, Emilee (our musically gifted child) was just a baby and I would sing to her, she would shake her head and say, "No sing, Daddy, no sing!"

But I was determined to be a solo vocalist on a major label. The question was: how? With literally thousands of talented people being turned down by record labels each year, how in the world did I expect to get a label to sign me?

Well, I had a game plan, and it depended on using all of the skills I'd learned from the first five stepping-stones.

First, I had to break the rules. If this was going to happen, I couldn't conform to the traditional wisdom of the record industry. I knew if I couldn't find a new angle I would be dead in the water. Sure, most people who recorded could sing or play an instrument. But who said that was the only sort of record people would buy? What about people like Bill Anderson who was famous for his "talking" songs? Anderson had created a fistful of "recitation" hits. And didn't guys like Tennessee Ernie Ford and Johnny Cash talk halfway through most of their songs? So, I decided to do recitations to music. Okay, that was a good plan so far, but how would I make this happen?

I had to write a recitation that had a great story—something with an unusual hook. It took months, but finally I had it. The song was "Flight 408." It was a story about a guy going to the airport to get his fiancé who was arriving on Flight 408. As he drove to the airport, dreaming about their wedding, the music on the radio was inter-rupted by a news report that Flight 408 had just crashed, and there were no survivors. The young man is totally devastated—his life is shattered. So, he turns his car around and heads back home. As he stumbles through the front door, the phone is ringing. He almost doesn't answer it but finally picks up the receiver.

On the other end, his fiancé says, "Honey, I'm sorry, but I missed the flight. I'll be flying out tomorrow on Flight 409."

Okay, pretty good concept. (I didn't say it wasn't corny.) But what was I supposed to do with it?

Well, I decided to keep on breaking the rules. One of the cardinal conventions of the music industry was that an artist should never have to pay for his or her own recording session. There were hustlers all over town who happily relieved unsuspecting suckers of their money. Often they promised to record their record, promote it, and turn them into stars—all for a price. The prevailing wisdom was that if you were good enough to get a record deal, some producer would recognize your talent and invest his own money.

This is where my Stepping-Stone #4 came into play. I had earned a lot of money selling books door-to-door, and I was prepared to spend it to make my own record. By borrowing from Stepping-Stones #1 and #4, I figured I was enough of a salesman to pitch my record to some big-time recording execs. If I could just produce a great record to leave them spinning like the records they made, I really believed I could get their attention (and a recording contract).

But first, there was another challenge to address. I needed a top-flight producer. So I started hunting for someone with a bona fide reputation in the music business. I didn't want one of the hustlers—I wanted a producer.

Finally, through a course of events, I met Ricci Mareno, one of Nashville's best-known producers who had a bucket-load of hits to his credit. During the time we worked together, he produced one chart hit after another. I convinced Ricci to take on the project. To his credit, he made it clear to me that he didn't think I had an ounce of talent. But if I was determined to spend the money, he would do the best he could to produce a decent recording. Besides, he sort of liked "Flight 408" and admitted it could be "a left-field hit." That was good enough for me.

For weeks, Ricci allowed me to come down to his demo studio after class each afternoon and practice. Boy, did we practice! Finally the big day came to do the master recording. I was thrilled. We hired top-drawer musicians, including D.J. Fontana, one of Elvis' drummers. We used the same hit-making studio where greats like Ringo Starr would later record. The day of the master session all the pros did a great job. On the other hand, I didn't do so well. Eventually, with the help of another producer named Bill Brock, we improved my vocal track enough to present it to some major labels. But surprise—none of the big labels wanted my record!

Ultimately, everyone gave up on "Flight 408" except me. I decided to pay the bill and press a thousand copies of the record. Then I did something that was almost unheard of in those days—I decided to use my sales skills to promote the record. This was long before most record labels spent a lot of time or money promoting their products.

I began showing up at area radio stations, asking the deejays to play my record. I prevailed on Ralph Emery, the legendary WSM country deejay. He was kind enough to interview me on his famous show that was heard all over the country. I asked him for an endorsement, which he was, again, kind enough to provide. Then I contacted Archie Campbell, a popular country star of the era.

Back under Stepping-Stone #2, I'd performed on stage with Archie when I was in high school. I dropped by his office in the RCA Records building one afternoon, and he was there—glad to give me another endorsement for my record. I also stopped by the offices of the Wilburn Brothers, who were hit artists in the 1960s. Doyle Wilburn was particularly warm. He listened to my record and liked it, so I asked him for an endorsement.

I also asked Doyle if he'd give me some record envelopes with his company's logo on them. In my radio days, I'd noticed that each week the stations got piles of records. Some came from major labels. Those were the ones we opened and considered. The ones with unknown names that arrived in nondescript envelopes were often pitched into the trash without being opened. I knew if "Flight 408" was going to have a chance, it'd better come in an envelope from a well-known company. And, since Doyle liked my record, he willingly allowed me to use his envelopes to mail my records to the stations.

With envelopes and endorsements in hand, I hired a buddy to come out to the airport and shoot some pictures of me boarding an airplane. Then I used his photos and the endorsements to make a promotional handbill. I also made a series of postcards that said,

> **"Warning! Steve Diggs is arriving on Flight 408!"**

It was late fall 1972, almost time for Christmas break from college. Since I would be back home in east Tennessee for three weeks at Christmas, I targeted about 30 stations in the area and started sending out my odd little postcards. A few days later, I sent the promotional handbill for "Flight 408," complete with my picture and all the endorsements. When I got home for Christmas, I struck out to visit the stations, hoping to get enough airtime to get my record noticed by a recording company.

At first, I visited the smaller rural stations. After I'd gotten my spiel down, I summoned the courage to go to the blowtorch of East Tennessee—WIVK Radio. This was the big time. If WIVK played my record, deejays might make it a "pick hit," and that might lead to it becoming a regional hit. Then, who knew what might happen?

But I wasn't going to just walk into WIVK and ask the on-air guy to roll my record. Oh no! The station was far too sophisticated for that kind of stuff. I knew the only way I had any hope of getting WIVK to play "Flight 408" was to get an audience with Bobby Denton, the program director.

As usual, I walked in without an appointment. (For better or worse, I always figured it was harder for someone to say "no" to my face than over the phone.) I asked if I could see Mr. Denton. The secretary wasn't particularly helpful, and Bobby sure didn't put me on his front burner that day. I remember sitting out in the lobby for what seemed like an eternity.

Finally, a bored looking Bobby Denton came out and asked what I wanted. I told him. He said, "Come on back here." I followed him to one of the station's production studios. He took my little record out of its sleeve and put it on a huge green felt fabric-covered turn-table. He turned it on and listened to it. When it stopped, he didn't say a word. Then he listened again. Then he looked at me and said, "I really like this. Would you like to get it on a major label?"

Whoa! I had hoped for some airplay, but a record deal? That was better than I'd dreamed. "Sure!" I said.

Within a few days, we were back in Nashville "sweetening" and upgrading the master tape—and out it came on Dot Records, a label that produced hundreds of major hits by artists from Pat Boone and Lawrence Welk to The Andrews Sisters and a fistful of contemporary country acts. And, to make it even better, Dot paid me for the rights!

Before I knew it, my career was launched. The label hired a publicity guy to encourage stations to run my record. There were television shows and radio interviews. I went to autograph parties. There were newspaper articles and even a polite mention in *Billboard* magazine. The record did chart in various areas around the country. But, in truth, there was one thing missing: People who wanted to buy my record. That's right. It never made the national charts. It was what is technically known as a "flop."

Stepping-Stone **7**
Back to the Drawing Board

No doubt about it. Striking out in the majors was painful. It took a while to get over the hurt and smile at the experience. It also took a while before I saw how the stepping-stones continued to lead across the river of my life.

In the coming months, I continued in radio. I worked at WATO in east Tennessee during the summer and learned more. I also worked to improve my skills in photography—a hobby I'd enjoyed since junior high school. As a matter of fact, I started a photography business in my college dorm room. I learned there was good money to be made in shooting weddings, freelance newspaper photos, and all kinds of stuff. If a singing group performed around town, I'd go and shoot their picture, then sell them copies.

Gradually, God was helping me build a path of important stepping-stones that he would use to lead me to a life of joy, excitement, and fulfillment.

Stepping-Stone **8**
The Day I Started an Ad Agency

It all had to start somewhere and that somewhere was a chance meeting I had with a college buddy during a school break. He had left college to run an optical and eyeglasses store in the Chattanooga area. As we talked, he complained that the business wasn't doing very well. But the owner had money and wanted to do some advertising, he explained. That was the moment for me to use all the stepping-stones I had crossed.

"I could help you," I said.

In the next few days, we fleshed out a plan. I would produce a jingle and start a radio and TV advertising campaign for the store. The store would pay me $175 for the jingle. Now that might sound cheap to you, but think about. I was an unproven commodity. I had no track record. These people were willing to give me a shot, and I think they did me a real favor. I used everything I'd learned about radio, recording, and selling. I asked a friend to write the jingle, and we hired some buddies to play on it. We rented a recording studio and popped it out! Next I had to shoot the television commercials, which stretched everything I'd ever learned about TV. Then, it was time to go to Chattanooga and put the commercials on the air.

I'll never forget a meeting I had with the salesman at WDOD Radio in Chattanooga. As I was placing the order, he said, "What's the name of your advertising agency?"

"What do you mean?" I said.

"Well, if you have an ad agency, I can give you a 15 percent commission," he said.

"Oh," I replied. "Is that how this works?"

"Yes," he said.

My middle name is Franklin, so it just seemed logical. "The name of my firm is the Franklin Agency," I said.

Within a year, the optical store's business had increased eight-fold. Eventually, it grew to have stores all over the region. We developed a symbiotic relationship—both helping each other achieve what we needed. I trust that the advertising we did helped the owners succeed. And I know their decision to let me work for them changed my life.

During the rest of my college career, the jingle and photography businesses continued to do well. And, because the college's administration trusted me not to squander the school's money, they allowed me to book, produce, and manage some on-campus shows. Still a victim of traditional "group thinking," I decided after graduation that it was time to get a "real job." I almost made the mistake of taking a job working for the school. It would have been okay. But, fortunately, they withdrew the offer, in part because my hair was too long to suit the president.

So there I was—only days before graduation and still no job. But thanks to a deacon in our church who owned a real estate firm, I went to work selling real estate. I did well and enjoyed it. I was able to set my own hours, which meant I didn't have to limit my opportunities for success to only 40 hours per week. The harder I worked, the more I made. No one determined my earnings except me.

Within two years, my broker told me I was in the top 5 percent of several thousand Realtors in Middle Tennessee. But my heart was still in advertising. I dreamed of owning my own full-service agency. Again, a stepping-stone appeared. My broker asked me develop a radio and television advertising campaign for his firm. This gave me valuable experience and the chance to learn more.

Stepping-Stone ⑨
Time to Grow Up

That's when life took an unexpected turn. Professionally, I was doing fine. I was making lots of money, helping manage the firm, and training new salesmen. My boss took me out of the pool of other agents and gave me an office with a big window. Sadly, I didn't handle success very well. To be truthful, I'd become a pretty cocky jerk.

That's when God gave me a wake-up call. Three years earlier, I had met the cutest little brunette ever produced in the state of Pennsylvania. Bonnie and I had our first date in February 1972. She wore a red dress and was the finest girl I'd ever dated. I was surprised (but filled with respect) when she wouldn't let me kiss her on that first date. As a matter of fact, it was on our first date that I told her I was going to marry her.

Sounds like a fairy tale, right?

Not quite. Over the next three years, I became increasingly ego driven and self-focused. I didn't show Bonnie the respect she deserved. It was all about me. To her credit, Bonnie tried to make it work. After graduation, she'd gotten an apartment in Nashville so we could be close enough to work on our relationship. But, eventually, she got tired of trying. When her mother died suddenly, leaving a father and an elderly uncle to care for, Bonnie packed up and moved back to Pennsylvania.

For a while, I tried to go on without her. But every day it became more and more evident that it was time for me to put up or shut up. If I was ever going to do it, now was the time to grow up and put some of those Christian principles I espoused into practice.

I closed my real estate business in Nashville and moved to Erie, Pennsylvania to rebuild our relationship. Things improved, and gradually Bonnie began to trust me again. On August 8, 1976, we were married.

My job in Erie wasn't going as well. I didn't have much of a plan when I moved. None of the ad agencies would hire me. After all, I'd never taken a single course in marketing, and I'd never worked at a "real agency." Eventually, I ended up selling cars. (Another job where I could control my own earning potential.) I put a ton of metal on the road, but hated every minute. "When will we be able to move back to Nashville and open the agency?" I wondered.

Again, God had the next stepping-stone lined up. I was driving back to the dealership after lunch one day when I noticed a group of people in a yard holding a real estate sign. One of them had an old 16 mm news camera. I immediately realized that they were trying to shoot a TV commercial. I stopped the car and headed toward the people in the yard. The sign said, "Lloyd White Realtors."

So, being the rocket scientist that I am, I asked if Mr. White was there. Someone pointed me to a wonderfully charming gentleman.

I stuck out my hand and said something like, "Hi, I'm Steve Diggs, and I'm an advertising man from Nashville. I think I can help you."

Over the next few weeks, Lloyd and I built a friendship. He asked me to come to work for him as his full-time, in-house ad man. Wow!

I'd hit the mother lode! I was finally in the advertising business, getting the experience I needed before I had the responsibilities of running my own Nashville agency!

Over the next six months, I used every stepping-stone I had crossed: my sales skills, my recording and TV experience, my communication abilities, my photography—everything! We built a dynamic ad campaign that made Lloyd White Realtors the best-known firm in town.

Stepping-Stone ⑩
Birth of a Business

In the spring of 1977, God relieved us of the responsibilities that had kept us in Erie and made it possible for Bon and me to move back to Nashville. Due to terrible spending habits, we'd wasted all the money we had earned, not saving a dime except for $4,000 that Bonnie's family and friends had given us as investors in Franklin Group, Inc. (To this day, I suspect some of my "investors" gave me that money so I wouldn't bring Bonnie to Nashville and starve her to death.)

In May 1977, we rented a six-hundred-square-foot office suite on Music Row, which needed to be remodeled in the worst way. By the time we opened for business a couple of weeks later, we had $1,900 left and the desperate hope that Lloyd White would keep working with us to the tune of about $300 per month.

For all practical purposes, we had no money and no clients. It would be an understatement to say the first few years were nail-biters. But at least no one was calling the shots except us. It was just Bonnie and me at first. She worked plenty of seventy-hour weeks, and I worked lots of ninety-hour weeks. It's tough to start a business! That's especially true when you start one the way we did.

Remember, I had never taken a course in advertising. I'd never worked at another ad agency—even as an intern. But if other people could do this, I reasoned, so could I! In those early days, I spent lots of time reading books and looking at what other people in the business did. I hung around pros and asked lots of questions. But it seemed to me that all I had to do was master three things:

1. Learn the basics.

I had to get my arms around the fundamentals of advertising. This was going to be a seriously steep learning curve. It meant I had to master the foundational methodology that all good advertising demands. In later years, I always got a chuckle out of it when I was asked to judge an advertising award show, speak as an expert on CNN, or teach college-level advertising courses. If only they knew how self-taught I was!

2. Apply what I knew about salesmanship to the advertising world.

Soon I began to understand that, conceptually speaking, advertising is pretty simple. It's nothing more than salesmanship to the masses. Since I was already a fair salesman, I decided to apply those techniques broadly to the public on behalf of my clients.

3. Know when not to listen to traditional wisdom.

Almost immediately, I noticed something smelled fishy about the advertising industry. There was a terribly high mortality rate within the business. Many ad agencies closed their doors within their first year. Even large agencies went down in flames. Something was clearly wrong. Many agencies overpriced and overpromised—and clients hated them for it.

So I decided to rethink things a bit. Why not keep overhead down so we could keep our prices below the competitors? And why not tell the truth? Instead of overpromising, we would simply try to deliver what could be reasonably expected. And, lastly, why not remember for whom we're working? Many agencies seemed to miss the point that the boss is whoever signs the checks. Too often agencies fixated on winning awards and accolades from their peers—while producing noneffective advertising for their clients. I was determined to live by the old adage:

> ## "It ain't creative if it doesn't sell!"

This isn't to say that I was allergic to awards. Over the years, our little firm employed dozens of people and won scores of awards, including a National ADDY Award. We were blessed to work with some of the finest clients anywhere. I believe we helped many of their businesses grow and flourish. Every day was new and adventurous. Over those decades, the business grew and grew. We became one of the leading firms in our region. Eventually, we owned our own office building on the same world-famous Music Row I had visited as a boy. Thankfully, we never had any major setbacks during our years in business. We never had a layoff. We never had a major cash flow problem. And we were always profitable.

Stepping-Stone ⑪
Going from Success to Significance

While I didn't coin that phrase, I do like it. As the years passed, I was finding myself increasingly restless—even to the point of burnout. A number of things happened to sober me. In 1986, my father died suddenly from a heart attack.

In 1992, at age thirty-nine, I found myself in St. Thomas Hospital undergoing five heart bypasses. I was becoming increasingly aware that life on this earth isn't forever. Maybe God had other plans for me.

Through the 1980s, Bonnie and I had straightened up our bad money habits. By the end of the decade, for all practical purposes, we were out of debt. We'd even paid off the house in 1990. I noticed that things were better when I didn't have debt. My car even seemed to drive better when I didn't have to make payments.

In the 1990s, I'd become a student of investing. Throughout the decade, I grew more and more aware that lots of people were struggling with money problems. In the mid-'90s, a publisher and I had discussed the possibility of me writing a book that dealt with family money issues from a Christian perspective. But I was too busy to do it, so nothing happened.

But in 2000, we sold the company. My shepherds at our church had been talking with me about becoming a shepherd. But I didn't feel the time was right. So, with the business sold, they offered me what I jokingly call my consolation prize. They agreed to let me join the staff as a minister and develop the *No Debt No Sweat! Christian Financial Ministries*.

This stepping-stone was a beautiful culmination of all the others. Over the years, we have developed books, curriculum, videos and a live seminar—all of which have reached thousands of people worldwide. I wake up in the morning excited. We've seen people all over the country get their money under control, get out of debt, restore romance in their marriages, and learn to give God's way.

What's Next?

I don't know what the future holds. But, like Paul, I know who holds the future. Maybe there will be more stepping-stones. I hope so. But what I want this book to do is help you identify the stepping-stones of your life. I believe that God has a special plan for each of us. That plan is as unique as your own fingerprints.

The beginning of wisdom is understanding God's deep interest in you and what you do with your life. Jesus told us that his "yoke is easy" and his "burden is light." When we find the stepping-stones of our lives, we can see how God's architecture works. Each stone leads easily and naturally to the next in beautiful, fulfilling harmony.

"For I know the plans that I have for you, declares the Lord, plans for welfare and not for calamity to give you a future and a hope. Then you will call upon Me and come and pray to Me, and I will listen to you. And you will seek Me and find Me, when you search for Me with all your heart." (Jeremiah 29:11-13, NASB)

Caution:

Beware of Missing the Big Picture

The problem with the ordinary is that it is, well, so ordinary. It's hard to see the big picture while living in a world where most people are small thinkers. We tend to start projects with high goals but somehow drift into the weeds of life, making it difficult to remember what's really important.

Take the story of Orville and Wilbur Wright, for example, who made their first airplane flight at Kitty Hawk, N.C. on December 17, 1903. On their fifth attempt the plane, under the control of Orville, embarked on a twelve-second flight. Wilbur rushed to the local telegraph office and sent the following message:

> "WE HAVE FLOWN FOR TWELVE SECONDS—
> WE WILL BE HOME FOR CHRISTMAS!"

Upon receiving the telegram, their sister, Katherine, went to the newspaper office and told the editor about her brothers' new flying machine. She informed him they would be home for Christmas if he would like to set up an interview. He promised her that he would put a mention in the paper about the boys.

On December 19, the editor ran the following headline on page 6 of the paper: "WRIGHT BROTHERS HOME FOR CHRISTMAS." It was the most important story of the year—man's first flight—and the editor missed it! The world will do all it can to force you into its pigeonhole. Fight that urge with all your might!

One Last Leg of the Journey

Alternative Success

In my office, there's a photograph on the wall that means a lot to me. It's a picture of Elvis Presley and his original band: Scotty Moore, Bill Black, and D.J. Fontana. The picture was a gift from Scotty, Elvis' first guitarist and bandleader.

Although I met him on a couple of occasions, I never really knew Elvis. But Scotty and I worked together on several recording projects over the years. I like Scotty. The picture includes an inscription from him that reads:

> *Steve, I worked with you and I worked with Elvis. I'm glad one of you made it! —Scotty Moore*

While I love the photo and laugh at Scotty's comment, I think he's wrong. Sure, I didn't make it in the recording business. For a period, I felt like a real failure. My dream was shattered. But years have a way of giving perspective. Frankly, I believe that my "failure" in the entertainment world was the hand of God in my life. I believe God knew that if I ever became a star, my faith in him would be toast! He loved me enough to protect me. Gaining the world versus losing my soul—I don't think so!

But I do believe that God allowed me to use every stepping-stone experience to eventually lead me to true joy. This is what I mean by "alternative success." Sometimes we see the hand of God in our lives only when we look at the stepping-stones we've already crossed.

If I'd been popular in school, I probably wouldn't have seen those greeting card sales ads in the comic books. If I had never learned to sell, I wouldn't have gotten my first radio show. If I hadn't gotten into radio, I probably would never have recorded that first jingle. Without that first jingle, I may never have considered a career in advertising. And without the success of the ad agency and the financial blessings it brought, I would probably have had no way to enter ministry and share the *No Debt No Sweat!* message. Without that, I likely would not have been invited to speak on thousands of occasions, do hundreds of TV shows, or write several books—all of which have helped struggling people develop life skills from a Christian worldview.

Remember:

There's Just One Best Way to Ride a Roller Coaster

Success is not determined by our hardware—it's usually determined by the software we're running. Most people have perfectly capable hardware (i.e., normal intelligence and decent health). The difference between winners and losers is in the software they run. By software, I'm referring to the things we tell ourselves, the way we choose to look at the world around us, and our internal motivation.

I've finally decided that life is a lot like a roller-coaster ride. People fall into two categories: the ones who hate roller coasters and the ones who love them. Those who don't enjoy roller coasters are usually afraid of them. Most of these people never even get on.

But if they do step aboard, it's three minutes of emotional torture. They grab tightly and push hard back into the seat as though it will prevent the inevitable downhill drop. They leave the ride ready to kiss the ground and vow to never do it again.

But for those of us who love roller coasters, it's a bit different. Sure, sometimes we have to muster the will to get on (especially if we've just downed a footlong hot dog and a shake). But once on board, we're jazzed! The juices start pumping; it's time for some real fun! These people don't hold anything back, and they certainly don't hold on.

When the big drop comes, they lean forward in their seats, raise their hands to heaven, suck in the fresh air, and squeal with delight as if to say, "Give me the best you've got!"

For many people, the worst regrets may be the things they never tried. We can use all of our precious life experiences to build new challenges and opportunities. The key to it all is to understand that you don't have to hit a home run to be a winner—it's a "win" to simply get up to bat in the majors.

My advice is very clear: never dismiss anything that God is doing in your life. Believe me, often it makes no human sense at the time. But, one by one, each stepping-stone will lead you closer to the goal.

Get Along With Other People
Effective Conflict Resolution

I fly a lot. It doesn't take long to size up a flight attendant's mood. This is an important skill because the flight attendant's mood is a good predictor of how enjoyable the flight will be. Recently, I was on a flight from Chicago to Nashville with an angry flight attendant. As a matter of fact, she bluntly announced, "I'm in a bad mood!"—and

> "Blessed are the peacemakers."
> – JESUS

she lived up to her billing. She was rude and didn't even offer to help the boarding passengers. It was so obvious that the pilot was out greeting passengers, trying to cover for her.

As she was slamming the compartment doors shut just before takeoff, I summoned the courage to walk up front, tap her on the shoulder and say, "I can see you're having a tough day. For whatever it's worth, I just want you to know that I care for you."

She seemed to ignore me. So, feeling a bit stupid, I sat back down. But apparently my comment sunk in.

As we were taking off, she sat in her jump seat facing me on the front row and began to cry, confessing, "I am having such a problem with my anger."

That got us talking. I told her it was okay.

"No, it isn't okay," she said.

I clarified, saying, "Well, I can certainly identify with how you're feeling. There have been a lot of times when I've done the same—and have been very disappointed in my own wife's husband afterward."

With the tension diffused, she said, "You must think I'm crazy."

"No," I replied, "I think you're struggling."

Later during the flight, she was like a different person. She apologized to me and couldn't have been kinder. It gave me a chance to give her my card and invite her to "call me anytime you wish."

> "Peace is not the absence of conflict, but the presence of creative alternatives for responding to conflict ...."
> – DOROTHY THOMPSON

Lest you think this is typical for me, it isn't. In far too many similar situations, I have used the other person's behavior as an excuse to act badly. I've left those situations worse than I found them. My blood pressure was up. The other person was still mad. And I'd blown my witness for Christ. Anger may help us see a problem—but it rarely helps us resolve it.

Wisdom of the Ages

"There is nothing new under the sun."

If he had never made another statement, this comment would have secured Solomon's place as history's wisest man. Each generation goes to great lengths to convince itself that theirs is the worst and most depraved one yet. But the fact is, human nature is pretty predictable. Conflict among humans has been around as long as there have been humans.

When the world began, it was Cain murdering his brother Abel in a jealous rage. Now, it's two angry, frustrated men in traffic, snarling at one another and speeding through an intersection—each trying to best the other. Then, it was Job and his malicious wife. Now, it's just one more three-month Hollywood marriage between a couple parading their private war before an insatiable public. Then, it was the Corinthian Christians embarrassing Jesus by taking their disputes before pagan judges. Now, it's a nation that files 10 million civil lawsuits annually—many of which take more than two years just to get into court. It's simply human nature to be … human.

Don't Ignore the Obvious

The 1950s was a good time for America. We had won the big war. The baby boom was in full swing. America liked Ike. We were feeling our collective oats. But not everything was as it seemed. In fact, we didn't know that several decades later we would look back on the 1950s as the Happy Days era. In reality, there was a lot of tension in the world at the time. The pressure to look perfect was intense. Dads hung smiling family portraits in their offices, and moms wore makeup and hose to the corner drugstore.

But people were scared. What about the Soviets? After all, this was the first time in history when an entire society realized it could be vaporized in a matter of minutes. Children grew up being taught to duck and cover. Parents dug fallout shelters. And for the first time in history, there was a new class of people: teenagers. Before World War II, there were essentially two age groups: children and adults. But now we had a new demographic who demanded the rights and privileges of adulthood, while still being sheltered from its responsibilities. This new teenaged population introduced another first—their own music. Even though Elvis rings with nostalgia today, we must remember that, in 1956, he scared parents to death!

In the midst of all this upheaval, young parents had few good resources. Of course, there was Dr. Spock and his best-selling child-rearing book, and Art Linkletter seemed to have a way with the kids. And, thankfully, entertainer Pat Boone bridged both sides of the generational gap, providing an alternative to the snarling Elvis persona. But few people dared admit their fears to others. It was simply safer to play bridge and make small talk. Overworked dads never considered leaving work early to play baseball with their kids. No "depressed" young mother dared to describe herself by that word. And psychiatrists—well, they were for the really crazy people. Even good, churchgoing people often received more ritual than renewal on Sunday morning.

So, what did all this varnish and pretense give us?

It led to the Timothy Learys of the 1960s who persuaded a generation of college students to drop acid by turning on and tuning out. It sparked a decade of wanton pleasure seekers who preached the message: "If it feels good—do it!" It ushered in a postmodern culture filled with despair that saw no absolutes. It gave us the highest divorce rate in the nation's history and left millions of young adults with no spiritual or ethical moorings.

Those of us concerned about these issues talked a good game. In the 1970s, we were told that anything goes—you're okay, and I'm okay. In the 1980s, bookshelves were loaded with "recovery" books telling us that we were all "dysfunctional." By the 1990s, the gurus encouraged us to "focus on self." Now, roll the clock ahead to this new millennium. Today we hear the phrase "self-actualization," and we're being systematically taught that greed and self-absorption are good for the soul!

But despite all this psycho-babble, our contemporary culture doesn't do a very good job at being open and honest. We don't get along well with one another. Yet for the early Christians, relationships were a top priority.

Their buzzword was "*koininia*." It expresses the concept of fellowship and openness—one with another. Done correctly, it leads to the "peace that passes understanding" that Paul wrote to the Philippians about. It results in the spiritual fruits of peace, patience, gentleness, kindness, goodness, and self-control that the apostle encouraged the Galatians to develop. Coincidentally, these are the same traits that lead to healthy interpersonal relationships.

To accomplish this openness we must start with a basic ingredient: transparency. Among other things, this means realizing that any group of human beings (whether it's a family, church, social or professional association, or business) is going to have conflicts. To deal with (and resolve) conflict, we must drive a stake in the heart of the 1950s mind-set that essentially says, "A problem ignored is a problem that doesn't exist." Simply put: It's time to stop pretending and get bone honest.

Conflict can bring out either the best or the worst in us. It can be a precursor to great gain. After all, wasn't your birth a conflicted event? There you were, inside Mom's tummy thinking, "Wow, do I really want to go through that tunnel? It's warm in here— lots of food and plenty of time to sleep." But without birth, think about what your future (not to mention your mother's) would have been!

Conflicts can open doors of unimaginable opportunities. Situations are rarely neat and clean. Frequently, when one finally deals with a conflict, it can lead to even more conflicts. It can be messy and uncomfortable. But with challenges come opportunities for growth. Our grandparents fought a war against Japan in the early 1940s. There was nothing good or glamorous about it, but most fair-minded historians don't question that it was essential. Today, Japan and the United States are close friends who share common interests. We respect one another and have grown mutually stronger through the conflict in our relationship.

Dealing With the Nasty "Now and Now"

If you're presently in the middle of a conflict, forgive me for wasting your time with the following section. In your case, the toothpaste is already out of the tube, and as the mother of any five-year-old knows, it's pretty hard to reinsert it.

But I want to begin by sharing a simple (yet overlooked) suggestion that can help us avoid many conflicts in the first place. Since

55

this is a preemptive move to help you sidestep conflict, it may not be of much help in your present dilemma. But you may find it useful because it may help you steer clear of future pain.

After this little digression, I promise to spend the rest of this chapter sharing some practical ideas that you will find helpful in understanding and overcoming conflicts. Since I come from the shallow end of the gene pool, this stuff won't be academic. My goal is to share strategies you can use right now to improve the situation and stop the bleeding. We'll look at the reasons most efforts to resolve conflicts fail. Then I'll share some insights that have proven successful in conflict resolution. Finally, we'll evaluate a fresh paradigm for conflict resolution that was first taught nearly two thousand years ago.

Conflict Avoidance 101

As I mentioned in the last chapter, Bonnie and I opened The Franklin Group, Inc. in the mid 1970s. Those first years were tough. We worked lots of eighty- and ninety-hour weeks. It was typical for me to start early in the morning catching up on paper-work, then to spend most of the day visiting clients and prospects. Since we didn't yet have an art department, a copywriter, or even a staff media buyer, I would work late into the night producing projects my clients had ordered earlier in the day.

By the 1980s, we had grown. We had a talented staff and a fistful of great clients. By then, we owned our own office building on Nashville's famous Music Row and, during that decade, we began winning awards. Local, regional, and even national trophies lined the walls of our conference room—in some cases three and four deep. We were a hot young agency, and we were growing fast.

By the early 1990s, the firm had been in business for about 15 years. I suppose we were feeling our oats. (That's a polite way of saying that I was becoming too self-sufficient and not walking as humbly before God as I should have.)

It was about that time that a local firm discussed its account with us. I quickly became convinced that I saw the whole picture and could easily develop a program that would fit the bill. I was courteous and made the routine visits, but, deep down, I was thinking, "I've got it covered—no problem."

The firm contracted with us to develop an advertising/marketing plan. "A good first start," I thought, "just wait until they see what we can do for them!" Over the next several weeks, we had creative meetings and discussed our strategies. We conceived designs and a slogan, building a "position" for the company's public identity.

Finally, it came: presentation day! As always, I was enthused. I couldn't wait to show 'em our stuff. After a couple of hours of razzle-dazzle, we concluded the meeting. They wanted to "think about it." Okay. But several days passed with no response. Finally, when I contacted one of the principals to see if they were ready to proceed, their answer was a real disappointment. They didn't want to go forward at all—at least, not with us!

I mustered enough courage to ask for a follow-up meeting. When we got together, I assured them that I didn't intend to push for a reverse decision. I simply wanted to know what went wrong.

"Do you really want to know?" One of them asked.

"Yes," I said, with a lump in my throat.

"You didn't listen to us! You had your own plans and agendas, but you never really heard us."

I was stunned. They were right. I apologized and left. After that episode, we renamed our conference room. We put a brass plaque on the door that contained two words:

Listening Room

You may be wondering why I included this story in a chapter on conflict resolution. Simple. Nearly forty years in the business world and ten years in the ministry have taught me that most conflicts are caused by (or at least fueled by) someone not listening.

"Nip It In the Bud!"

To quote the great 20th-century philosopher, Mayberry's Deputy Barney Fife, one of the best ways to avoid conflict is to do the right thing in the first place and simply, "Nip it in the bud!"

Succinctly put, conflict often happens because people tend to be gutless. I've heard it said, "If you want to have less conflict, have more of it." I think that's profound. When we meet conflict head-on (not pretending that problems don't exist), we become healthier for it.

For instance, suppose you're the manager of an insurance company, and you learn that Jill, a young adjuster, is using her company computer to buy family Christmas gifts. You know, and she knows, that it's against company policy to use the firm's computers for non-company purposes. You may hope the problem just goes away. You like Jill and want her to evolve into an important part of your team. "Besides," you tell yourself, "unlike most of the other adjusters, she has great people skills and communicates well with the clients. Sure, she's breaking policy. But what's the big deal? Christmas will be over soon. It's not impacting her work." Yet in your heart of hearts, you know what she's doing is wrong.

Now, suppose a month later you learn that another adjuster is using his computer to download porn. But this time, the stakes are higher. This time, that person is Eric, the head of the department—and he's being wooed by a competitive firm. If he were to leave, he'd probably take several key accounts with him. The bottom line is you don't want to lose him. Now, what do you do?

With a gut load of righteous indignation, you summon Eric into your office and demand, "Why are you doing this? You know it's against company policy to use your computer for non-company purposes—and besides, what you're doing is immoral!"

This brazen young man, however, isn't operating on your moral compass. He looks at you and stealthily decides to argue his case based on the merits of your first complaint, claiming, "Everybody in the department knows that Jill uses her computer to buy gifts online!" Now what? You're on the defensive (just where Eric wants you) and forced to argue your case based on his abstract comparison rather than on the immorality of his behavior.

The fact is, this problem with Eric might never have happened (or at least could have been dealt with much more succinctly) had you been courageous enough to have kindly, but firmly, dealt with Jill earlier.

To successfully handle conflict, it's wise to win the little inevitable battles first. That way, you may be able to avoid many of the wars. Understand the pressure valve concept: By dealing with the little tremors as they arise, we're more likely to miss the big earthquakes.

Some of my greatest regrets from the years I spent running businesses are the times I pretended not to see a problem. Pain came when I ignored a situation I should have confronted: the times I looked the other way, the times I "ducked and covered" instead of "stood and dealt," the times that I failed to "nip it in the bud!"

Dogged Pursuit

In his first letter to the Corinthians, Paul tells the ancients *"God is not a God of confusion but of peace."* (I Corinthians 14:33) Confusion, chaos, and turmoil are all the stock-in-trade of Satan. I'm convinced that most of life's struggles, defeats, and broken relations can ultimately be traced to the common root of selfish individualism. Most of what we see in our popular culture reinforces this worship of self. However, people who are truly successful (defined here as those who surmount conflict) see beyond this cultural smoke screen and doggedly pursue true relationship.

Defining Conflict

Just like the advice given to Dorothy and Toto as they began their trip down the yellow brick road to Oz: The best place to begin any journey is at the beginning. For us, the beginning is to define conflict. Conflicts fall into two categories. For the purposes of this book, I will refer to them as *immediate* and *prolonged*.

Conflict occurs when two or more parties have different views about the same issue. It usually happens because at least one feels threatened or misunderstood. That person fears he or she may lose something of importance. This fear of loss, however, may not necessarily reveal itself as the surface issue. Sometimes this fear can manifest itself as an issue of pride or prominence or something else equally distinct from the matter at hand.

An additional ingredient in many conflicts is the sense of power-lessness. In most conflicts, one person feels (whether true or not) less powerful than the other. The conflict frequently comes to a head when that person overcompensates. Often the issue at hand (the *immediate* conflict) is only the tip of the iceberg. What the parties may actually be dealing with is a *prolonged* conflict suddenly brought to the surface by a pressing issue.

Jessica and Rachel may be debating whether this year's vacation Bible school should be three or five days long. But it's likely the immediate conflict has its basis in years of prolonged conflict between the two.

Maybe Jessica and Rachel never played well in the sandbox together. Maybe they were school rivals. Maybe they dated the same guy. Maybe Rachel just feels that the church leaders "like" Jessica more. Maybe Jessica has come to see Rachel as a crybaby who sulks and whines anytime she doesn't get her way.

To resolve any conflict, you have to know what the actual conflict is. Is it an immediate or prolonged issue finally coming to the surface?

It's important to keep our eyes on the ball. The goal of conflict resolution is simple: to achieve a desired goal and maintain healthy interpersonal relations in the meantime.

Why Conflict Resolution Fails

Now, let's get into the how-to steps. Whole books have been written on this topic, but allow me to summarize the reasons why people frequently walk away from conflicts feeling even more conflicted.

1. Rabbit chasing

The easiest thing to do in a dispute is to get off message and begin chasing rabbits. If two account executives, Ron and Janice, are feuding over how to best court a prospective new client, little is accomplished if Ron launches into a diatribe about how Janice's hiring was done to fulfill a gender quota mandate from the home office. Rabbit chasing is usually counterproductive. It strikes at the very heart of the relationship we need to maintain in order to overcome a conflict. The bottom line: Stay on message. Unless it's vital to the goal of resolving the dispute, rehashing old issues is rarely wise.

2. Small-mindedness

Often when people are in the midst of a dispute, they fail to see the ocean of options lying before them. As the disagreement continues, they become more and more rigid. We sometimes refer to an elderly person as being "set in his ways." Believe me, being set in your ways has nothing to do with age, lap blankets, or drool cups! Some of the most "set-in-their-ways-people" out there are barely old enough to suck air! What about two toddlers fighting over the same toy—while an even more enticing one sits right behind them? What about the husband and wife who are stressed and worried about the credit card collectors calling six times a day? Mom is at home with the kids (where she really prefers to stay), but she insists on getting a job to pay off the debt. Dad believes he should be the provider and that the children need their mother at home. He refuses the whole notion.

Days turn into weeks. The couple stop speaking—except to make nice in front of the kids (who are smart enough to know something is wrong.) Since the space in the middle of their king-sized bed has become a no-man's-land, the marriage has lost its intimacy. This makes Dad even angrier and more determined not to back down.

By this time, it's become more than a dispute over Mom's job. Now it's the fear that one of the two will lose his or her power and self-worth by giving in. All the while, the old dilemma is still there—and the bill collectors are still dialing for dollars! What if the couple's small-mindedness had paved the way for some creative, out-of-the-box thinking?

Just last week, I was talking to a mother who had the worst of both worlds. She was working to help her family pay off a $16,000 debt. But it meant spending a large amount of her earnings to warehouse the kids in a day care. Since she and her husband were up to their hips in alligators, it was tough to do effective out-of-the-box thinking.

But for me—an objective third party observer—there seemed to be several solutions that would earn the money needed and keep Mom and the kids together. One idea: change jobs. Go to work at the day care where the kids stayed. That way she would be near her children and bring home more money to get out of debt sooner. And in the process, Dad's concerns would be alleviated.

3. Allowing perception to replace reality.

We all react based upon our perceptions. Not all perceptions, however, are correct or accurate. Objectivity is sometimes slain on the altar of past experiences, prejudices, and other life situations. Misconstruing a situation can cause us to respond incorrectly. Many conflicts could be avoided or more readily resolved if we made a sincere effort to approach them with an accurate perspective and as little emotion as possible.

4. Failing to see the positive potential of conflict.

We all tend to avoid certain things. I'm no fan of snakes, licorice, or conflict. But, in truth, they all have their upsides. Sometimes the challenge is to look beyond the immediate havoc for the long-term potential for gain. Snake venom has medical value. Licorice can turn a six-year-old boy's mouth into a color that will keep his sisters out of his bedroom. And conflict, if correctly approached, can be the beginning of greater understanding, renewed vision, and the accomplishment of unexpected goals.

5. Confusing the real enemy with the imagined one.

When a soldier is confused for the enemy and shot by a fellow soldier, the military calls it "friendly fire." In our lives, conflict often erupts at the moments of greatest emotional and physical pain— times when we don't perform at our best. Researchers tell us that one of the leading causes of divorce in America is money problems. Many otherwise loving couples make bad financial decisions that lead them down a road of destruction.

Before they know it, those credit card-financed vacations and "I-have-to-look-cool" car payments have swamped their boats. Instead of locking arms and facing the problem together, each tends to blame the other. As the credit card collectors' phone calls increase exponentially, so do the accusations. At the very time the couple needs each other the most, they're blaming each other!

6. Picking the wrong time and place.

Little good is ever accomplished when we are tired, stressed, ill, or focused on too many other issues. Sometimes the best thing to do is schedule an exact time for discussing a conflict.

7. Failing to offer release valves.

Any organization will always have some conflict within the group. The genius of our democracy is that it allows for this reality. Americans are allowed to vote for their leaders. We're encouraged to write letters to the editor. We can protest and make our feelings known. We're not forced to tow the company line. Maybe this is, in part, why the great American experiment has lasted for more than 200 years—during which time scores of dictatorships around the globe have come and gone. When people are given avenues for redress, conflict will often evaporate.

8. Believing we must agree on everything.

It will not come as news to our friends that Bonnie and I do not always agree. As a matter of fact, there are some issues on which we remain in separate camps—even after thirty-four years of marriage. (Bon has always been charitable enough to allow me to be wrong.) If our relationship required us to agree on every point, it would be boring—and probably long over. I respect Bonnie, and she respects me. That respect (and belief that we're both pulling in the same general direction) allows us both to flourish and be ourselves.

But there were a lot of years in our marriage when this wasn't the case. It was either my way or the highway. This, to say the least, diminished our love for each other. As I've grown and matured, I'm amazed to see the depth and perspective Bon brings to our relationship. So many times I would stand at the front door of a problem, trying to break it down to get in. All the while, Bonnie was quietly walking to the back of the same house, finding an unlocked door, and opening the front door for me from the inside!

9. Forcing the point.

Proving one person right and the other wrong may be okay in a courtroom, but it accomplishes little when it comes to conflict resolution. Actually, leaving one party embarrassed and unprotected can do more harm than good. It might incite the person to act like a cornered animal, which can lead to volatile and unnecessary situations. Phrases like "win the battle and lose the war" come to mind.

What the Pros Know

Through the years, I've listened and learned from some wise people. I've also had my share of experiences trying to find common ground with, and for, people with different agendas. There seems to be a similar set of values among those who seek and find peaceful solutions. Let's take a look at the skill sets that define these people.

1. They pray.

I would be dishonest here not to share my heart. As a Christian, I approach my circumstances and the events of my life from a Christian worldview. Accordingly, I'm deeply committed to prayer. Why? Because some of the worst mistakes of my life have been made in a prayer vacuum. Some of the best results of my life have happened when I spent serious time on my knees before the event occurred. So it will come as no surprise when I tell you that I believe one is not serving himself or herself well (or those with whom he or she is dealing) without first spending serious time with God. Recently, I was asked to lead a conflict resolution discussion. A lot was on the line. If this situation worsened, much could be jeopardized, including family relationships, economic security, and the health of an entire organization's leadership. Although I did the typical things needed to prepare for the meeting, the most valuable time I spent was before God asking for his presence, direction, and wisdom.

2. They care.

Arguably the most basic common denominator among successful conflict resolution specialists is that they care about the welfare of others. First and foremost, they tend to be kind, gentle, and thoughtful. One of the most temperate, caring people I know is Larry Bridgesmith. His ability to step into a highly charged situation and infuse a sense of calm has amazed me for years. Though he was a partner at a major law firm, Larry left that career to return to academia. Today, he serves as executive director for the Institute of Conflict Management at Lipscomb University.

3. They love "deal making."

In another world, most conflict resolution specialists could be great salesmen because they love to see a meeting of the minds where everyone walks away better for the experience. Note, I didn't say that everyone is necessarily happy. But they work toward an agreeable atmosphere where both parties leave with their dignity intact.

4. They are articulate.

People who excel at conflict resolution have an effective command of the English language. They understand that words mean things. Often conflict resolution boils down to using precise language and understanding the nuances of different words. Many conflicts really aren't conflicts. Both sides generally agree. They share similar goals. But they are using different words. Sometimes it comes down to semantics. Resolving a dispute is often a matter of regrouping a set of words and rephrasing what you are trying to communicate.

5. They listen.

Although I touched on this earlier in the chapter, it bears repeating: Effective conflict resolvers are good listeners—they make it a point to hear what is being said. As we discussed earlier in the chapter, most people in failed relationships can trace their difficulties to non-listeners who would vow that, in fact, they are great listeners. Much of the conflict I have experienced could have been avoided if I had simply been willing to shut up and listen to the other person. Despite my best efforts to camouflage the truth, when I don't listen it's generally not because I'm too busy or urgently needed elsewhere. More often than not, I fail to listen for one of two reasons: I'm arrogant enough to believe I know more than the other person, or I simply don't care enough about that person to pay attention. Hard to admit but true!

To resolve conflict, you need to understand what's going on. This means it's wiser to do more listening than talking. I've noticed that most successful people are good listeners. Simply put, they are good with their ears. They know that often the three most important things they can do are listen, listen, and listen.

6. They are open to new ideas and unexplored pathways.

Open minds trump open mouths about 90 percent of the time. I still remember a meeting I participated in several years ago. It involved the staff of a sizable metropolitan church. All the players were godly, loving people. But, like every other life-form that sucks air, these people were not perfect.

As the meeting progressed, a dispute began to grow between the senior minister and a staff minister. The staffer simply refused to open his mind to the possibility of doing something differently than it had been done in the past.

Finally, out of frustration, the senior minister asked, "What if I showed you in the Bible that this is a perfectly fine thing for us to do? Would that change your mind?"

Without missing a beat, the staff minister replied, "Nope!"

Whew! Where do you go from there? It's been said before: Sin can be forgiven; stupid is forever!

This relates to the point I made earlier about how small-mindedness is at the epicenter of many needless disputes. There is no place for mediocrity here. If we are seriously going to reflect Jesus, it requires a passion for excellence. It means that we must become creative thinkers—people who refuse to stay inside the box. After all, is God the Great Creator? And, if we are his children, isn't it logical to expect us to reflect his traits? Why not look at things from different directions? Why not explore untried options? Why be afraid of doing something different?

On the next page is a visual illustration of what I'm discussing. This is a little trick that some readers may have already seen, but it still illustrates the point that there is always a solution—provided we are willing to "get out of the boxes" of our preconceived notions, prejudices, and previous practices.

Here's the challenge: Connect all nine of the dots on the next page using only four straight lines. In case you can't figure out how to do it, turn to the last page of this chapter to see what some nontraditional thinking can accomplish.

7. They know they are not the message.

If you're not one of the parties in the conflict, remember: It's not about you! You're the facilitator—not a participator. Rarely do the fans in the stands notice the refs in a pro football game. That is, unless one of them makes a dumb call or trips over a player. Then they notice him—and it's for all the wrong reasons. The same is true with conflict resolution. You cannot afford to become the message. Leave your baggage at home. Effective conflict resolution specialists are simply good conduits who help the two sides hear what the other is saying—not always with words but with their heart.

This is why the ability to use nuanced language is critical. When one party begins to get off track and the veins on the side of his neck start to bulge, that's when good conflict resolution specialists will step in. They may need to rephrase the comment. For instance, they might say, "Rob, maybe instead of 'lazy,' what you meant to communicate to Josh is that he tends to produce fewer widgets during his shift than

9 DOTS PUZZLE

Connect all nine dots using only four straight lines.

Turn to the end of the chapter for the answer

the other employees do—right?" Or they may need to change the pace by suggesting a coffee break. Or if the situation is getting unduly heated, they may suggest adjourning the meeting and rescheduling a follow-up meeting when, presumably, tempers will have cooled. I think of this as emotional

> **Your goal:** Facilitate what two parties want to communicate in a way that won't further aggravate, exasperate, or frustrate the situation.

rebooting. Conflict resolvers are not the solution—they are just the catalyst for the solution. As a general rule, the less of you there is, the better.

8. They avoid "stinkin' thinkin.'"

Author and motivational speaker Zig Ziglar was the first person I heard use this phrase back in the 1970s, but it has stuck with me ever since. Many of life's problems result from one form or another of "stinkin' thinkin.'" As a person attempting to help resolve a conflict, it's your job to set the ground rules early. Help both sides understand that there is validity in each person's views. Neither should begin conflict resolution expecting to leave with a single winner and a single loser. Winner versus loser thinking sets both sides up for failure. The apostle Paul had to remind the warring factions in the early Corinthian church that when Christians sue each other, both sides lose. (1 Corinthians 6)

Note that in all of this conversation, I'm deliberately avoiding the use of the word "religion." Religion, for religion's sake, doesn't fix problems. And, no, I'm not disrespecting Christianity or suggesting it isn't a religion. It is. As a matter of fact, Christianity is the only perfect religion there is. But I reassert the truth: Religion doesn't fix problems! If it did, the Middle East would be the most peaceful place in the world. Religion brought us 9-11! Religion doesn't stop litigation. I'm told that Salt Lake City, the center of Mormonism, has as much litigation per capita as any other city in the country. The only permanent solution to a problem between people or human institutions is to create a mutually satisfying relationship between them.

Do you remember what Jesus taught about this in Matthew 22:33 (ff)? Loosely paraphrased, when crowds asked Jesus what it took to be right before God, he essentially said, "Are you serious? Do you really want to know? Okay, I'll tell you. If you really want to be right with God, it's going to take two things: First, learn to love God with everything you have inside—from the DNA out. And, secondly, learn to love other people the way you already love yourself."

Accordingly, if a conflict is to be resolved, the goal must be to establish a beachhead of relationship—an environment from which both parties come to see the situation from the perspective of the other. They have a clear goal, and that goal is to unite. Do you remember Jesus' prayer in the garden on the night he was to be murdered? In John 17:21-23, his prayer was:

"The goal is for all of them to become one heart and mind—Just as you, Father, are in me and I in you, so they might be one heart and mind with us. Then the world might believe that you, in fact, sent me. The same glory you gave me, I gave them, so they'll be as unified and together as we are—I in them and you in me. Then they'll be mature in this oneness, and give the godless world evidence that you've sent me and loved them in the same way you've loved me." (The Message)

Notice the reason why Jesus asked God to bring unity. It was so mankind could clearly see that he was sent by the father. It was so the outside world would be able to glimpse the fingerprint of God.

Paul reminded the Corinthians that, at its very core, Christianity is "a ministry of reconciliation." (2 Corinthians 5:18) What a church to bring that message to! The Corinthian church was overwhelmingly divided. Members argued over women's roles, fought over how to observe the Lord's Supper, and debated worship styles. In general, this was not a happy-clappy church. Yet Paul saw their potential. He exerted the effort. He dealt with people where they were and believed that conflict could lead to consensus.

Time-Tested Strategies

As we wrap up this chapter, I want to share three strategies to help you avoid or reduce the conflicts that life brings. Most of life's lost relationships are the product of not having a predetermined strategy. Without these strategies, life is spent constantly reacting to external stimuli. That's bad! But with strategies already in place before a crisis arises, you can be proactive. The net result is less conflict—and better relations. Bulls in the china shop don't enhance the value of the inventory. Finesse is an underappreciated life skill. The person who plans (or strategizes) is usually the one who comes home with the prize.

Let me share three strategies you may find helpful. The first one we'll explore is the "3 D's of Conflict Avoidance." Then, not to carry the alphabet soup thing too far, I will show you the "5 C's of Conflict Resolution." Finally and most importantly, we will look what I call "The Jesus Approach."

The "3 D's" of Conflict Avoidance

Jesus encourages us to be "peacemakers." Although I've frequently failed in my efforts, it has always seemed appropriate for me to strive for peaceful relations with others. So, that means a divisive conflict that never happens is better than one that must be resolved. One foundational strategy that has been time-tested is what I call the "3 D's of Conflict Avoidance."

Earlier this week, I got a call from Greg, a twenty-eight-year-old youth minister at a large church. I have known Greg all his life. He accepted Jesus at the age of eight. He has always loved Jesus and has a passion for ministry. Greg is well educated and has extremely good people skills. However, his call this week wasn't a pleasant one.

Greg told me that he was depressed and discouraged. As a matter of fact, he would happily leave the ministry and live on an island all alone. "What," I asked, "is wrong?"

Greg began to tell me a story that is far too typical in ministry. (Note: This goes a long way in explaining why so many of our best and brightest become cynical, apathetic, or simply leave the ministry altogether.) During Wednesday evening classes, Greg had been bombarded by one disgruntled person after another. People who should have supported him didn't. And mature Christians who should have been problem solvers were the problems. People with conflicting views were pulling at Greg—both parties were unhappy and expecting him to "fix" their problems.

As our phone call evolved into a two-hour long counseling session, I decided to acquaint Greg with my 3 D's of Conflict Avoidance.

1. Defer

Greg had told me about a couple who had interrupted his work with a group of kids to pull him aside and complain about a situation. Caught off guard and unprepared, it had left him flustered and confused. I explained to Greg the importance of deferring. I told him he needed to establish boundaries—and refuse to allow inconsiderate people to cross them.

I suggested that the next time something of that sort occurred, he should simply say, "Bill and Pam, I appreciate your interest in this matter. But I'm presently involved with these children. Why don't you call me tomorrow morning between 10 and 11, and we'll schedule a meeting to discuss your concerns in-depth?"

This would have served Greg in several ways. First, most people are lazy. They like to complain, but when asked to do something productive, they usually don't. Odds are Greg would never get that phone call because Bill and Pam would have already forgotten the issue or gone on to annoy someone else. Second, even if they do call to set the appointment, Greg will be prepared to give it his full attention and not simply agree to something he may later regret. Additionally, if he deems it wise, he could ask another minister or a church elder to attend the meeting with him. Also, this meeting will be on his "turf." Strategically speaking, there's a lot to be said for having the meeting in the minister's office instead of the hallway.

2. Deflect

Far too many people, especially those of you who tend to be in ministry or caregiving, find it hard not to shoulder everyone else's problems. Obviously, God tells us to *"...weep with those who weep."* (Romans 12:15, NASB). But the point here isn't to become a toxic waste dump for everyone who has a complaint.

There is a good and appropriate time not to get involved. For instance, part of what Greg was dealing with were different parties who were upset with the behavior of the other. My suggestion to Greg was to deflect. In other words, instead of attempting to be a conduit (and making enemies on both sides in the process), why not bounce the problem back to the troublemakers? What Greg could do was simply say to each party, "That's an interesting concern you have. Why don't you speak directly to Connie about it?"

This way he would encourage two Christians to do as Jesus taught and talk directly with one another. In the process, he could avoid the stress of being put in a lose/lose situation. Another way of deflecting involves "passing the buck." Now before you get mad at me for even suggesting this tactic, think about it. Aren't there times when it is better to "pass the buck?"

In the military, there are lots of decisions a colonel cannot make because they are above his pay grade. So, what does he do? Doesn't he pass the decision up the line to the general? It was exactly the same for Greg. Some of the junk he was dealing with wasn't under his authority. It would have been totally fine for him to say, "This isn't my decision. We really need to get our shepherds involved."

3. Delegate

One of the toughest things I ever had to learn in the business world was to delegate. I'm not sure why. Maybe it was ego—I thought I could do things better myself. Maybe it was fear—I thought anyone else would fail. But because of this flaw I was miserable until I changed some things. My final suggestion to Greg was to focus on delegating. When someone approaches him with a complaint about how something is, or isn't, being done, why not say, "That's an interesting idea. Why don't you develop an attack plan? Then, after we review it, you can run with it?"

This way, Greg has no downside. In most cases, as I mentioned before, people are lazy, and they won't follow through. But, in the event they do, great! Now they're personally involved and invested—and Greg doesn't have more work on his plate!

Postscript: Greg called me back a day or two later to say how excited he was. He had already implemented part of the 3 D's of Conflict Avoidance, and he told me it was helping. But, as I had cautioned him already, he was also realizing this is a learned skill. It will become effective and successful only with lots of practice.

The "5 C's" of Conflict Resolution

To deal with conflict, we must understand its different forms. More importantly, we must choose our battles very carefully.

A few days ago, I was counseling a children's minister at a church in a Southeastern state. She was terribly upset because a program in which she had invested a lot of time and energy was being re-thought. She was hurt and angry. Though this young woman happened to be in the ministry, her disillusionment was not unlike that experienced by many of us in ministry, business, or any other organizational work.

In reality, both sides of the debate had valid points. Those who were unhappy included good-hearted people who were concerned about the benefit the program would have for their children. On the other side were the majority of parents who wanted to go forward with the program. The church's leaders were caught in the middle, trying to keep everybody happy. The children's minister felt unsupported by the leaders. From her vantage, they were being weak—folding like a cheap card table. She began our conversation by saying, "I'm tired of all the politics."

The truth was, (she began to realize), there were no bad people here. Everyone was doing what seemed right. The trouble was a good program was about to be harmed, and the minister was frustrated. I've long believed that the two greatest enemies to a productive, enjoyable life are apathy and cynicism. That's why it is important for leaders to insulate and mentor young employees, ministers, and salespeople.

The important thing to remember when a conflict develops is: Your response generally determines how the conflict will end. This is where you may find these "5 C's of Conflict Resolution" helpful. While I've stylized these five points, the foundation for the remaining material in this chapter borrows heavily from Dr. Randy Lowry. In his work as an attorney and now as the president of Lipscomb University, this good man has spent much of his professional life dealing with and teaching others the techniques of effective conflict resolution. I thank Lipscomb University for its training and permission to share some of these insights. Much of what I

> For those of you interested in in-depth training in conflict resolution, visit **www.icm.lipscomb.edu.**

have learned and share with you in this chapter is directly from, or an adaptation of, the university's Institute for Conflict Management.

1. Circumvent

Many conflicts don't have to happen in the first place. Some occur between our ears. Others are the product of too much personal investment or a failure to be open to other options. We can avoid many of life's struggles by just walking away. That was the case with the conflict I just shared with you. Instead of a confrontation, the minister could have reasoned, "These are all good-hearted people with different ideas. The fact is, while I have a preference, either approach will bless this church's children. My shepherds aren't being wishy-washy—they are simply trying to keep the peace. Even if all my work is scuttled in preference of another approach, we're all on the same team here. This is no reflection on me. They aren't rejecting me—they are simply rethinking the approach we've selected. And, besides, I am being paid to work at the pleasure of these shepherds—it's their right to change their minds. They are dealing with all sorts of issues and personalities—only a small percentage of which I'm aware. This is a good time for me to keep my powder dry and simply promote whichever plan is adopted. Because one day there may come a 'battle' I must win. Besides, there is really no downside here. If this different approach works—great! If not, people will remember that I championed the other option. My credibility will be higher the next time something of this sort occurs."

Circumvention/avoidance is founded on biblical precedent. Can you recall an instance when Jesus used circumvention to avoid a problem? How about when a group of Jewish fans tried to make him their king? Jesus could have accepted. But that would have been wrong. He hadn't come to be an earthly king. He could have lectured the crowd on how terribly wrong their theology was. But what did he do? According to John 6, he did nothing. That's right. Jesus, the flawless Son of God, did nothing. He circumvented the situation by slipping through the crowd and walking away.

2. Be Cordial

Sometimes the best thing to do in a conflictive situation is to be cordial. Please don't misinterpret what I'm saying here by suggesting that I'm recommending we prostitute our convictions merely for the sake of maintaining peace. Certainly there are times when we must stand and be counted—even if that causes conflict. But the question is: when? Maybe the answer comes only with honest self-examination. Often what I claim is a position built on principle is actually, in part, based on my own pride, prejudice, and personal preference. There are times when it's simply best to go along to get along. Sorry if that doesn't sound as idealistic as you would wish—but my nearly 60 years of living have taught me that it's true.

Again let's ask, "Did Jesus ever do that?" As a matter of fact, I believe he did. Do you remember the story in John 10:22 when Jesus went to the Jewish Feast of Dedication? (This is what has come to be known as the annual celebration of Hanukkah.) Now why would I bolster my point with this event in the life of Jesus? Because God never instituted the Feast of Dedication. As a matter of fact, you can search the Torah (the first five Old Testament books, which contain the laws and ordinances God gave his people), and you'll never find the Feast of Dedication mentioned. This was a celebration of human origin. Yet, when invited, we don't see Jesus condemning those who were going, and it seems fairly evident from the passage that Jesus went, too!

Wow! What does that do to some who feel it is their God-ordained job to criticize other Christians who worship God in different ways? What about those who are critical of Christians who celebrate December 25th as the birthday of Jesus or Easter as the day he arose? If you don't believe me, check out Romans 14. Paul builds a solid case that it's wrong for one Christian to have the audacity to tell another that he or she should (or shouldn't) hold one day above another to celebrate God.

3. Be Competitive

A third option during conflict is to become competitive, even combative. As humans, this is too frequently our first response. In most cases, becoming competitive costs more than it delivers. But there are times when this is the right thing to do. Again, Jesus exemplified this behavior on several occasions during his ministry. Think of the times he stared down hypocritical Pharisees and challenged their fundamental, core belief systems. He had some brusque words even for his own disciples, when they tried to deny the children access to the Savior. Remember the scene in the temple with the money changers? In John 2, we read about an angry Jesus who actually made a whip and started flipping tables over as he chased the money changers from the temple. Granted, there have been passive Christians through the ages who have suggested that the whip was merely to run the animals from their stalls. Yeah, right. I suspect that if Jesus didn't hit those money changers with his homemade whip—it wasn't because he wasn't trying! There are times when it's appropriate (and required) for Christians to grow a spine—and make a clear, tough stand.

4. Compromise

This is what many of us consider the goal of conflict. We have been conditioned to think that if we can just achieve a minimal degree of mutual unhappiness—all will be well! Granted, there are times when compromise may be the best we can accomplish. And, in truth, a half a loaf is better than none. But healthy organizations are those that hesitate to settle for second best. Their reasoning: What if there is a better way?

5. Find Consensus

This is the ultimate—the gold standard. What if both sides in a conflict could walk away with a win? What if we could use the principles I've shared in this chapter to set the highest goal of all-consensus? Wouldn't that make Satan's worst nightmares come true? As an example of how effective conflict resolution can lead to true consensus, let me share the modern-day parable.

The Story of Sister Gladys and the Teenagers

Inspired by an illustration I heard Lipscomb's Dr. Lowry share with an audience, let me tell you the story of ninety-year-old Sister Gladys and the teenagers.

Sister Gladys had been a Christian since she was baptized in 1933 at the church her parents had started in their home. Through the years, she had poured herself into this sweet church. When members constructed a building, Gladys helped paint the walls. As she grew into young adulthood, she taught classes, visited the sick, and always made food for families in need. This was the church in which she was married.

As a widow in more recent years, Gladys was still the first to arrive and the last to leave most Sundays, and she appreciated Randal Franklin's sermons. To her delight, the church had recently been enjoying a real growth spurt. Dozens of college students had found this little out-of-the-way congregation. They were breathing new life and bringing lots of their friends into what had become a dying church. Someone was accepting Jesus almost every week.

So, you can appreciate the surprise the minister felt the morning Sister Gladys told him, "Brother Franklin, I believe I will begin attending services at another church next week."

"Why, what in the world for?" the stunned preacher asked. "Is something wrong?"

"Yes, there is. Ever since those college students starting coming, everything has changed," she complained. "I'm glad they're here, but things aren't like they used to be."

"What have we changed?" Randal quizzed.

"We don't sing any of the old songs anymore. All they sing are those new songs the kids like. They haven't led 'The Old Rugged Cross' in twelve weeks—I've counted!"

Fortunately, this wasn't new territory for the minister. Calmly he asked, "Would you mind if we get together this afternoon with some of the teens and talk this over?" Sister Gladys agreed that would be fine.

Later that afternoon, Sister Gladys, the minister, and about a half dozen of the students sat down together in one of the classrooms. Randal began with a prayer asking that God's Spirit be the unseen host as they visited.

Then he began by saying, "The reason I invited you to be here is because I love and respect all of you. Sister Gladys has been a faithful Christian for many years and has blessed hundreds of people in this community with her selfless work. You college students have been a welcome breath of fresh air. You are reaching people for Jesus and blessing the entire congregation. But there is a concern. Those of you with the college group have brought us a lot of new songs. We know you enjoy singing them. But Sister Gladys has been troubled that she no longer hears the songs she is familiar with. Sister, why don't you tell the college students how you feel about this?"

"Well," she began slowly, "I don't intend to hurt anyone's feelings, but these days it feels like a different church to me. I can't understand the words to the new songs. They are all so different—it confuses me. Besides, what you young people don't know is this is the very church my family began. I grew up singing all the great old songs in the hymnbook as we struggled through the Depression. As a matter of fact, they sang 'The Old Rugged Cross' on the day I was baptized."

Without another word from Randal, the college students locked eyes around the table. Finally, with tempered words, one young man spoke for the group, "Sister Gladys, we're sorry. We can see that you feel invaded. We all were suddenly here, and without meaning to, we sort of took over. That was never our intention. As you were speaking, I turned to 'The Old Rugged Cross' in the songbook."

He read the lyrics of the iconic song to the group. One by one, as the timeless words sunk in, the young people realized the timelessness (and timeliness) of the message.

"Wow," said the youngest girl in the room, "I never knew there were songs like that!"

The young man continued, "Sister Gladys, the main reason we sing the new songs is because they seem to 'speak' to our unsaved friends. And it's our goal to bring as many of them to Jesus as we can. But, now that we understand your concern, we'll be happy to stop singing our songs if that will bless you."

By this point, Sister Gladys' face was moist with tears. After a long silence, she spoke again, "I, too, am most sorry. Of all the people in the room, I'm the one who should have understood this best. You are using these new songs to reach your friends much like my family supplied vegetables from our garden to witness for Jesus when I was a child. Please forgive my narrow-mindedness. And, please, keep singing those songs!"

Today, that little church isn't so little. And you can be sure that, every Sunday morning, there will be a beautiful blend of old and new songs as the Christians praise God—by loving others. That, my dear friend, is conflict resolution by consensus. It happens only when there is true relation to others.

The Jesus Approach: A Different Paradigm

Dr. Lowry has also suggested that it's possible we may have misunderstood Jesus' teaching in Matthew 18. Maybe instead of using this passage as an instruction manual to show one Christian how to disfellowship another, could it be that Jesus was actually doing just the opposite? Could he be laying out a paradigm for personal reconciliation here? Maybe this is the foundation of effective conflict resolution.

"If your brother sins against you, go and show him his fault, just between the two of you. If he listens to you, you have won your brother over. But if he will not listen, take one or two others along, so that 'every matter may be established by the testimony of two or three witnesses.' If he refuses to listen to them, tell it to the church; and if he refuses to listen even to the church, treat him as you would a pagan or a tax collector." (Matthew 18:15-17, NASB)

Let's dissect this strategy and talk about how it might look in today's church. If there's a problem, Jesus tells the offended individual to deal with it: *"Go and show him his fault …"* Notice that Jesus didn't say to ignore or gloss over a problem. Much conflict could be avoided if we would simply be honest and up front in the early stages, but we resist this. It's not comfortable to talk about negative things—at least directly to the person involved. So we begin a slow burn. We avoid that person. We don't like to share the same space. Eventually, we begin to justify our behavior by building a case for it. This is when the gossip begins. We don't really mean to. But it's just easier to let off steam by sniping and talking about (instead of to) another person.

Conflict resolution requires that we get out of the sandbox and step into the grown-up world. We must leave our comfort zone and get involved. A final note: Jesus said to go privately, *"…just between the two of you."* Our goal isn't to put a notch on our belt or a mounted head on our wall. We shouldn't attempt to aggrandize ourselves. Our goal is to bring resolution and reunion of spirit—or as Jesus put it, to conclude by having *"won our brother over."* If that fails, Jesus says, *"But if he will not listen, take one or two others along, so that 'every matter may be established by the testimony of two or three witnesses.'"*

If our private meeting is not successful, Jesus tells us to include one or two others in the conversation. This is distinctly different from sharing it with all our buddies. Involving a couple of spiritually focused Christians (who know how to keep a secret) is key here.

I make a point of this because I have noticed that "good" Christians have their own way of gossiping. They don't actually "talk" about someone else. They ask the whole class to "pray for Jason who is struggling with his wife and an embezzlement issue at work." Or, as any self-respecting Christian knows, if you're going to gossip outright, it's vital to begin the conversation with the Southern phrase, "Bless their hearts." As in, "Poor Lauren, bless her heart, she just can't seem to stop that late-night running around. It really is causing problems between her and Ronnie—bless their hearts."

Then, proper etiquette requires that you gently cross your hands in your lap and look grief-stricken to have had to reveal such a confidence. With enough practice, you can become most convincing using this little technique.

If all else fails, Jesus says to use the power of community. *"... If he refuses to listen to them, tell it to the church ..."* Finally, with other options running out, it's time to take it before the entire church. Note: With this comment, Jesus is assuming there actually is community. In his mind, community was a precious relationship that no one would want to lose.

Sadly, this doesn't play well in today's consumer-oriented society that puts a high premium on rugged individualism. Many of today's institutions (whether we think about churches, families, or businesses) are little more than loose configurations of people with varied agendas who interconnect occasionally. Maybe this explains the phenomenon I call "church divorce." In far too many cases when people get upset about something in their home church, they simply leave (because there's really no community to break) and move to another church. Problems remain unresolved, and ill will festers.

Finally, with all other options exhausted, Jesus says, "... and if he refuses to listen even to the church, treat him as you would a pagan or a tax collector." Now, I'll bet I know what some of you are thinking. You're thinking what I used to think, "There, that'll teach that hard-hearted so-and-so a lesson!" Right?

Maybe, but maybe not. This might be a good time to step back and ask the question, "Exactly how did Jesus treat pagans and tax collectors?" Didn't he deal which such people on two levels—based on their individual situations and the openness of their hearts?

Sadly, there were times when Jesus finally gave unrepentant sinners over to their misdeeds. When it's a "brother" who is living in open sin, there comes a time when the brother-to-brother relationship is no longer an option. But this doesn't mean the compassion must stop. When the rich young ruler rejected Jesus, the ruler did the walking away. Jesus never moved. He was there any time the materialistic yuppie wanted to come back. Jesus was always available for relationship—but he refused to compromise his core principles.

In my experience, conflicts are never resolved by the righteous simply accepting evil as though it doesn't exist. If, in fact, evil is evil, ultimately it can never be the source of lasting life, healing, and joy.

Andrew, a minister friend, recently told me about a teenage boy he had worked with several years ago at another church. This young guy made it his job to disrupt the whole youth group. He was in ongoing sin with drugs and alcohol. Nothing Andrew did seemed to get him refocused.

Finally, when he caught him trying to sell pornography to other kids in the youth group, Andrew had to put his foot down. The damage this kid was doing to the rest of the group was too great to ignore. Andrew decided to confront the situation. He met with the boy and his parents. He told the teen that he was welcome to continue attending church and sitting in the pew with his parents, but he could no longer attend the youth activities. I wish I could tell you that the boy immediately repented and mended his ways. But it didn't work that way. In fact things got even worse, and he fell into even deeper sin. Several years later, however, Andrew got a call from the young man. He was calling to apologize and tell Andrew he had come back to the Lord. The seed Andrew had planted years earlier had sprouted!

Jesus aggressively chased after pagans and tax collectors. Why else would he tell the parable about the father (God) running headlong to welcome his sinful son (us) home? (Luke 15:20) Or why select a woman of Mary Magdalene's probable pedigree to be among his closest friends? What about Zaccheus? There he was in a tree, looking over the heads of the crowd, to get a glimpse of Jesus. (I've long suspected that this short, Jewish tax collector knew how hated he was, and that mingling with the crowd would be a good way to get elbowed black and blue!) Yet, Jesus stopped the whole procession and took time to "do lunch" at the little guy's house. In the process, he won Zaccheus' heart. Speaking of tax collectors, wasn't one of Jesus' own apostles a tax collector named Matthew?

Actually, Peter emphasizes Jesus' point in this passage above, when in verse 21, he asks, *"Lord, how often shall my brother sin against me and I forgive him?"* Jesus effectively goes on to tell Peter he should never be unwilling to forgive. Curiously, this passage says nothing about withholding our forgiveness until the sinner asks for forgiveness. Apparently, Jesus wants his followers to simply have forgiving hearts—ready for reconciliation at a moment's notice.

Does This Stuff Work All the Time?

The short answer is no. But these principles do work some of the time. I could fill a book with stories of times when I have not performed at my best. As I've admitted, I don't always practice what I preach. Let me share an incident that just occurred where I did my best to resolve a conflict—and failed. As I write this, I'm at 26,000 feet in the air returning to Nashville on an early morning flight from a *No Debt No Sweat! Seminar* we just concluded in Ohio. The old phrase "physician, heal thyself'" occurs to me. Though I have now presented this seminar more than 350 times nationwide and abroad, I have rarely done it in a more unsettling situation. While the host organization was excited to have me come, I learned several months ago that there was one high-profile individual who wasn't a bit happy about it. I believe he felt threatened by me and somewhat competitive.

To give a little context, in the *NDNS! Seminar*, I teach a godly approach to money management. This particular gentleman was an accountant and financial products salesman who was already teaching similar material using another curriculum.

The organization's leaders had warned me about the situation and asked me to call this man to try and build a bond prior to the seminar. When I called, he was cordial but not particularly friendly. He suggested that my material wasn't necessary and went on to say that he disagreed with my position on some issues. Being familiar with the curriculum he was teaching, I knew one of our points of difference was on the topic of credit cards. He believed people should not have credit cards at all. While I'm no fan of credit cards, I don't prohibit their use. I regularly refer to them as "monsters in our pockets." But to blame credit cards for our bad spending habits is like blaming Burger King because I eat too much—and come out looking like a Whopper!

When I arrived to begin the seminar, the directors and I met to discuss the possibility of using the *NDNS! Money Boot Camp*—our follow-up study. But as I learned how territorial this man was, it became evident to me that there was more to be lost than gained by adopting our curriculum. Besides, the curriculum he was already using is a good study that has helped thousands of people. So I recommended that we not even offer the *NDNS! Money Boot Camp* as an option. Instead, I suggested that they recommend that attendees use the curriculum the accountant supported.

In the course of those two days, I determined to do everything within my control to make a friend of this gentleman. On at least a half dozen occasions, I made it a point to get into close proximity, hoping he would speak to me. He didn't. More than five times during the seminar I recommended him and his curriculum to the audience. He never thanked me.

Finally, on the second night just before the last session, I approached him. "Rex," (not his real name) I said, "we need to get to know each other and visit after this is over."

"Well, I don't know if I can hang around much longer since I have to be up at four in the morning," came his response.

Not to be deterred, I said, "Well I have an early flight, too. But I think we need to talk."

Since I knew he wanted to promote his follow-up study, I said, "Why don't you come up and tell the audience about your program at the end of the session?"

Actually, I had three goals with this. First, I wanted the people to know about it. Second, I wanted to offer him a warm fuzzy. But, also, I figured this was the best way to keep him from leaving early. At the end of the seminar, I made another positive comment about Rex and his program and then invited the audience to bring him up with their applause.

I wish I could tell you that we ended the night as best friends but that would be a stretch. As a matter of fact, he never approached me at all. So after the crowd had begun to thin out, I approached him. We had a hospitable conversation. He was warm and communicative. When a couple of people from the audience came up for advice, I deferred to him. As he answered their questions, I was able to agree with him in front of his peers.

We ended the evening on a friendly level. And, more importantly, I left knowing I had done everything in my power to follow the admonition, *"If possible, so far as depends on you, be at peace with all men."* (Romans 12:18, NASB)

Turning the Other Cheek

Throughout this chapter I've alluded to it, but thus far, I haven't said it in so many words. For some readers, I suppose it has been conspicuously absent. So before we conclude, let's remember that many cases of conflict can be resolved by simply applying Jesus' directive to "turn the other cheek."

"Oh, I've heard that since I was a kid," you may object. "I bought this book to get some new ideas."

Like it or not, Jesus' advice is flawless. It's easy to comprehend, but not easy to apply. Simple, yet profound. So why do most of us resist it? Could it be because from the world's perspective, it doesn't promise us a "win"? Yet I've noticed something curious about the people who apply this simple teaching as a lifestyle: They live peaceful, joyful lives.

Recently, I had lunch with a group of church leaders. One of them said, "I suppose you've heard that we had some troubles in the church a year or two ago. Actually, we lost about 20 families."

As I listened to his story, I was impressed by how kind he and the other leaders seemed to be. The dispute that caused the problem wasn't even of any real consequence, but it was splitting a church. It was damaging the body of Christ. It was diverting the church's attention from important things like sharing Jesus with lost people. How did these leaders resolve this problem and restore peace? They did something totally unexpected—something that, humanly speaking, was ridiculous. They turned the other cheek.

My friend told me, "It occurred to us that we had a building fund of about $50,000. So we met—both sides."

There was stress in the air. Tension ran high, until these good shepherds said, "Folks, we understand that you disagree with the direction we are taking in this matter. And we understand that you cannot continue to worship with us in good conscience. Another church could really bless this community. Why don't you start one with our blessings? And we'll give you the $50,000 in our building fund to get you started."

There was an immediate, almost palpable change in the room, my friend said. People calmed down. The tension melted away. It was a bad day for the devil!

When we begin to apply the Jesus Paradigm of Conflict Resolution, amazing things happen. People with the most divergent backgrounds and viewpoints can find common ground. Skin color doesn't matter. Black and white (and blue, pink and polka-dotted) Christians learn to love each other. Rich Christians are accepted by (and accepting of) poorer Christians. People in Armani outfits sit next to orange-haired skateboarders in cutoffs.

As we focus more on "being Jesus," we draw closer and closer to Jesus. And as different people with different ideas and agendas draw closer to Jesus, they cannot help but become closer to each another.

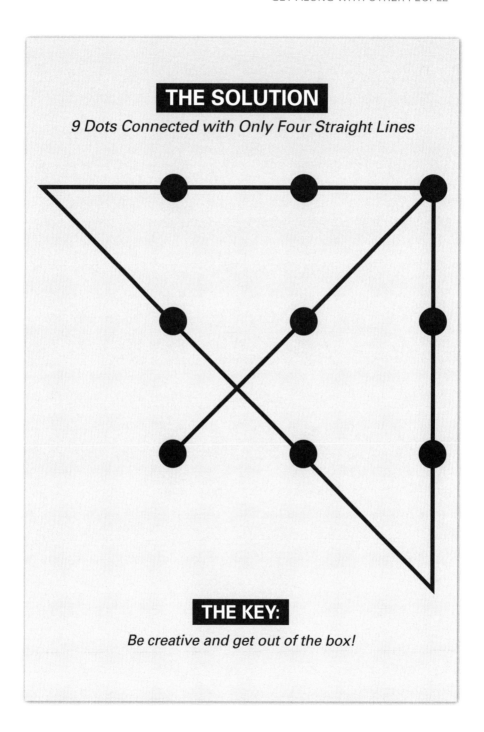

THE SOLUTION
9 Dots Connected with Only Four Straight Lines

THE KEY:
Be creative and get out of the box!

Get What You Both Want
The Art of Successful Negotiating

Have you ever heard someone (maybe yourself) say, "I hate buying cars because I don't like to haggle"? Or, "Just let them have their way, it's better than getting into a fuss"? How about, "Let's just all get along and do what they want"?

If so, you need the message of this chapter. As a matter of fact, this chapter is a first cousin to the previous chapter on conflict resolution. Conflict resolution and effective negotiating skills go hand in hand. Most conflict resolution takes a bucket-load of effective negotiation.

> "Most people spend more time and energy going around problems than in trying to solve them."
>
> –HENRY FORD

Many of us resist the idea of negotiating because it terrifies us, or we associate it with being a manipulator. But effective negotiation is the building block of any civilized society, peaceful home, or productive business. As to its importance in resolving difficult church-related situations—don't even get me started.

I know some of you are probably skeptics who aren't buying this. After all, didn't Jesus tell us to simply "turn the other cheek"? Sure, he did, but let's be careful here. While the purpose of this chapter isn't to analyze and dissect what Jesus was trying to teach in that passage, no competent biblical scholar would suggest he was saying that we should never attempt to find common ground with others. As we saw in the last chapter, there were clearly times when Jesus' prescription wasn't to run from a conflict.

In fact, he appreciated the importance of negotiation. In the Sermon on the Mount, he taught us to, *"Settle matters quickly with your adversary who is taking you to court. Do it while you are still with him on the way, or he may hand you over to the judge, and the judge may hand you over to the officer, and you may be thrown into prison. I tell you the truth; you will not get out until you have paid the last penny."* (Matthew 5:25, 26, NIV)

> "Listening, not imitation, may be the sincerest form of flattery."
> –DR. JOYCE BROTHERS

In one of my earlier books, I shared much of the message of this chapter. Several years have passed since writing that book. In the years since, my conviction has only increased that our culture (and Christians are certainly part of it) is woefully lacking in this most important skill set. All over the country, I visit businesses, schools, and churches where much good is not being accomplished because people simply do not understand the importance of negotiating a solution that will benefit both sides. It's far easier to simply get mad and retire to separate corners than to face, discuss, and negotiate a better existence.

Some people, however, are starting to hear me on this. Just this week a woman rushed up to me at a retreat and said, "Steve, I've been using your negotiating skills and they're saving me money. I just got a hotel to reduce its price!"

That made me feel great! People who study the art of negotiating report the same thing. In one study, more than 65 percent of respondents said they had tried to negotiate with sellers. And, among that group, more than 85 percent had successfully negotiated a better price. Sadly, more than 30 percent of the respondents said they had never even tried to negotiate for a lower price.

"Mr. Gorbachev, Tear Down This Wall!"

Decades before becoming our fortieth president, Ronald Reagan had preached his message on the strengths of the free enterprise system and the evils of communism. So it was no surprise to anyone that he brought those same convictions with him to the White House. On June 12, 1987, near the end of his presidency, Reagan confronted communism head on.

In hundreds of meetings and thousands of hours of negotiations, the governments of the United States and Soviet Union had begun to find common ground. Over the past few months, President Reagan built a true friendship with Soviet General Secretary Mikhail Gorbachev. To do this, the men had implemented some of the techniques I'm going to share with you in this chapter. They used these strategies to surmount what generations on both sides had grown to believe was an inevitable scenario: At best, a stagnant, unceasing cold war; at worst, nuclear annihilation.

As in all successful negotiations, there comes a moment of truth. In the sales world, it's called "closing the sale." This is when the salesman has to decide whether he's going to ask for the order—or simply be a professional visitor. In a much grander, more significant way, that's what happened on that June day in 1987.

Everything was on the line. Despite what an uninformed observer might think, what President Reagan said was not spoken rashly or expressed as a thoughtless, emotional outburst. The two nations had negotiated. Lower level diplomats had forged the basis of a lasting peace plan. But it was going to require one person to grow a spine and ask for the sale. It was calculated. It was planned. It was the right moment in time.

On that day in 1987, President Reagan had traveled to West Berlin, Germany. Standing in front of the Brandenburg Wall, he delivered a 2,703-word speech that was arguably as consequential as Abraham Lincoln's Gettysburg Address. This was, in many ways, the culmination of all Reagan had worked, prayed, and negotiated for throughout his political life. Though the speech was delivered to the free people of West Berlin, it was also audible to the enslaved people on the eastern, communist side of the wall.

After extolling the benefits of human dignity and freedom, President Reagan commended the Soviets on the healthy, productive steps they were taking toward this awakening.

Then he "closed the sale," culminating the negotiations with this statement, "General Secretary Gorbachev, if you seek peace, if you seek prosperity for the Soviet Union and Eastern Europe, if you seek liberalization: Come here to this gate! Mr. Gorbachev, open this gate! Mr. Gorbachev, tear down this wall!"

Many of Reagan's advisors were stunned and quaking in their Gucci's. But the president was undeterred. He had built the relationships. His people had negotiated terms. It was time to kindly, but candidly, speak his mind—and close the sale.

At their fourth and final summit in Moscow in 1988, the Russians treated Reagan like a celebrity. A journalist asked the president if he still viewed the Soviet Union as "the evil empire."

"No," Reagan responded, "I was speaking of another time, another era."

At Gorbachev's invitation, Reagan stepped up to the platform at Moscow State University and gave a speech on free markets.

At the end of this chapter, I'll return to this and share, as the late Paul Harvey used to say, "the rest of the story."

Hard Lessons to Learn

It's been about three decades since the Soviet Union imploded. In the years intervening, I've had several opportunities to visit ex-Soviet countries. It's always a thrill for me to visit in these peoples' homes, churches, and universities. I've had some unforgettable experiences sharing Jesus and teaching in their universities. These people are anxious to know what has made America great. They're intrigued by our marketing and sales techniques. They're fascinated by how Westerners do business.

But one common trait among many of these people is how distrusting they are. I suppose that's what happens when you're never sure which of your neighbors is working for the secret police. Seventy years of communism didn't inspire much in the way of trust or goodwill. Today, many great business and economic opportunities are missed because so many ex-Soviets fear someone is trying to take advantage of them. Former communists simply find it hard to believe anyone else cares about them. They really think everyone is out to get them.

This point was brought forcefully home to me a few years ago during a visit with Peter and Janis. Janis, an American, had been married to her ex-Soviet husband, Peter, for more than thirty years. They had been a missionary couple in Peter's homeland for more than twenty-five years. This dynamic duo had built a church in one of the Eastern Bloc's most important regions. Together, they advanced the cause of Christ.

But on this particular day, Janis was pouring her heart out. She shared a very real problem in her husband's life—one she didn't know how to help him with. She explained that because of his past, Peter had a difficult time trusting people.

"He simply doesn't understand that two people can negotiate an agreement in which both come out ahead," she said. "Peter believes that in every negotiation one person takes advantage of the other."

As I have reflected on that conversation, it has occurred to me that there was really nothing unique about Peter. This certainly isn't a trait exclusive to old ex-Soviets. It's very common. Most people have a warped idea of what negotiating is all about. As I mentioned earlier, many people hate the thought of negotiating with someone else. When the word comes up, it's typical to hear comments like,

> "I don't want to be confrontational."
> "I'm not a manipulative sort of a guy; after all, I'm a Christian."
> "I don't want to beat anything out of another person."
> "I can't lie with a straight face."

What Negotiating Is *Not*

If the thought of negotiating makes you queasy, rest easy, my friend. This chapter is for you! I want to show you the benefits and blessings of a great negotiation. But before we delve too deeply into this, I want you to understand four things good negotiating is not:

1. Good negotiations are not confrontational. A good negotiation can, and should, be handled with dignity and respect.

2. Good negotiations are not manipulative. Successful negotiating sets up a win-win atmosphere where both parties come out ahead. The goal should always be to help everyone involved get what he or she wants. This includes maintaining personal dignity!

3. Good negotiations are not dishonest. Good negotiators do not lie to gain the advantage; they tell the truth. There is no place for deceit in the negotiating process.

4. Good negotiations are not emotionally painful. Negotiating should be fun for both parties.

Back to the Basics

Some people have the ability to complicate a crowbar. Many books filled with long, scholastic definitions have been written about negotiation. That's all fine and good. But for our purposes, let me share a concise definition of negotiating. Simply stated: Negotiating is the process by which two or more parties get some, or all, of what they want through the process of open, transparent, and creative communication with one another.

Opportunities Missed

I'm convinced that most people go through life settling for far less than what they want (and could easily have) because of fear and ignorance. Sometimes, it's the fear of being rejected or told "no" that keeps Person A from asking Person B to work together to find a common solution or reach a common goal. Other times, it's because neither Person A nor Person B knows how to go about it.

So, what happens? Nothing. Every day there are:

› Car salesmen who fail to sell cars to people who really want to buy them.

› Husbands and wives who go to bed angry with each other, leaving lots of wasted real estate in the middle of the bed.

› Churches that are filled with hurting people who don't know how to communicate and resolve disputes—or get on with the business of sharing Jesus with the lost.

› Employers who don't give jobs to people they really want to hire. Why? Because neither party had the guts or the knowledge to initiate the necessary dialogue to negotiate a mutually satisfactory solution.

Negotiation in Action

My daughter Emilee learned the anatomy of negotiation while on a trip with me to Europe several years ago. While traveling to Germany to visit a missionary family with whom we were close, we spent several days in London and Paris. The trip paid for itself with one lesson Emilee learned about the benefits of effective negotiating.

We were staying at London's beautiful Rembrandt Hotel. It was an unusually hot day when we checked in. Unlike in America where every motel has air-conditioning, many European hotels don't.

This was a real problem for me. Partially because of the medications I take and partially due to preference, I like my rooms cool. Strike that. I like them cold! Think "meat locker." When I learned that the hotel didn't have air-conditioning in every room, it concerned me. I was told it was available, but they charged an extra 35 pounds for an air-conditioned room. Something had to be done, but at the exchange rate, I hated to pay so much extra money. So it was time to do some negotiating. I knew that our room price included two complimentary breakfasts. So I spoke to the manager and convinced him that the cost of putting us into an air-conditioned room would be less than the cost of the two breakfasts—which I offered to trade for the air-conditioning. He agreed. (Fact was, we were leaving for an early flight and wouldn't be able to eat breakfast anyway.)

How to Get the Most for Your Money

As I get into techniques for effective negotiating, I'm going to frame these strategies in economic terms. I'm doing this to keep some focus and clarity.

Since many of our negotiations revolve around what we pay for the things we buy, this is a universal reference point. But remember, this isn't just about saving money. The basic methodology I'm sharing applies to all sorts of interpersonal relationship negotiations, whether they take place in your marriage, church, business, civic group, etc. Depending on who you are and what your current situation is, adopt or adapt these principles to fit your needs. While individual situations may vary, these methodologies don't.

One thing is certain: You will either control your circumstances, or they will control you. Part of effective money management is realizing that your money will go to whomever wants it the most. If you don't value and appreciate your assets, someone else will get them. One of the most fundamental ways to avoid "asset evaporation" is by controlling spending. This can be done in two ways: You can simply buy less or pay less for what you buy. In this chapter, we'll focus on ways to achieve the latter.

Bear in mind that just because someone puts a $100 price tag on something he's trying to sell doesn't mean it's worth $100 to you.

Your job as a negotiator is to find the lowest price at which the seller will happily trade what he has for your cash.

Remember, your first negotiation will be the toughest, scariest, and most daunting. But trust me: With several successful negotiations under your belt, you'll be ready to tackle almost anything.

19 Secrets of Great Negotiators

When you read through these, you may say to yourself, "Well, that was obvious." That's because many of these suggestions are rooted in common sense and the idea of "loving our neighbors." When we treat other people the way our Heavenly Father would have us treat them, the situation usually works out to everyone's advantage.

1. Use time to your advantage.

The less of a rush you're in, the better. Car salesmen can tell when you have "car fever." People know when you're more anxious to buy than they are to sell. Avoid this temptation. Take your time. Be patient. Usually the less passion you invest in a negotiation, the better.

2. Figure out what the other guy wants out of the deal.

This isn't always obvious. Frequently, the other guy doesn't tell you what he really wants to accomplish. For instance, he may say, "I'm selling this car because I need $5,000 cash." If you take his comment at face value and don't ask questions, you'll probably assume that he has a $5,000 financial need and won't sell the car unless he gets that much money. Since you can only afford to spend $4,000, you shake his hand and leave without either one of you getting what you really wanted.

Maybe the deal didn't have to fall apart. This is where the art of negotiating becomes valuable. With some open conversation and friendly communication, you may have learned that the truth is a little different. He's really selling the car because he doesn't drive it anymore, and he's tired of paying insurance on something that stays parked in his garage. (The $5,000 is a figure he would like to get, but more than he thinks the car is worth.)

3. Get into the other guy's skin.

Always try to look at the deal from his side of the fence. This will help you craft your comments so they aren't offensive. Sincerely try to structure a transaction that's as good for him as it is for you.

4. Leave the other guy with a graceful way to escape.

Most people think negotiating is the art of winning arguments. Not true! If your negotiation becomes an argument—you've already lost! One of the best ways to leave the other guy a graceful way out is to avoid putting him in a corner in the first place. For instance, instead of asking how much he wants, sometimes I like to tell him what I want to pay. Here's why: If you begin the negotiation by asking, "How much does it cost?" he may give you a price that's more than he would be willing to accept and definitely more than you're willing to pay. At that point, you're left with three unappealing options:

- You could accept his price.
- You could pass on the deal.
- You could ask him to reduce his price.

At first impulse, the third option (asking him to reduce his price) may not seem so bad—but it could be a deal breaker. The minute you ask for a lower price, you infer that his is too high. He may feel offended and become defensive. That's not the response you want!

Instead, you might say something tactful like, "I don't know how much this item is worth to you. It's obviously very nice. But I'm on a budget. Would it be all right if I make an offer?" Suddenly, the table is turned, and you're the one establishing the price. Of course, he's free to accept or reject your offer, but at least he knows what you feel is a fair price.

5. Never be discourteous or condescending.

Some people mistakenly think that they can get a better price by pointing out flaws in what the other person is trying to sell. There are rare occasions (i.e., where someone is trying to unload defective merchandise) when the prospective buyer has to call the seller's hand, but usually it's bad strategy to criticize the other guy's stuff. Typically a buyer does this to convince the seller to lower the price. But it usually makes him mad instead. Once he gets mad, two bad things happen simultaneously: He begins to build even greater value into his merchandise, and he starts to dislike you.

6. Employ your best ally: Knowledge.

Never go into any important negotiation without doing your homework. One of the first rules of being a lawyer is to never ask a question to which you don't already know the answer. The same holds true for good negotiators. A little "pregame" research will pay huge dividends. Learn all you can about the prices for which similar products are currently selling. Study the competition. Do a Google search or go to eBay. Get smart. Be prepared to conduct an informed conversation.

7. Remember: Negotiation is a process—not a battle.

Go into a negotiation with goodwill and true empathy for the other party. Try to win a friend first.

8. Be a good communicator.

Learn to use words clearly and precisely. Speak loudly enough to be heard. Avoid using technical or professional jargon that may confuse the other party or make him or her feel patronized. Stay focused. If you're going to make a lengthy presentation, practice it in the mirror first.

9. Get to the decision maker.

One of the first things I used to teach young account executives at my ad agency was that no presentation for a new account would be successful unless they were talking to the person who could make a final decision. Nothing was more frustrating than to work for weeks on a major advertising campaign, only to realize that the point person we were working with had no authority to "green light" the project.

The same holds true when you are negotiating. Before you start the conversation, ask, "If we reach a mutually agreeable price and term, can you give the final okay?" If the person says no, then go up the line as far as you must to get to that all-important decision maker. This is especially important when you're buying a big-ticket item like a car. Nothing sours a deal faster than for you to reach what you think is a final price, only to have the salesman get up from the table and announce that he has to take it to his manager for approval. Yikes!

10. Remain focused—don't bring other problems or issues into the negotiation.

Forget about peripheral issues that might cloud the negotiating process. Stay on message. I would even encourage you to check your emotions at the door. If you begin to act on your emotions (such as anger, fear, excitement), you may be facing certain failure. During negotiations, you must think with your head and not your heart.

11. Check your body language.

People "listen" to more than just your words—they also "listen" to your body. Some studies have suggested that our words make up less than 10 percent of the message we send to others. The vast majority of our message (much of which comes through our tone, facial movements, and body language) can send a message that's completely opposite from the words coming out of our mouths.

When negotiating, use friendly, inviting gestures. Lean forward, smile easily, and be open. I try to be very relaxed. Sometimes, I lean back in my chair and put my hands behind my head. It's always wise to avoid "closed" body postures like crossed arms and legs.

Of course, you can find entire books written on this subject, and there's no way to cover all of the various body language techniques in this chapter. Generally speaking, effective body language is a matter of common sense. Think about the other person. How will he or she read your body language? Will your gestures be seen as warm and inviting or cold and aloof?

As I write this, I'm thinking of two preachers I know. They're both wonderful men. They both know the Bible and have a passion for lost souls. But they each have a body language problem that hinders their effectiveness. One of these men rarely makes eye contact when he converses with people. His tendency to look off in other directions causes those he's talking with to wonder whether he's paying attention. The other man was a preacher I knew as a boy. I always dreaded shaking hands with him because he had the classic "dead fish" handshake. You know the one; it's where the other guy sort of limply lays his hand in yours and waits for you to let go. **Yuck!**

12. Use gentle words.

Remember, negotiating isn't a game of "one-upmanship." It's a process of connecting with another individual in the hopes of reaching a common goal. To achieve your goal, choose your words carefully. Avoid using words that sound harsh or gruff. Stay away from words like "never," "no way," and "you must." Instead, try to use phrases like "maybe this would work," "there's no rush," or "is there a more convenient way for you?"

13. Pay attention to the other guy's nonverbal communication.

Watch for body language and facial expressions that tell you if the other person is responding favorably or negatively. Often you can learn as much from someone's nonverbal signals as you can from his or her words. Pay attention to smiles, frowns, glances, and the like. For instance, when a person puts his hands in his pockets, it may indicate hesitance or resistance. If someone refuses to look you in the eye, be slow about believing everything she's saying.

14. Find out the reason behind the sell.

It's always wise to know what is motivating the other person. Don't be so focused on your desire to seal the deal that you forget to learn from (and about) the other person. Ask why he wants to sell the item. Use questions to your advantage. Look around. Consider the surroundings. When you learn why the other person is motivated to sell or buy, you will be better able to tailor your own comments to the situation.

15. Stay calm.

Ignore personal insults—that's not why you're here. If the other person gets ugly or emotional, be kind in return. This is absolutely the time to be "turning the other cheek." I prefer to assume that a negative response from someone stems from his or her own fear of negotiating. A kind, gentle, nonthreatening response to even the most vicious comment can save both the deal and your witness.

Scripture reminds us, *"A gentle answer turns away wrath, but a harsh word stirs up anger. The tongue of the wise makes knowledge acceptable, but the mouth of fools spouts folly."* (Proverbs 15:1-2, NASB)

16. If the seller reneges, don't panic or become angry.

Sometimes a person will get nervous and try to back out of a deal. Don't respond emotionally. Slow down, take a breath, and be gentle.

One phrase that has helped me in such cases is to simply look the other person in the eye and kindly ask, "Were you sincere when you offered to sell me your item at such and such a price?"

At that point, he must either honor his earlier commitment, clarify a misunderstanding I may have had, or admit he isn't going to live up to his word.

17. Enter a negotiation with one or two alternative plans.

By doing some pre-negotiation thinking, you'll be able to antici-pate the most likely objections to your offer. Be prepared. Suppose, for instance, you're talking with a neighbor about buying his riding lawn mower. It's late August, and through conversation, you learn that he's planning to move into a condominium in September. Common sense tells you that he won't need the mower at his new home, and a quick sale to you will save him from having to hunt for another buyer. Still, you are $100 apart in price.

Why not make an alternative offer like, "Bob, if you're willing to sell the mower for what I can afford, I'll do two things to sweeten the deal. First, I'll share the mower with you until you move so you won't have to pay someone to cut your grass. Second, on moving day, my son and I will help you load the truck."

Assuming he likes your alternative offer—you have a deal. (Now all that's left is a little negotiation with your son.)

18. Be a good listener.

I'm convinced that most unsuccessful negotiations fall apart because at least one of the parties was too busy talking—and not listening.

Being a stoic philosopher in ancient Greece may have been a dull life, but Epictetus hit the nail on the head when he said, "Nature gave us one tongue and two ears so we could hear twice as much as we speak."

19. Always tell the truth.

Need I say more on this point? There is an old adage: "The first casualty of war is the truth." Unfortunately, this is sometimes true of the negotiating process, too. No prize is worth selling out our integrity. As Christians, we must maintain our honor whether we win or lose. Jesus said it this way, *"For what will a man be profited, if he gains the whole world, and forfeits his soul?"* (Matthew 16:26 NASB)

The Proof Is in the Pudding

Designing a book's cover is always a big job. Publishers and authors work hard to create covers that "speak what the book speaks" and attract "shelf attention."

I recall planning the cover design for one of my most successful books, *No Debt No Sweat!* As we planned the cover, one of the first considerations was the author's (that's my) photo. When we decided to add this dubious decoration to an otherwise attractive cover design, the next question was, "What would I wear?"

One thing was for sure, I wasn't going to wear a suit! That's just not me. After wearing coats and ties seven days a week for some twenty years, I'd had enough! These days you just about have to die to get me into a suit. As a matter of fact, I like bright shirts—the tackier, the better. I wear them everywhere. If you've ever been to one of my live events, I was probably wearing a loud shirt. All around the country, women come up to me to talk about my shirts. Usually, they make one of two very divergent comments. Some say, "Steve, I love your shirts—I sure wish I could get my husband to wear shirts like those." Others say, "Steve, if my husband ever wore a shirt like that one—I'd kill him!" (As I write this, I'm on a plane heading to an engagement in Missouri wearing a shirt adorned with colorful popsicles! I think it makes me look cool. I know, bad joke.)

So when it came to selecting a shirt for the cover of that book, I was determined to dress like I usually do. It seemed best for me to wear a long-sleeved shirt, but that's where the problem came. I didn't have many long-sleeved shirts. But because this was a special book, it deserved a special shirt. A few weeks later in California, I found the right shirt! I loved everything about it—except the price. No, I'm not going to tell you how much it cost, except to say that I could have bought a nice sports coat for the same amount. For an old boy with a bunch of $25 shirts in his closet, this shirt was too much.

"But," I reasoned, "I'm out here, and I've found what I want. Why not try out some of those negotiating skills I teach others?"

So I did. I'm happy to report that I bought the shirt on the back of that book for less than 70 percent of the marked price! In that one little deal, I saved enough to buy several of those cheap shirts.

Yes, Virginia, these negotiating tips really do work.

The Most Important Key of All

I have separated this last key—what would have been the 20th secret of the great negotiators—because it's too important to be just one point on a longer list.

Earlier in this chapter, I relayed the story of President Reagan's successful challenge to Soviet leader Mikhail Gorbachev. Now, let me share the backstory. This, in great part, will explain why President Reagan was able to succeed. If you remember nothing else from this chapter, I hope you will remember this most fundamental of all keys for a successful negotiation.

President Reagan didn't just stroll up in front of international news cameras and challenge Gorbachev unexpectedly that day at the Brandenburg Wall. Based on James Mann's wonderful book, *The Rebellion of Ronald Reagan* and recently declassified memoirs at the Reagan Library in Simi Valley, I now believe that Reagan had spent years building a bridge with Gorbachev. He had taken the time to earn the right to be candid with him, exposing his soul to the Soviet leader.

The story begins in 1985 with the first of four summit meetings between himself and the general secretary. Reagan went into that meeting with his mind made up to discuss his faith. He felt this might render fruit, as he had heard Gorbachev use the phrase, "God bless," which he hoped might indicate a deeper faith. According to note takers at that meeting, the president attempted to persuade Gorbachev of the existence of God. That meeting soon turned its attention to "peaceful coexistence" and human rights.

As Gorbachev began to see the president's heart, negotiations proceeded into new territory. Gorbachev accepted a list from Reagan of Soviet citizens America believed were victims of repression. Once the two were alone, the president continued his plea for religious tolerance in the Soviet Union. He thanked Gorbachev for his overtures of friendship toward the Russian Orthodox Church. He stepped further into unchartered territory by suggesting that Gorbachev allow people to practice their faith openly and go to church. Gorbachev deflected the requests, but, I suspect, they penetrated the exterior of this crusted cold warrior. As a matter of fact, Reagan's openness proved effective when Gorbachev made a startling comment.

Although he claimed to no longer be a believer, note takers recorded that he told the president that "he, himself, had been baptized." With the door beginning to open more widely, Reagan shared more from his world. He told Gorbachev that his son, Ron, was also an unbeliever. According to Mann's declassified minutes of the meeting, "The president then concluded that there was one thing he had yearned to do for his atheist son. He wanted to serve his son the perfect gourmet dinner to have him enjoy the meal and then to ask him if he believed there was a cook."

It's debated whether Reagan was actually trying to convert the Soviet premier or simply be more congenial and less tactile. But whatever the motive, Reagan's pure, unadulterated authenticity won the day. Like few negotiators, he understood the most important aspect of negotiating: Keep it real.

The results? They speak for themselves. *"Perestroika"* (restructuring) and *"Glasnost"* (societal openness) won the day. Soviets were given historic human rights. Churches that had been boarded for seventy years reopened their doors. Along with thousands of other Americans, I was privileged to share the news of Jesus in universities, churches, and even one casino in Russia. Thank God for a president who knew how to negotiate.

5

Make Every Minute Count
Powerful Time Management Strategies

My best male friend is my son, Joshua. As he grew up (and to this day), Josh has always shared his heart with me. The two of us are living proof that iron sharpens iron. We talk about everything; and for some reason, he still seeks my advice quite often. Awhile back, Joshua paid me a high compliment. I'm sharing it here not to brag but because its sentiment might serve as an inspiring challenge as you manage your time.

> "If you want to make good use of your time, you've got to know what's most important and then give it all you've got."
> – LEE IACOCCA

Josh's e-mail said, "Dad, here's a quote that made me think of the way you've tried to live your life. By the way, a 90-year-old woman sent this to me." The quote beneath Josh's note read, "Life is not a journey to the grave with the intention of arriving safely in a well-preserved body, but rather to skid in broadside, thoroughly used up, totally worn out, and loudly proclaiming, 'Wow! What a ride!!!!'"

Learning to Appreciate What We Have—While We Have It

As I've discussed, my early life was absorbed with the entertainment world. I drooled at the thought of being on the radio or in a recording studio. From my teen years on, I never missed an opportunity to visit a station or go to Nashville, where I made a total nuisance of myself stopping at practically every recording studio on Music Row. Of course, as I've also written, these visits were the inspiration that helped me get a major label record deal and, eventually, begin my own radio and television production company.

> "It's not enough to be busy, so are the ants. The question is, what are we busy about?"
> – HENRY DAVID THOREAU

By 1970, I had moved to Nashville to start college. In those early days, I made a lot of afternoon and nighttime trips to the studios. I loved them. My nostrils flared when I looked at those huge consoles. I felt cool hanging out with the musicians. I'll never forget those gigantic speakers that blew the hair right off my head! When I went into a studio, I was as happy as a dog slurping up melted ice cream in the back of a Wal-Mart!

One of my favorite places to go was the old RCA building, where I worked and hung out a lot. That building had it all! The third floor was where legends like Chet Atkins, Porter Wagoner, and my friend, Archie Campbell, all had offices. My producer, Bill Brock, was on the second floor. Downstairs were the studios. Studio A was huge—big enough to accommodate a large orchestra. Then there was Studio B, which is famous because Elvis cut a lot of his tunes there.

One of the most interesting rooms in the building was at the end of the hall, just past the engineers' office. It was deceptively called the vault. Although it was filled with hundreds of master tapes produced by the biggest country artists in the world over multiple decades, there was nothing "vaultish" about it. There were no bars. I recall it had no reinforced concrete walls. If there was a lock on the door, it didn't matter because it never seemed to be closed! There they sat—tapes containing some of the biggest hits in the business. I remember some of Elvis Presley's master recordings being in that room. These tapes sat on shelves with no security. Anyone could have walked in and gone home with an Elvis master! It was incredible.

Of course, today, I assume things are different. Hopefully at some point, there was a high-powered meeting with all of the Nashville, New York, and LA execs, which concluded with an official note in the minutes, "Duh, this is dumb. Somebody could steal our tapes! Buy a padlock."

Reducing Our "RQ" (Regret Quotient)

Today, I suspect those tapes are stored away in steel and concrete, but back in the early 1970s, no one really appreciated their value. After all, Eddy Arnold was still around. He could always record another record. And as some of you may recall, Elvis was not nearly as big of a star in his last years as he became after his death.

But before we criticize RCA too much, maybe we should do a little soul-searching. Do RCA's underappreciated master tapes have a modern-day application for me? I have personal regrets about things I didn't appreciate fully before they were gone. Don't you? For instance, I wish my Dad and I had spent more time together. I wish I had visited more with friends like Alton Howard, Ira North, and Archie and Margaret Boone before they passed away. But I didn't—and now it's too late to go back.

If we don't spill the milk in the first place, we won't have to cry over it. This chapter is designed to help you have fewer regrets. One day, if Jesus doesn't come first, we will all assume room temperature. It's important to squeeze every ounce of opportunity out of the apple of life before we hit the core. To do this, we must understand and maximize one of our greatest (but most underappreciated) gifts: time.

As I was researching this chapter, I realized that I first wrote on this topic some twenty years ago in my second book, *Free To Succeed*. "Whoa!" I thought. "Wonder how much my thoughts will have changed." As I perused the older book, I was struck by two things:

How similar some of the "new" material is to the old; and how the past twenty years have helped me nurture, massage, and mature my thoughts. As a matter of fact, I have decided to mix some of that earlier material with the new.

Where It All Began for Me

The point I'm trying to make here is simple: If you don't understand the value of time, you probably won't appreciate the gift. God has given each of us a certain number of days. My passion for the topic of time management is personal. I've written about my heart disease elsewhere in this book, but let me share how and when we first learned about it. When I was twenty-seven, I noticed an ache in my left arm when I walked for a distance. By chance, I mentioned this to my doctor during a regular checkup. Fortunately, he was paying attention and encouraged me to get an immediate arteriogram. The results showed that I had coronary artery disease. Over the next twelve years, I took medication and did a little more exercising.

In 1992, at age thirty-nine, we learned that the disease had progressed significantly. A few days later, I was in the hospital being diagnosed with extensive artery disease and undergoing quintuple bypass surgery. Although I wish this hadn't happened, in a strange way I'm grateful for it, because I believe this disease caused me to realize the value of time much sooner than most of my peers. Suddenly, I felt very mortal. I took things more seriously than many of my friends. Granted, I probably overcompensated, but every day became a race to see how many projects I could complete each hour. It probably spurred me to squeeze life a little tighter than I would have otherwise and appreciate every moment even more.

Granted, I'm a little obsessive compulsive when it comes to time management. I tend to multitask too much. Just a couple of hours ago, I caught myself brushing my teeth while simultaneously filling my water cup for the twenty-something pills and vitamins I take each day. And it's typical for me to be at the office talking on the phone and checking my e-mail, while clipping my nails. I'm ashamed of some of the things I have done while driving a car—including reading books! But suffice it to say, I put a high premium on time.

Managing Our Vanishing Inventory

In the advertising business, there are two types of media. One is better than the other because it doesn't allow for waste. This first type includes newspaper and magazine ad space. It's what I call "produced inventory."

If, on a given day, a newspaper publisher has twelve pages of news and ten pages of advertising, he simply prints a 22-page newspaper. Then if he sells four additional pages of advertising the next day, he easily (and profitably) prints a newspaper that is four pages longer. Structured this way, a publisher can always produce the right amount of inventory and never spend money printing empty, unprofitable pages.

It doesn't work this way with most other media. For instance, in the radio world, there are twenty-four hours in every broadcast day. In each hour, a certain number of minutes are allotted for advertising. Any of that available time that is not sold to advertisers is gone forever. The time may be used for music or talk; but it's wasted because it goes unsold and produces no income for the station. This is what I call "vanishing inventory."

When you boil it down, our lives are more like a radio station than the newspaper. Each day we are blessed with 24 hours, or 1,440 minutes, or 86,400 seconds. No more and no less. This vanishing inventory is the great equalizer of humanity. Rich and poor get the same amount. Educated and ignorant are given an equal stash. The fundamental question is how each of us will choose to use our vanishing inventory. The more we understand this truth, the more our lives will count.

Too often we minimize what the Bible teaches on the topic of stewardship. Frequently, when we hear that someone will be discussing stewardship, our first thought is, "Great. Another talk about frugal living and giving money to the church." I would certainly agree that God expects us to be good stewards of the money with which he blesses us. But what about all the other gifts he gives (that's spelled l-o-a-n-s) us? If you have a high IQ, isn't there extra responsibility to educate yourself fully? If you have the ability to sing, shouldn't you use your voice to bring praise? Wouldn't the same theory apply to how we use, or steward, our time? And since we all have the exact same amount of time, isn't time management the perfect principle on which Christians should encourage each other to focus?

I still remember a conversation with a dear friend who was around ninety years old at the time. This man was a godly saint. Occasionally when I would visit him and his wife, he would open his heart to me about personal struggles and concerns. I still remember the day he looked at me and said, "Steve, one of my regrets is that I've spent so much of my life watching television." For a long time, I thought, "Well, nuts, what else is a ninety-year-old going to do—go mountain climbing?" But it has since occurred to me that he "got it." There he was, in his last months, still wanting to make the minutes count. I'm close friends with his son, one of the most famous entertainers in the world (as well as a successful businessman and philanthropist). Maybe Dad underestimated himself and his example because to this day, his son, who is now in his seventies, accomplishes more with his time than most people half his age.

I'm convinced that godly stewardship includes how we use our time. This seems to be exactly what was on Paul's mind when he wrote his friends at the church he had established in about 55 AD at Ephesus.

"Don't waste your time on useless work, mere busywork, the barren pursuits of darkness. Expose these things for the sham they are. It's a scandal when people

waste their lives on things they must do in the darkness where no one will see. Rip the cover off those frauds and see how attractive they look in the light of Christ. Wake up from your sleep, Climb out of your coffins; Christ will show you the light! So watch your step. Use your head. Make the most of every chance you get. These are desperate times! Don't live carelessly, unthinkingly. Make sure you understand what the Master wants. "(Ephesians 5:11-17, The Message)

Through the ages, our best thinkers have understood the value of time used wisely. In the mid-1800s, Henry David Thoreau lived a life of inner reflection. Although we may not agree with all of his conclusions, no one can deny that Thoreau spent a lifetime learning how to use his time with frugality. The Harvard Business School Essentials reports a story of how Thoreau found that time could be both managed and appreciated on the cheap. He observed that he could walk the 30 miles between the towns of Concord and Fitchburg, Massachusetts and enjoy the trip through the country—all in less time than would have been required to earn the money to buy a train ticket for the same trip.

In the last century, we have seen a lot of change. We've gone from calendars to clocks to computer chips. By the 1950s, we were losing control of our time. While many of us remember the '50s as the happy days of rock 'n' roll, soda shops, poodle skirts, and Howdy Doody, reality doesn't reflect those rose-colored reviews. The '50s ushered in an era when we lost control of our time. Time began to manage us. It was the beginning of what I call the age of "Turbo Time." Busyness and stress were taking their toll. In the '50s, the divorce rate increased, families began to crumble, heart attack rates surged, mental disease became a national epidemic, and church services got accommodatingly shorter. We tried to anesthetize the pain by listening to the lies our culture told us. We were told that Winston tasted good like a cigarette should—but never shown the dying patients in the cancer ward. Television shows convinced us that a martini was the perfect way to start a party—but never showed us the aftermath of alcohol-related car wrecks. We were told that happiness was in direct proportion to the size of our car's tail fins—but never warned that our next-door neighbor would probably have the newer model within six months. In our rush to acquire the good life, we became slaves (rather than masters) of our time.

So today we are left with a misunderstanding about time management. Today, time is sold like a commodity. We're sold pills that "work fast," food blenders that "save time," and food that is "instant."

Understanding how to effectively manage our time is important because it allows us to reclaim our destiny. Proper time management allows us to pre-act, so we don't spend our lives having to re-act to everything that occurs.

Hearing the Noise—But Missing the Symphony

Of course, the trick here is learning to hear the music over the noise. To use our time most productively and enjoy it to its fullest, we must properly categorize the various things we want and need to do. The goal here is to hear over the *noise* of life so you will have the time to write your life's *symphony*.

The things that absorb our time fall into at least three categories:

1. The Now's. These are the duties that are most time-sensitive and should be done immediately—as in right now!

2. The Necessary's. These are tasks that absolutely, positively must be done.

3. The Neat's. These are things that would be fun and neat to do, but they are not vital to our existence.

Here's where it becomes a bit more complex. Categories 1 and 2 (the *now's* and the *necessary's)* may, or may not, be one in the same. There are some things that are urgent (a *now*) but not absolutely *necessary*. Suppose I'm interested in sociology, so I decide to take a class at a local college. A theme paper is due by week's end, but I already have job commitments that will claim the rest of the week.

120

Today the family will be gone, so I could spend the entire day at the computer working on the paper. This task needs to be done *now* because it is urgent, assuming I want to pass the class. But it's not absolutely *necessary*. Sure, I'd like to learn more about sociology—but since I'm an accountant, what real difference will it make?

Conversely, there are tasks that are *necessary* but not urgent *(now's)*. For instance, your doctor might suggest that you come in at a convenient time for a routine follow-up test for cancer you dealt with several years ago. Since you have a history of cancer, you would consider this a *necessary* task. But if your doctor says there is no rush since he expects no problems and considers this a preventative medical practice, you might not feel any tremendous pressure to do it yesterday. But suppose that tonight as you drive home, a truck careens into the side of your car, breaking your left arm and two ribs. Suddenly, getting medical help becomes a *now* task. Considering all of the other things presently going on, the cancer-screening test (while still totally *necessary*) is not a *now* task.

Let's put a sharper point on all of this. What happens when the *now's* and the *necessary's* converge? For instance, what if, in the stress of the car accident, you had a heart attack when your broken ribs punctured your lungs? By the time the ambulance pulls up to the hospital, you have already flatlined twice, and the paramedics are ventilating you. Triage will have to make a tough decision since both conditions are *now* and *necessary*. Both of those tasks suddenly move to the top of the to-do list!

Finally, let's look at Category 3, the *neat's*. These are items we'd like to accomplish but agree are not totally essential. *Neat's* fall into two subcategories: *neat/now's* and s*imply neat's*. Suppose I've been looking for a new suit. There is a sale in progress at my favorite store, but it ends tonight at nine o'clock. If I'm going to save a few bucks, this task needs to be done *now*. But in fact, it is not *necessary*. Sure, I'd like the new suit, but if I don't get it, I have other suits in the closet.

Finally, there are tasks that are *simply neat*. These are things I want to do someday, but they can wait. Someday, for instance, I'd like to read a book about William F. Buckley. But there's no rush—he's still dead. I'll get to it when I get to it.

Three Great Time Management Truths

I have found the following three truths to be effective in reclaiming and managing time.

Truth 1

To Manage Your Time, You Must First Know What You Want to Do With It

It seems so simple, but it's rare to meet someone who can explain in clear, concise terms exactly what he plans to do with his time. Granted, we are not the captains of our own ships. As I've already said, we are only stewards of the time God allows us. Assumption is the height of foolishness. None of us knows what tomorrow (or even the next five minutes) will bring. Jesus shared a parable that points out the folly of becoming overly assumptive:

"The land of a rich man was very productive. And he began reasoning to himself, saying, 'What shall I do, since I have no place to store my crops?' Then he said, 'This is what I will do: I will tear down my barns and build larger ones, and there I will store all my grain and my goods. And I will say to my soul, "Soul, you have many goods laid up for many years to come; take your ease, eat, drink and be merry."' But God said to him, 'You fool! This very night your soul is required of you; and now who will own what you have prepared?' So is the man who stores up treasure for himself, and is not rich toward God." (Luke 12:16-21, NASB)

As James tells us, all of our planning is at the pleasure of God. *"Come now, you who say, 'Today or tomorrow we will go to such and such a city, and spend a year there and engage in business and make a profit.' Yet you do not know what your life will be like tomorrow. You are just a vapor that appears for a little while and then vanishes away. Instead, you ought to say, 'If the Lord wills, we will live and also do this or that.'"* (James 4:13-15, NASB)

But even in view of these Biblical mandates, the scripture doesn't absolve us from the responsibility of stewarding and managing our time. In Colossians 4, Paul talks of the importance of "redeeming the time." It falls squarely into each of our laps to "redeem" our time wisely. Other words for redeem might include "exchanging," "cashing in," or even "emancipating" our time.

Like they say: Sin can be forgiven, but stupid is forever. There are many people who go blithely through their years with no plan. As I write this, I'm thinking of just such a person. This man, today in his eighties and in poor health, is living out the last days of a wasted life. He began without a plan, and he is ending the same way. He spent his young adulthood aimlessly. Then for several decades he worked at a job and supported a family he didn't appreciate. Today, after three unhappy marriages and grown children with whom he's distant, he lives a hermit's existence. What a waste! Begin by establishing an agenda. Ask yourself, "If I only had one hour today what would I do with it?" Then build out from there.

The wisest guy to ever grace this planet was Solomon. He understood and wrote about the importance of diligence:

"Whatever your hand finds to do, do it with all your might, for in the grave, where you are going, there is neither working nor planning nor knowledge nor wisdom." (Ecclesiastes 9:10, NIV)

The world is a tough place. Many of us face daily battles. As the warriors of old knew, it was important not to go into battle without their suits of armor snugly affixed to their bodies. Effective time management involves understanding the importance of starting each day correctly. Bonnie and I have found the value of starting each day with a firm appointment with God as we read our Bibles, pray, and meditate. My friend Cal Thomas, author and Fox News commentator, likes to say that he begins each morning by reading two things: his Bible and the *New York Times*. That way, he explains, he gets both sides of the story! Seriously, whenever you decide to do it, you will find real value in spending daily time in meditation, prayer, and Bible study. I have found that this practice makes the rest of my time more productive. Even Jesus seemed to find this a necessary part of a well-managed life. Over and over, we read of Jesus slipping away from the pressures of life to spend quality time with his Father. As I've discussed elsewhere in this book, I know from too much personal experience that when I drift away from this vital discipline, my time becomes less and less productive.

Truth 2

It Doesn't Count If It's Not on Paper

I'm known nationally as a financial coach. Everywhere I go, I tell people that a fundamental building block for financial security is to have a written budget. I jokingly tell audiences that I get rattled when I'm counseling a couple, and I ask, "So, do you have a budget?"

And the guy looks at me and says, "Yep."

"Well, can I see?" I ask.

"Nope."

"Why not?"

Then as he points to his forehead, he proclaims, "Because I keep it right here."

Well, dear friend, it's the same with time management. You can't manage your time if you don't have a plan. Until it becomes a habit, your to-do list should be in writing. I don't care whether you're talking about a to-do list, a new law, or the constitution of a nation—it's nothing more than a bunch of free-floating thoughts in open space until you put them in writing. The written to-do list is the fireman that's going to get you out of the middle of the burning house of confusion and mismanaged time.

Granted, once you have learned to manage your time, you may not need a written list every day for the rest of your life. Once you establish good habits, you may find that you don't always need a written playbook. But for now, let's focus on the advantages of having one. My friend Paul Winkler, a professional investment advisor, tells of a university that learned that only 3 percent of the school's graduates had committed their goals to paper. That three percent, however, earned more than the other 97 percent combined!

Eventually, you may wish to develop two to-do lists: one for the immediate tasks, which we will deal with in the next paragraphs, and a second list that outlines your long-term goals. The second list is less about time management and more about life management—so we won't spend a lot of time discussing it in this chapter. My purpose here is to address how to manage our time in the present. Suffice it to say, your long-term goals list will be fun. It will become both a dream list and a list that reminds you of things you hope to do. This is what many people call their "bucket list"—all those things they'd like to do before sucking their last breath of air. Based on decades of experience doing this stuff myself and teaching it to others, let me make some suggestions on how to give legs to this effort.

› **Conclude every day by writing tomorrow's to-do list (your "TTDL").** Late afternoon is the perfect time because today's activities are still fresh in your mind, and you can visualize exactly where you need to pick things up in the morning. Write down everything you need to do tomorrow. Then prioritize each one. Unless there's something absolutely more urgent, I suggest starting your TTDL with the number one thing you least want to do! Why? Because by "eating your problems for breakfast," as one author put it, you turn a day of dread into a day of anticipation. The forgotten secret of the last two generations is the joy of deferred gratification. By always insisting on having what we want, when we want it, we have raised two generations of spoiled losers.

Immediate Gratification:
The Anatomy of a Meltdown

For years to come, economic students will study the economic meltdown that began in 2008. But at its core, the crisis was not about financial theory. The heart of the meltdown was the direct result of decades of immediate gratification. Many experts point to the housing crisis as the snowflake that began the avalanche. We're told that it was those greedy Wall Street types and their under-collateralized, mortgaged-backed securities that caused the problem.

True. But that's like saying that the people who perished on the Titanic died because of too much water in their lungs. Also true, but it doesn't really tell the whole story. The reason that some 2,000 souls perished on that fateful cruise was because of missteps and faulty assumptions that began years earlier. Issues dealing with the ship's design, overconfidence in untested theories, and assumptions that an iceberg would never drift so far south all contributed to that disaster.

Certainly, dishonest financial practitioners should share the blame for the resulting economic troubles, but the real problem is much deeper. It has more to do with the sense of entitlement that has become the mantra for many Americans. Once we were a people who paid as we went, buying only what we had the cash to pay for.

Remember the old "layaway" system? I do. As a boy, I worked at J.C. Penney's. Layaway allowed buyers to select what they wanted at department stores. Then, every week, they would come in and pay a few dollars toward the total. Finally, with the last dollar paid, they took their item home. Seems a far distance from where we are today, doesn't it?

In my *No Debt No Sweat!* book, I call this the culture of "Stuffaholism." It has led us to the precipice of ruin. By early

2009, millions of American home buyers were in a mess. Many of these people, kindly referred to as "subprime home buyers," had no business buying a house in the first place. (Within financial circles, "subprime" is closely associated with being a deadbeat.) But liberal politicians had learned they could "buy" votes by lying to the ignorant and telling them that everyone "deserved" their own home.

Greedy lenders realized that they could make a fortune by selling lousy loans and then reselling them to unsuspecting investors. But to make this whole Ponzi scheme work, home buyers had to be part of the fraud. They had to become as greedy as the lenders. Although many have since claimed to be mere victims, the truth is many of these "subprime" home buyers signed their names to long documents that were terrible. Some of these loans allowed for lower monthly payments by applying nothing to the principal. Then there were "signature loans" (also known as "liar's loans") that allowed people to claim whatever income was necessary to get their loans without offering any proof.

To manage time wisely and efficiently, you must grow a spine and accept the hard truth: It's best to do the tough things first, then enjoy the fruits of your labor. Otherwise, you may be condemned to a "subprime" existence forever—always dreading the tough jobs ahead. In the long run, it's much less painful to do the painful things first! Living a life of deferred gratification makes everything ahead seem more special, and it comes without the baggage of bad past choices. It would be impossible to calculate how much pain and energy is spent in the course of a typical person's life simply dreading the future. Do the tough stuff first!

› **Find a format that works best for you and stick with it.** Some people prefer to keep their TTDL on their smartphones;

127

others like computers; and there are still some of us old dogs who like to keep ours on paper. I do keep some of my scheduling (especially the long-term schedules, which I'll discuss more later) on computer. But I prefer the old pen-and-paper approach. Why? Because it's simple. Unlike the electronic gizmos, a pad and pen can be in action in two seconds. They weigh less. And the batteries never die at the worst moment. You techies can laugh if you wish, but I used the primitive pad-and-pen method for more than twenty years to build a multimillion-dollar business. It's worked for me!

Sketch It Out

Personally, I usually do my to-do lists on yellow pads. I like these because they stand out visually. They're easy to see. Also, since they're in written form, I can pop my pen out and add anything I wish, anywhere, any time. Finally, it makes prioritizing simple. I frequently use a check-mark approach. I look over the completed list and put one check beside the things that are important; two checks besides those that are urgent; and three beside the items that failure to do will cause the end of the world! Another cool advantage of a handwritten list: It gives me a real sense of accomplishment—or reinforcement, if you will. Every time I complete a job, I strike a line through the completed task. This is a steroid-packed emotional boost that makes me eager to do more.

To bottom line it, it doesn't matter how you compose your TTDL. It only matters that you do it.

› **Don't get discouraged if you don't get it all done.** If you're worth your salt, you can always identify more jobs than you can realistically get to. That's a good thing. It means that you're thinking and you're a productive person. Just don't become obsessive compulsive—a slave to your list. The cool thing about having prioritized your TDDL is that you get the most difficult and urgent jobs done first. Besides, whatever is left over becomes the beginning of tomorrow's TTDL!

Truth 3

It Pays to Be Paranoid: Time Thieves Are Everywhere!

Built into the universe is a devious plot to steal your most valuable asset: time. Those who deny or ignore this great truth will never learn to manage their time. The fact is, either you will manage your time, or the people and forces around you will manage it. As with any battle, to be victorious, it's crucial to clearly identify the enemy and develop a battle plan. The following is a list of the "10 Most Wanted Time Thieves."

 Time Thief 1

People With Small Buckets

When I first entered the business world in 1974, I was just out of college and as green as the giant who sells the vegetables. My boss at the real estate firm was Dave Floyd. For some reason, he took a liking to me and determined to round out my real-world education with real-world advice. He shared important life strategies that have served me well to this day. Every now and then—maybe when he noticed me paying too much attention to other agents who were too lazy to suit him—Dave would tell me the "Bucket Story."

He explained it this way, "Steve, everyone has a bucket in life. And everyone tries to fill his bucket. The difference between people isn't so much whether or not they totally fill their buckets. The real difference is in the size of their buckets. Some people have very small buckets and are pleased with the status quo. They fill their buckets quickly and don't aspire to greater things. Other people have large buckets. For them, life will always be filled with new challenges and opportunities. It's not that they aren't content. It's that they find joy and contentment in the journey itself. These people with big buckets may not reach all their goals, but they will end the journey with lots of cool things in their buckets. Steve, it's up to each of us to select a bucket. Don't settle for one that's too small."

> **Your Battle Plan:** Beware of people you work and worship with who have small buckets. It's a safe bet that when they fill their buckets (which doesn't usually take very long), they will have too much time on their hands and will begin to impede you on your journey.

It's easy to spot small-bucketed people. They're the ones who have time to sit around the house watching reality shows. The ones who steal extra time at the watercooler instead of prepping for the afternoon meeting or turn their computer screens away from their office doors, so others won't see them surfing the Web while supposedly doing company business. Watch out for these people because they will feel intimidated by your work ethic and try their best to suck you into their mediocrity. Don't waste time in their world—or at their watercooler. Bring your own bottle of water to work and stay focused. After all, one day you'll probably be managing them.

⭐ Time Thief 2
Complainers, Fault-Finders, and Negative People

I call these people the Negavites. Although in context I believe Paul's point reached much deeper, he spoke to the Corinthians about the dangers of hanging out with the wrong people. He warned that nothing good comes from running with the wrong crowd: *"Do not be deceived: Evil company corrupts good habits. Awake to righteousness, and do not sin; for some do not have the knowledge of God. I speak this to your shame."* (1 Corinthians 15: 33, 34, NKJV)

There will always be more negative people than positive people in the world. Being a realist, I'm not suggesting that we need to be blind to the difficult side of life. Pollyanna made a great story, but I'd hate to depend on her in a jam! That said, to appreciate our time and use it productively, we need to avoid people who always seem to have 19 reasons why every plan will fail.

Be warned: Running with people who are better at excusing their failures than finding productive solutions is dangerous.

 Time Thief 3

Procrastinators

The motto of the procrastinator is: "Today's greatest work-saving device is tomorrow." To revisit an earlier point, this is why I encourage people to start each day by doing the thing they least want to do. Get it over with and the day improves dramatically. This way you will tend to look forward to the future with optimism and hope instead of the dread that's the procrastinator's fuel.

 Time Thief 4

Perfectionists

The fear of failure is the great paralyzer of the good. When you think about it, the devil really doesn't have much to work with. After all, if we really believe that God is the Good Creator, it means we accept three foundational facts:

 1. God made the world.
 2. God made everything in the world.
 3. Everything that God made is good.

So if this is all true, those who fear failure should ask, "What does the devil have left to work with?" Actually, all the devil has is the good stuff God has made. Satan simply takes the good and twists and perverts it just a bit. Then he tries to sell it back to us. Sex is good when it's within marriage. But sex outside of marriage is wrong. Ambition is good if it inspires us to strive for excellence. But if ambition becomes our excuse to crawl over others to get what we want, that's bad.

In a similar way, fear has its place. When we see a car cross the center line, fear spurs us to hit the brakes. When we notice an intruder break a neighbor's window, fear directs us to dial 9-1-1.

But the devil is the master of fear mongering. He's the one who constantly whispers fears and doubts into our ears. He's the one always ready to remind us of past failures. He's the one who stands ready to fill us with doubt every time we consider stepping out of our comfort zone. This inappropriate fear causes many to misuse, waste, and lose one of their richest resources: time.

⭐ Time Thief 5

Slow Starters

I still remember a man I worked with years ago. He was a skilled, creative person who helped us develop hundreds of successful projects. He had an eye for the unique and distinctive way to best serve a client. But Robert (not his real name) had a flaw. He was a perfectionist. On the surface that sounds admirable, but in his case, it was a real burden. His office was always a mess. It was so over-filled that I didn't dare go in without a tether tied to my foot! It wasn't that Robert liked a messy office. His office remained sloppy because the only time he would clean up the mess was when he could spend the hours (or days) necessary to meticulously go through every trade journal and piece of mail and file them, one by one.

A lot of people never learn to properly manage their time because they can't find the starting line. Sometimes the best place to start a project is right where you are. Instead of wasting forever trying to find the best way, settle on 90 percent of "best" and get busy! I understand that, in theory, there may be a more perfect way to do it. But until some action happens, it's nothing more than a theory. Check out Matthew 25. You'll notice that Jesus didn't condemn the one talent servant because he wasn't as gifted as the five-talent servant. He condemned the old boy with one talent because he refused to try! He took his talent and buried it. I'd much rather go down swinging with some misses than to go down without even striking a blow.

In my experience, sometimes when I'm not totally sure where to start a project, the best thing I can do is simply start kicking up some dust! Usually once I've forced myself off the starting block, I can see more clearly how to complete the task. The old adage holds true: The best way to eat an elephant is one bit at a time! So, start chewing!

⭐ Time Thief 6

People Pleasers

This is an especially difficult one for me. I'm a pleaser. I want people to like me. But the truth is, no matter what I do or how well I perform, some people will still go away shaking their heads.

The trouble with trying to be liked by everyone is that it sucks up our time. We're so busy trying to get the approval of others that we leave the more important things undone. And, ultimately, we become little more than their punching bags. The more we try to please, the more demanding others become.

This is a special problem for those of us in what I call "high touch" careers. These are people whose jobs require constant interface with others. Ministers, entertainers, health-care givers, and middle-level managers have high fatigue and burnout rates because they have frequently never learned to draw lines and simply say "no" to many of the requests made of them. Learning to say no is an art. The devil will use all his powers to persuade you to add "just this one more duty to your schedule." But the fact is, no one but God can be geographically, emotionally, and intellectually everywhere all the time. Watch out. Don't turn virtue into vice. Stop overcommitting.

 **Time Thief 7**

Meeting Mongers

My advice for going to meetings is: avoid, avoid, avoid! I hate meetings. In many organizations, more time is wasted in meetings than anywhere else. Often they're little more than a collective pooling of ignorance. But if you must meet, maintain certain guidelines:

› **Never begin without a leader or moderator.**

› **Set a clear agenda.** Usually it's best to prepare and circulate the agenda prior to the meeting. Then when the meeting starts, insist that everyone stays on message. Avoid chasing rabbits, reminiscing about the "good old days," and passing around family photos.

› **Expect everyone to come prepared—no excuses.** Remember, if you are in a meeting with ten people participating and one person wastes fifteen minutes—he's stolen two-and-a half-hours (10 people x 15 minutes each = 150 minutes) of company time. Hold attendees responsible.

› **Start with a predetermined and agreed-upon stopping time.** One of the reasons meetings are so often unproductive is because there is no sense of urgency. If we agree that time is a vanishing inventory, then we shouldn't waste it. Having a clear stopping time helps people remain focused and involved. Also, there is a malaise that sets in when people don't have a clue when they'll finally get back to their desks. A stopping time is as important as a starting time.

⭐ **Time Thief 8**

Wheel Spinners

Untold amounts of time are wasted every year because of what I call "wasted motion." I remember having a store boss when I was a kid who always expected us to look busy. Since I worked in the linen department, whenever I saw him coming, I started refolding the same towels I had just folded on his previous pass through the department. Think before you invest time. Avoid a plane trip when a conference call will do the trick. For some of us, this won't be possible. I take more than a hundred flight legs every year. I may be a professional speaker, but I'm not a very good one. So far, I haven't been successful enough to get my audiences to come to me, so I have to go to them. But I make my air time count. In past years, I've been contracted to write more than thirty print articles and do dozens of television segments each year, I did much of my writing and scripting on my flights. Significant portions of this book were written at 30,000 feet.

Look for other ways to avoid "wasted motion." Depend on e-mails and texting when feasible. Usually an e-mail is faster than a personal visit or even a phone call.

 Time Thief 9

Micromanagers

This is one thing I've never done well. One of the greatest regrets of my adult life has been my failure to delegate better. I can still remember a day about twenty-five years ago when our media buyer, Sunny Hersh—a delightful lady who was old enough to be my mother—sat me down for a talk. Although she worked for me, she didn't hesitate to speak her mind. One day, when she'd seen enough, Sunny landed on me for my failure to delegate more effectively. She made a great case, and I did improve some. But to this day, I still have a hard time practicing what I preach on this topic.

At least intellectually speaking, I believe that learning to delegate can be one of your most effective weapons against the time thieves. Although I still struggle to delegate jobs to others, I have learned to delegate at least some of the things I'm not particularly good at or interested in doing.

Everyone who knows me well knows I have very little mechanical ability. When I run out of gas, I start thinking about trading for another car! Okay, that's a bit of an exaggeration, but I'm not adept at car repair, carpentry work, or most anything else that requires similar skills. I learned a long time ago that it makes no sense for me to spend two hours changing my car oil when I can pay someone $40 to do it in ten minutes while I sit in the car and catch up on phone calls or computer work. Efficient time managers also tend to be effective, aggressive delegators.

⭐ Time Thief 10
The Habitually Late

It's amazing to me how much time can be wasted simply waiting for someone else to get to an appointment. Frankly, it tires me to have to wait for someone else who has already agreed to (and often been the one to set) an appointment. I have secretly admired the guy I heard of who docked his doctor's medical bill for being late. The fellow set a 10 a.m. appointment with his doctor. The doctor finally came into the examining room at 11 a.m. When the man received the doctor's bill, he paid it, minus the hourly rate he charged his own clients. While I don't know if that story is true or not, I suspect that if it is, it got the doctor's attention. I've never been that bold, but I did finally dismiss my physician some years ago, in part, because of his failure to be punctual.

Let me share a technique that has saved me lots of time over the last thirty years. A long time ago, I realized something important: When I set an appointment for 1 p.m., the other person often felt totally comfortable arriving at 1:10 or 1:20. So, to remedy this, I began setting appointments at "off times." Instead of suggesting that we meet at 9 a.m. or 2:30 p.m., I would recommend meeting at 9:05 or 2:40. I got some double takes, but it sure did help the get the appointments started on time!

Snooze Buttons Are for Losers

Scripture condemns slothfulness. God expects his people to be diligent. That's why I don't like snooze buttons. People with things to do aren't likely to hit their snooze buttons often. The Bible urges godly people to live diligent, industrious lives. Consider these verses:

"Go to the ant, you sluggard; consider its ways and be wise! It has no commander, no overseer or ruler, yet it stores its provisions in summer and gathers its food at harvest. How long will you lie there, you sluggard? When will you get up from your sleep? A little sleep, a little slumber, a little folding of the hands to rest—and poverty will come on you like a bandit and scarcity like an armed man." (Proverbs 6:6-11, NASB)

" The soul of the sluggard craves and gets nothing. But the soul of the diligent is made fat." (Proverbs 13:4, NASB)

Centuries later, Paul had harsh words for the Thessalonica church when he learned that a number of the young Christian converts had quit their jobs in anticipation of what they expected to be the imminent return of Jesus. While politically incorrect by today's cultural standards, Paul's words to them are nonetheless divine, *"For even when we were with you, we gave you this rule: 'If a man will not work, he shall not eat.'"* (2 Thessalonians 3:10, NIV)

I still remember the summer of 1970. As I mentioned in another chapter, a friend and I were selling books door-to-door in south Georgia. You may be familiar with the Southwestern Company of Nashville. For more than 100 years, the company has trained thousands of college students in the techniques of salesmanship and self-reliance. Some of America's most successful businesspeople are Southwestern alumni.

One of the most important lessons I learned was the culture of hard work. With Southwestern, you're paid exactly what you're worth, not a penny more or a penny less. Why? Because a student's income was entirely based on commissions he earned from the books he sold. It won't surprise you to hear that this wasn't a typical 9 to 5 summer job. The Southwestern culture encouraged us (that's putting it mildly) to work at least eighty-hour weeks. This meant getting up early, doing our morning prep, getting dressed, and knocking on doors by 8 a.m. After the first few days when there seemed to be far more rejections than interested buyers, it got increasingly difficult to crawl out of bed. So my partner and I devised a plan. At bedtime, we set the alarm clock and placed it across the room at an equal distance from both of us. Then we each put a $20 bill under the clock. The rule was simple: In the morning, the first one to turn off the clock got to keep the $40.

Diligence vs. Workaholism

Finding a Balance

So I won't be misunderstood, allow me to draw a clear, sharp line between healthy diligence and workaholism. Granted, there are plenty of people in our postmodern culture who sincerely believe it's a badge of honor to be called a workaholic. Some twenty years ago, I heard about a young man who regularly arrived at his office at two in the morning! I can only wonder what toll that lifestyle took on him, his marriage, the relationship he had with his children, and if he ever found quiet time to be alone with God. I wonder where he is today.

I am a recovering workaholic. In my earlier years, there were plenty of ninety- to hundred-hour workweeks. There were lots of missed vacations. And there was far too little time spent with the family. Even when I was at home, my mind was on the business. So, if you're like me—overly driven and ambitious—please ignore some of the tougher points I make in this chapter. They're not aimed at you. Taken to an extreme, this material can be like pouring gasoline on an open fire. If you are persistently working seventy-five-hour weeks (unless it's for a specified period of time with a specified goal, such as paying off outstanding debt), you need to take a chill pill and cool your heels. It's not worth it.

An inordinate work schedule is wrong. Too many Christians in our society have allowed legitimate diligence to become vain striving.

In Psalm 127:2, the writer warns, *"It is vain for you to rise up early. To retire late; to eat the bread of painful labors;* **For He gives to His beloved even in his sleep.** *"* (emphasis mine, NASV)

Note especially the promise in the last line. God is the Father of Lights. He is the giver of all good and perfect gifts.

Time management (like all the other skills taught in this book) demands that vital ingredient I spoke of earlier: balance. Somewhere between the eighty-hour-a-week workaholic and the thirty-hour-a-week goof-aholic that balance exists. Your prayer life and study of the Word will help you find it.

A Worthy Investment

Like most of the topics I discuss in this book, time management takes a strong dose of self-discipline. Sometimes we confuse sloth-fulness with meekness. We tend to excuse laziness and second-rate performance rather than demanding the very best from ourselves.

Christians, more than any other group, should strive for peak performance. We should applaud and appreciate the time and talents God has loaned us. We, of all people, should be the best at investing the time God has allowed us because, just as with all of his other gifts, one day he will ask for an accounting of how we redeemed our time.

Control Your Money
How to Get It, Give It, and Grow It

As this book goes to press, I will have spoken to live audiences on this subject more than 1,500 times throughout America and in Europe. My book, *No Debt No Sweat!*, was on this very topic. In addition to the dozens of radio and television appearances I've done, I spent two years doing a weekly on-air segment as a TV money advisor. (My kids were the only ones on the block whose dad had a makeup kit!) I've written hundreds of articles about personal finance. On average, I speak to audiences more than 250 times yearly, teaching people how to handle their money. So it's fair to say that I've got a real interest (and some experience) in this area.

> "When your outgo exceeds your income, then your upkeep will be your downfall."
> – *UNKNOWN*

The Cold, Hard Facts

It's possible (and actually probable) that a young person can go through twelve years of school and four years of college—supposedly being taught what she needs to know to be an educated, productive member of the culture—without ever being shown how to balance a checkbook, do a budget, or avoid a bad credit card deal! In my years of teaching on money, I've marveled at how some of the most educated people out there (i.e. doctors, government workers, lawyers, etc.) are often dummies when it comes to their finances. These facts should give us all pause:

› Personal bankruptcy is a huge problem in America. In some recent years, there have been about 1.5 million bankruptcies. In some of those years, we have had more bankruptcies than undergraduate college graduates. Think about that: more bankruptcy decrees than college degrees!

> "Money is a wonderful servant but a terrible master."
> – UNKNOWN

› Presently the average household debt in America, not counting mortgage debt, is roughly $15,000. But, remember, that's only an average. When you factor in the number of people who live responsible lives with no debt, it means that many others are in a world of hurt. I counsel people regularly whose short-term debts exceed their annual income.

› Americans are presently carrying most of a trillion dollars of credit card debt. Many people think nothing of buying this week's groceries on a credit card and paying for them over the next twenty or thirty years. It has been estimated that, depending on terms and interest rates, if you're are carrying a credit card balance of $4,000 and are paying only the monthly minimum, in many cases it may take more than twenty years to get rid of that debt!

› The average fifty-year-old has less than $40,000 of total wealth, including his or her home. (To have any real hope of stockpiling $1,000,000 by retirement time, that fifty-year-old may need to start saving at least $25,000 every year. And even that may not be enough to hit the goal!)

› As I write this, the unemployment level in America stands at about 10 percent. Many job hunters are spending more than eight months hunting for a new job.

› Although many students leave college with more than $20,000 in student loan debt (that doesn't count the credit card and car loan debt), many depart the ivy halls without a job. So they become convinced that the solution is more education, which leads to even more debt. Eventually, with multiple sheepskins in hand, they hit the hard, cruel world, only to realize that their chosen major doesn't produce jobs that pay enough to allow them to aggressively kill their student loan debt. They spend their adulthood trying to catch up—constantly fussing with their spouses and unable to relax with their children. Twenty years later, they have nothing saved for their kids' college or their retirement.

› As of 2009, there was about twelve trillion dollars in outstanding mortgage debt, which represents roughly fifty million home loans. Since 2007, millions of Americans have lost homes because of terrible loan products they signed for between the late 1990s and 2007. Predictably, there is a lot of finger pointing. The fact is: As I mentioned in another chapter, everyone is at fault! I blame the government for aiding and abetting, the lenders for lying, the real estate sellers for their greed, and the rating agencies for turning a blind eye. But most of all—I blame us!

Many of the homeowners who are blaming everyone else for their problems today should take a close look in the mirror and admit that they really didn't read the loan documents (or get an attorney's help) because the deal sounded "so good." Most of the "interest only" loans and adjustable rate mortgages were terrible products. Worst of all were what I call the "wink and grin" loans. These were commonly referred to as "no documentation loans," or, as I referred to in the last chapter, "liar's loans." People were allowed to claim whatever income they needed to get a loan—without having to prove anything. People who dishonestly or greedily committed to such loans bear much of the responsibility for their pain.

My experience convinces me that more than 70 percent of all Americans are in financial pain—living from paycheck to paycheck.

And that number is growing. Many people who always considered themselves middle-class citizens made bad decisions that, today, are costing them dearly.

We Interrupt this Chapter
for a Special Word to You Married Folks

It frightens me when a couple tells me they've never fought over money. I figure if they will tell me that, they'll lie about other stuff, too! So before I go further, I want to speak to those of you who are married. I'm convinced that money issues destroy more marriages than practically anything else. One survey indicates that more than 55 percent of divorces claim that money trouble is the leading cause. At this very moment, some of you married folks believe you are sleeping with the enemy!

The truth is, your spouse is the best friend God will ever give you. The enemy is not the money—or your spouse. The enemy in all of this is Satan himself. He's the one who smiles when you're in pain and laughs when you fight. He's the one who whispers, "You'll never get it right."

As I'll discuss more fully later in this chapter, the Bible tells us the devil's stock-in-trade is in lies. If he can convince you that you'll never work through the money issues with your spouse—guess what? You won't. And you will become increasingly convinced that the two of you are "wrong for each other." Remember, whatever is wrong can be made right with God's help, provided you're willing to do some important things the right way.

It's not until husbands and wives see the enemy for who he really is that their finances will begin to improve. It's time for couples to fall back in love with each other—and start making love with each other! Many can trace the day their relationship changed for the better to the day they decided to get on the same side of the money fence.

As I've mentioned before, I've taught these principles to a lot of people. And I've witnessed some pretty staggering things. But some stories stand out.

Jim and Joyce (not their real names) live in the Dallas area. When I came to their church to present the *No Debt No Sweat! Seminar*, Jim was a thirty-four-year-old architect, and Joyce was the church secretary. Jim thought he had no money worries—at least none he cared to admit.

He paid $521 a month to lease a Ford Exhibition. Even with gasoline prices rising he filled up frequently because he got only 17 miles to the gallon on his 80-mile round-trip to work. He ate lunch at restaurants most days and thought nothing of using his credit card to finance outings to the gourmet pizzeria or the Chinese buffet. This was a real problem for Joyce, who handled the money and paid the bills for their family of four.

On Sundays, Jim would throw a few dollars in the collection plate, never thinking about the fact that he'd spent more on a backyard "pet butler" to clean up after the family's dogs than he'd given to God.

About the only financial stress Jim would acknowledge was the constant "nagging" from Joyce. Joyce was fully aware of her husband's $40,000 of school debt, their $10,000 of credit card debt, and her $5,000 of medical bills due to chronic migraines and rheumatoid arthritis. The fact was, their money problems were growing by the day, and Jim didn't seem to get it!

"Every time she'd talk about finances, I'd get angry or upset," he said. "I don't know if it was because I didn't want to know, or because I felt she was coming down on me."

That was their situation when Jim and Joyce attended our seminar. Along with the material I taught in those sessions, I reminded the audience that, by making only the minimum payment on debts—as the couple had been doing—it could take twenty to thirty years to pay them off. One comment, in particular, stuck with Jim. I told the audience, "Some of you have made credit card payments this month on meals that you ate during the Reagan Administration!"

Apparently, that hit a nerve. Jim later explained, "I had never realized that eating out, putting it on the card, and just paying the minimum makes that about a $200 meal."

Sometime after that Dallas seminar, I got the following e-mail from Joyce:

"I am a rejoicing woman, and I have you and God to thank. Something in the lessons you gave here at (name of church) reached my husband, and we are beginning a new life. Praise God ... You will never know how much you have impacted our lives."

While Joyce's comments were kind, all I had done was turn a flashlight on and point to the pathway out of their pain. The rest was up to God and them. The point I hope to leave you with is this: No matter how tough your present money situation is, it doesn't have to be a marriage buster. In all likelihood, the two of you can—with enough unselfishness, love, and a laser focus—kill the debt monster and enjoy the life God means for you to have.

By the way, if you have a disinterested spouse, don't give up. Ask him or her to sit down and read this chapter with you. (Note: There's nothing wrong with a little necking while you read!)

The Money Lies We Believe

According to an ABC-TV news report called "The Mystery of Happiness," in a survey of 49 of *Forbes* magazine's richest people, 37 percent reported lower than average happiness levels. It seems obvious that money does not make people happy. Money is just that: dollars and cents—nothing more, nothing less.

But that is not what many of us believe. Sure, the wisdom of the ages has warned of the dangers of riches. The news regularly reports stories of wealthy people who live lives of pain and despair. We see rich starlets and overpaid athletes arrested because their lives remained empty while they were trying to fill the holes in their hearts. Sadly, many of us Christians (who are called to be the "salt of the earth") have lost our savor. Many of us are in the same mess as the rest of the world. Even those of us who would criticize others who abuse drugs and alcohol think nothing of anesthetizing the pain we feel when the credit card bill arrives by going back to the mall!

We live in a culture that constantly sends the message that personal happiness is directly proportionate to how much we acquire. Pop culture tells us that happiness depends on how much money, stuff, and sex we have. Granted, most of us would not admit, "Yep, that's my philosophy of life!" But, in truth, don't we live like we believe that message? Be honest. Haven't you been convinced (at least upon occasion) that one more raise, a new boat, a cooler car, or a bigger house would make you happy? I have. That's hard to admit. But, I'm human, and I sin.

At the heart of it all is the belief that God was wrong. In fact, the borrower is not the slave of the lender. We buy the lie and dig an even deeper hole of debt, believing we can eventually build a mountain of wealth. We live in a culture saturated with "stuffaholism." Didn't the apostle John warn of the dangers of loving the things of this world?

"Do not love or cherish the world or the things that are in the world. If anyone loves the world, love for the Father is not in him." (1 John 2, AMP)

 We have fallen for the lie from the pit that says: stuff, sex, money = happiness.
Okay, let's ask the hard question. If the world's equation is correct:

Sex + Money + Stuff = Happiness

Then why aren't the happiest families in America all in Hollywood?

There are three lessons that might turn this predicament into a fruitful learning and growing opportunity.

Lesson 1

Jesus' half brother, James, put a high premium on wisdom. (see James 1:5, NIV) Today, there seems to be confusion between wisdom and knowledge. They both have their place, but they are not synonymous. Knowledge is what tells us that a tomato is a fruit. Wisdom is what tells us not to put a tomato into a fruit salad. Today's world has plenty of knowledge but a dearth of wisdom. The smart people of today's financial world have had their turn at things, and now we are in trouble. Maybe it's time to rethink the fundamental tenets of our beliefs. Wisdom speaks to this. It says whenever someone gets something for nothing, there will eventually be a disproportionate price to be paid.

Lesson 2

Solomon, King David's number one son, was fond of saying, "There is nothing new under the sun." It seems to me that there is nothing "new" about our contemporary culture. While I would agree that the names and players are different, the root cause is the same. It pivots on the three things that John warned the early Christians to guard against, *"For all that is in the world, the lust of the flesh, and the lust of the eyes, and the boastful pride of life, is not from the Father, but is from the world."* (1 John 2:16, NASB)

Lesson 3

We would serve ourselves well to remember that the best financial teaching is in the Bible. I call it "Money 101." It comes from a man who knew how to live with, and without, prosperity. Paul shared with his young protégé Timothy the secret to dealing with money in 1 Timothy 6:17-19:

"Command those who are rich in this present world not to be arrogant nor to put their hope in wealth, which is so uncertain, but to put their hope in God, who richly provides us with everything for our enjoyment. Command them to do good, to be rich in good deeds, and to be generous and willing to share." (NIV)

Note the three things Paul tells rich Christians to do. (By the way, if you have a bathtub in your home—comparatively speaking—you're a rich Christian.)

1. Don't be prideful and arrogant. Wealth doesn't make one person better than another.

2. Don't put your trust in your 401(k) plan. As we've all seen, dollars in the bank do not guarantee anything.

3. Enjoy your wealth, but be ready to share it at the drop of a hat.

You may be thinking, "That was fine in the day of well-drawn water and one-room houses with no electrical outlets, but it is far too simplistic for our modern, complex world."

I disagree. Paul's words from the ancient world are every bit as relevant as the headline on the *Wall Street Journal* sitting next to my computer. His teaching drills to the very core of who we are and how we think. It gets back to what I mentioned a moment ago: appreciating the difference between knowing (knowledge) a lot about wealth and being wise enough (wisdom) to use our wealth properly.

Seeing the Eternal Through the Temporal

I would submit that the difficulties our nation is experiencing may not necessarily be a bad thing. Most humans look up only when we have been sucker-punched and are lying on the floor flat on our backs. That's when we tend to see the eternal through the temporal.

As you read this, the financial markets may be shooting toward the moon, or they may be in the tank. Historically, stock market investments go up roughly 70 percent of the time. Over the last 100 years, stocks have gained value in most every ten-year period. The question laid squarely at our feet is how will we respond to the tempests in the teapots of our lives in view of eternity? What if tough times caused Christians to again become salt? What if we, again, led by example? What if we bought fewer "extras?" What if we paid off our credit cards and purchased only cars we could afford? What if we saved more than we spent? What if we always had money to give to others and were truly ready unto every good deed? What if we got serious about being all we could be as God's witnesses before the world?

"Dear friends, I urge you, as aliens and strangers in the world, to abstain from sinful desires, which war against your soul. Live such good lives among the pagans that, though they accuse you of doing wrong, they may see your good deeds and glorify God on the day he visits us." (2 Peter 2: 11-13, NIV)

Three Reasons Why People Who Are In Debt, Stay In Debt

As I write this portion of the chapter, I'm on a plane returning home to Nashville from a *No Debt No Sweat! Christian Money Management Seminar* that we concluded last night in Montana. The church was filled with sweet, godly people. But many of them were struggling with their money. I was especially touched by a couple of situations where the people felt hopeless. I've learned several things through the years as I've taught the seminar around the country, and one of those lessons is that people who are in debt stay in debt for three reasons:

1. They feel hopeless.

In truth, they are usually not hopeless. Most people who follow what we teach in our seminars can get out of personal debt (not counting their homes) in a one- to four-year period. Granted, there are huge benefits to starting this process early rather than later in life. But if you're already in your late forties, fifties, or older, it's not too late. There are people who start savings plans in their seventies and still see helpful results. Remember, it's never too late to start doing the right thing. (By the way, in addition to the financial implications in that comment, there are also some profound theological implications. The God we serve is not only the God of the second chance—He's the God of the ten thousandth chance, too!)

2. They feel all alone.

This is where Satan does his best work—he convinces a person that he is the only one with the problem. So, naturally, he's embarrassed and tries to hide it by putting on his mask and pretending like everything is okay. Yet, inside, he's dying. His spiritual vigor is gone. He's fighting with his spouse. He doesn't have time for the kids. He can't sleep at night. He's depressed.

The truth is, if you're in debt, you're not alone. As I've mentioned earlier, I'm convinced the majority of Americans are only one paycheck away from trouble. It's been estimated that many of us are spending 20 percent of our income paying off short-term, high-interest rate debt. As long as the devil keeps us convinced that we're the only person hurting—he wins!

I've about decided that the devil is nothing more than a roach. Have you ever gone into a dark room, turned on a light and seen a roach in the middle of the floor? What does it do the second the light hits it? That's right—it runs for cover! Dear reader, the devil is a roach. When we begin to shine the light of Jesus on him, he scrams!

What we need to do as Christians is develop the "*koininia*-style" fellowship that the Bible tells us to develop. We need to become each others' best friends and confessional partners. When we start to talk openly with each other, things change. Church is much more than sitting for an hour looking at the bald head in front of you! It should be the place where we develop our closest friends and confidants.

But to be painfully pointed here, the church is sometimes its own worst enemy. In many churches, "that sort of thing just isn't done," some Christians might say. After all, if we're God's kids, aren't we supposed to have our acts together? Sure, we can admit to some of the socially acceptable sins: "I wish I didn't lose my temper so easily" or "I spend too much time at the office and not enough at home with the kids." But that's where we draw the line. After all, many of us are "people of the mask." When we come into the church building, our neckties are straight, our dresses are in fashion—and our lives had better appear to match up. Maybe it's time to shine the light of Jesus on that old roach!

When we become involved and invested in one another—and start telling the truth—we'll begin to open up. Some of you guys need to begin a weekly men's prayer breakfast so you can cultivate this kind of atmosphere. Some of you ladies need to get gut honest in your prayer circles. Some of you husbands and wives need to invite another couple over, pop some corn, and start the conversation.

If you don't know what to say, try something like: "I'm sitting bolt-upright in bed at three o'clock in the morning scared about my debts;" or "My wife and I are at each others' throats;" or "I haven't given anything at church in six months." I believe if you try a stunt like that you'll be surprised at how the conversation will flourish. And you know what the neat thing is? There's a high probability that the other people will breathe a sigh of relief and say, "Me too!"

3. They feel dumb.

It's amazing how often when I'm talking to people about their debts, they'll stop and look at me and say, "I feel so stupid" or "I'm such an idiot." Here's the fact: Being in debt and being dumb are two entirely different things! Sadly, it's possible to be totally out of debt and still be a dumb person! But, seriously, the opposite is also true. It's possible to be in debt and not be dumb at all! I could share a number of stories with you of people I've known who were smart business leaders but got themselves into terrible debt troubles.

Granted, most of our debt dilemmas are the result of dumb decisions. But making a dumb decision and being a dumb person are two totally different things!

We All Have Butterflies in Our Stomachs
The Key Is Getting Them to Fly in Formation!

Here's the good news: Your past does not have to dictate your future! As long as the devil can keep us believing that we are somehow mentally inferior to others, he wins. The reason I make such a strong point of all of this is because the devil uses this lie to destroy us.

In Scripture we see Satan as he really is—the great accuser of God's children. This is how he is depicted in the book of Job when he accuses Job of doing his good deeds for selfish purposes. The devil pulls the same trick again in Zechariah 3:1:

"Then he showed me Joshua the high priest standing before the angel of the LORD, and Satan standing at his right side to accuse him. The LORD said to Satan, 'The LORD rebuke you, Satan! The LORD, who has chosen Jerusalem, rebuke you!'" (NIV)

The name, "Satan," is closely akin to the Hebrew word, *Satan'el*, which means "accuser." This is Satan's stock-in-trade. He is the celestial prosecutor who never forgets our sins and mistakes. Every time I fall down spiritually and try to get up again, it's Satan who whispers, "Steve, you know who you are. Maybe you've fooled these people and they think you're spiritual, but we know better don't we? Don't you remember the TV show we watched the other night when no one else was looking? Don't you remember that guy whom you vainly flattered to get a better price? And how about those thoughts you had when that young blond crossed her legs at the party?"

It's only when we accept the reality of God's grace and peaceful forgiveness that we will be equipped (or even motivated) to change and improve. Many of us feed on the guilt of past mistakes and, in the process, miss a better future. Forgiveness comes when we repent and ask for it. After forgiveness happens, any further worry is simply wasted effort. It comes from the devil himself. God's righteous conviction results in godly improvement and a realization that, as Paul says, *"…one thing I do: forgetting what lies behind and reaching forward to what lies ahead, I press on toward the goal for the prize of the upward call of God in Christ Jesus."* (Philippians 3:13b-14, NASB)

When all that your past mistakes accomplish is an ongoing sense of worry, dread, and a lifestyle of inactivity, you can bet that those emotions are not from God. The truth is, God is pulling for you. The Psalmist says, *"This I know: God is on my side!"* (Psalms 56:9, NLT)

God is the one who wants you to turn off the tube, get off the couch, put away the chips, and get busy for him! Specifically in the context of this chapter, that means we're not going to allow past dumb money mistakes be our excuse for future dumb money mistakes. It's time to fearlessly get up and get going! To paraphrase the late Coach Bear Bryant: The road to success is dotted with too many parking spaces. It's time to get the car out of park and into gear.

The truth is that anyone with enough gray matter between his ears to crawl out of bed, brush his teeth, and drive to work also has enough smarts to get out of debt and get ahead. It's a matter of learning some basic (pronounced, s-i-m-p-l-e) strategies, then determining that you're sick and tired of business as usual!

In *No Debt No Sweat!*, I was able to go into much greater depth than space permits here. As a shameless plug for that book, I would strongly recommend any reader who has an interest in his or her money (whether you're struggling with debt; trying to get ahead; wanting to learn the basics of sane investing; interested in developing healthy giving patterns; or teaching your children about money) to get a copy. In the following portion of this chapter, I want to share thirteen keys that need to become part of your financial lifestyle, if you ever hope to manage your money instead of allowing it to manage you.

⌐🗝 Key 1
Learn the Importance of Thrift

I hesitate to mention this one. Not because it isn't important—but because I can sense that many of you are already rolling your eyes and saying, "Which century does that guy come from?" Admittedly, I'm approaching the time of life when I can comb my hair with a towel and my teeth are the shade of a camel, but I unapologetically stick to my guns on this old-fashioned (and nearly forgotten) principle.

When you boil it down to basics, there are two ways to have more money. (Actually, I suppose there is a third, but it involves using a mask and gun—probably not a good plan.) Seriously though, I still remember a meeting with our business' accounting firm many years ago. I suppose the monthly numbers hadn't been great and probably without thinking, I stupidly asked, "What do we need to do?" Before I could retrieve that idiotic question, my accountant said, "Earn more or spend less."

It's still true. That's how the people who get ahead—get ahead. But, today, thrift is a forgotten art. Maybe it's because we're too many generations removed from the Great Depression when people didn't know where their next meal was coming from. We think it's bad today when we can't afford a new Apple computer. In the 1930s, people were just trying to afford an apple for dinner!

My father grew up in the Great Depression, and after World War II, he and my mother married. A few years as a teacher convinced my dad that he needed to do his own thing. So he began an insurance firm that became very successful through the years. My father always dressed in a coat and tie. We lived in a modern house with all the niceties of life, but I can still remember my father picking up pennies when he walked down a sidewalk. He really didn't need them, but he was thrifty. He understood the value of money—and the effort it took to get it. (Similarly, I was told that someone once calculated that it would be a waste for Bill Gates to stop and pick up a $100 bill, because the $100 would be worth less than the few seconds it would take him to retrieve it!)

Practically applied, thrift means we watch our money carefully. Remember, if you don't care enough about your money to keep an eye on it, someone else will! This means we must aggressively look for ways to cut our cost of living. Sometimes it's simply a matter of being thoughtful: turning off lights when we leave the room, setting the thermostat lower and wearing a jacket, planning our errands so we avoid needless driving, and so forth.

But more and more in our self-indulgent, got-to-look-cool culture, this will require that we depart from the pack. It means doing stuff our friends won't do, like:

- Refilling our water bottle from a filtered tap rather than spending two dollars for a hip brand at the store.
- Reusing our cups. Did you know that if you bring your own cup, many convenience marts will let you refill it for up to 50 percent less than the cost of buying a new cup?
- Clipping coupons.
- Buying our kids' clothes at the next-to-new shops. They'll outgrow them before they outwear them anyway.
- Selecting a car for transportation rather than to impress people you don't know!

⊙⇒ Key 2

Avoid the Credit Card Sinkhole

Having spoken to thousands of debt-ridden Americans, I'm convinced that credit cards are the most misused financial product in the country. I see more pain, sin, and mental illness due to credit card problems than any other single source. But I disagree with people who say that no one should own a credit card. Credit cards can be helpful in a number of ways, such as:

› If your credit card is stolen and used fraudulently, you'll likely have fewer problems retrieving the loss than you would if your cash was stolen. In many cases, your liability limit is $50 per card.

› Some credit cards offer extended product warranties.

› Credit cards offer a good way to manage your money.

› If you have a dispute with a merchant, your credit card company can often be of assistance.

But there should be a skull and crossbones warning here, too. While they're promoted as plastic prosperity, credit cards are plastic explosives for millions of Americans. I would agree that some of us shouldn't touch them. I believe there are three things that anyone using a credit card should do:

1. Never buy anything with a credit card that you wouldn't buy with cash. If you don't have money in the bank to pay for it, don't buy it. Studies show that people often spend 12–40 percent more when they're using plastic!

2. Have a "Love Number" with your spouse. Agree with your spouse beforehand on a maximum amount you can spend with the credit card—and don't exceed it without first talking to each other and agreeing on it.

3. Pay every single penny every single month. If you notice a couple of months passing with an unpaid balance, it's time to pay it off or get rid of the card! Never, never, never carry a balance! It's a witch's brew for trouble.

Beware of the Minimum Payment Trap

As a follow-up to number three, let me say a word about the minimum payment trap. Millions of Americans think they're doing just fine as long as they make the minimum payment each month. But, believe me, if that's all you're paying you've already got one foot in the financial grave and the other on a banana peel!

Credit card companies love people who make the minimum payment and let the balance go unpaid month after month. Conversely, credit card companies don't like you very much if you pay off the entire amount each month—because you're only making them a little bit of money. Most of these companies make a huge percentage of their profits from interest and various late charges and service fees. As a matter of fact, if you pay your entire balance every month, the credit card companies call you a deadbeat!

Let me illustrate how this works. Suppose you have a credit card balance of $4,000 (that's only a half or a third of what many families carry), and you decide to pay just the minimum each month. Now let's assume that your credit card company's minimum monthly payment is 2 percent. (That's more than some cards require. But let's use this figure since the more you pay—the faster it goes away.) At that rate, we'd send in the first monthly payment of $80. Depending on the interest rate and various other details of your contract, some experts estimate that it could take more than thirty years to pay off your $4,000 debt!

🗝 Key 3

Avoid Borrowing for Depreciating Assets

"What," you ask, "is a depreciating asset?"

It's anything that goes down in value after you buy it. This is why I urge people to avoid borrowing money for furniture, appliances, and even new cars. At the top of this list is a vacation. Think about it. Where's the sanity in taking your credit card on vacation and giving it a tan—then having to work and worry for the next year to pay off that vacation?

Remember, when Christians start listening to Madison Avenue, Detroit, and Wall Street, that's when we get into trouble and lose our honor. Suppose you become convinced that you just have to have that brand new motorcycle—because the slick ad says, "You deserve it." So you borrow the $15,000.

What happens ten months later when you lose your job and still owe $13,000 on the motorcycle? Now it's worth only $11,000. How do you sell the motorcycle for $11,000, pay off the $13,000 you owe, and still maintain your honor? How does the calculus of that work? When Christians listen to the wisdom of the world, we're headed for trouble.

The Bible encourages running aggressively from the debt trap. It challenges us to look to the ant (whose IQ starts with a decimal point) and consider our own need to plan ahead.

"Free yourself, like a gazelle from the hand of the hunter, like a bird from the snare of the fowler. Go to the ant, you sluggard; consider its ways and be wise! It has no commander, no overseer or ruler, yet it stores its provisions in summer and gathers its food at harvest. How long will you lie there, you sluggard? When will you get up from your sleep? A little sleep, a little slumber, a little folding of the hands to rest—and poverty will come on you like a bandit and scarcity like an armed man." (Proverbs 6:5-11; NIV)

⚷ Key 4
If You're In Debt Now—GET OUT!

I frequently meet people at speaking engagements who make similar amounts of income but who are in very different situations. For instance, Family A and Family B are both earning $60,000 a year. But, while Family A feels hopelessly in debt, Family B has money in the bank. Why is that? More often than not, it's because Family B has murdered its debt. Getting ahead with a burden of debt is like trying to build a skyscraper while simultaneously digging a hole to China—pretty tough to do!

When we think of King Solomon, we think of wisdom. But according to the biblical record, Solomon was possibly also the richest guy who ever lived. (He could have bought and sold Bill Gates twice in a day's time with the change that fell through the holes of his tunic!) This ancient "moneyman" summed debt up in one line: *"The rich rule over the poor, and the borrower is servant to the lender."* (Proverbs 22:7, NIV)

Arguably, a better translation of the word "servant" would be "slave."

Nothing feels as good as having no debt. All the things we buy to help us feel good pale in comparison to the peace we experience when we don't have credit card bills due, a car payment to make, a school loan that's always there, or even a mortgage payment.

So, the question is: How do you get out of debt? I recommend two tactics to get you started: Steve's 3-Point Steroid Kit and an aggressive plan of attack.

Steve's 3-Point Steroid Kit

To accomplish our plan of attack, you're going to need some money. Let me share three things this is going to require. Before I start, let me cut some of you off at the pass. There are lots of folks who think what I recommend is too radical. They wonder, "Isn't there an easier way to do this?"

In my experience, unless you've just signed a $6 million dollar record deal or a pro baseball contract, the answer is usually, "No." What I'm about to recommend are three things that each of us already knows but few are willing to do. It's important to remember that there are always a thousand excuses for failure, but for those who truly want to succeed, there is a path. So, here we go with my 3-Point Steroid Kit:

1. Sell stuff.

That's right. You're going to sell everything you don't need. You're going to have garage sales, post items on eBay, figure out where the consignment shops are—whatever you have to do. Lots of people make thousands of dollars selling their junk to others who see it as treasure. Also, remember that there are two ways you can sell: the good way and the great way. The good way is anytime you sell something and get extra cash. The great way is when you sell a boat, a storage shed full of junk you aren't using, or a car you don't absolutely need to keep. Then, not only do you get the cash from the sale, but you also get rid of other expenses like insurance, maintenance, and upkeep. The net result is that you bring down your overall cost of living. So get busy selling stuff!

2. Cut expenses.

What does that mean? That means we lower our standard of living. It's time to go from the lifestyles of the rich and famous to the lifestyles of the poor and forgotten! This means we're going to apply those points of thrift that I mentioned in Key #1. When we put $40 of gas in our car—we're not going to put $4 of sodas and chips inside of us! It means we aren't going to the restaurant—we're going home to eat leftovers. Simply put, when we're in debt, we can't afford five dollars for 50-cent cups of coffee, period!

3. Learn how to work.

This is the one that gets the most resistance—but I believe it's the most important of all three steroids. In 1938, the United States government told us a lie. They told us that forty hours of work each week was the same as being fully employed. I'm telling you that that isn't true! When we're in debt, fighting with our spouse, and the collectors are calling—lying on the couch, eating chips, and watching Oprah ain't going to fix it! It's time to get busy. Think about it, we all get the same 168 hours each week, right? The only question is, "How are you using your hours?"

If you're an average adult, you probably need to spend at least fifty-six of those hours in bed. If you're a parent, you need to spend time with the kids. I was told of an old study that indicated many parents spend less than twenty minutes a day with their kids. But suppose you want to be a good parent, so you're going to spend two hours playing with the kids every day. That's fourteen hours—which brings us to seventy total hours. Now, how about another fourteen hours for personal stuff (running errands, jogging, etc.). Also, kick in another two hours daily (fourteen per week) for church and Christian activities. By my count, that totals 98 hours of our 168-hour week. And, also by my count, that leaves seventy hours when we could be working.

My point is simply that when you're in debt, get another job, or two, or three—and start murdering the debt. For most people, there is nothing wrong with working fifty- to eighty-hour weeks for a limited period of time to kill the debt that is killing them.

Now to Kill the Debt

Now it's time to put our action plan into action. The first thing to do is get the biggest, meanest crowbar you can find and go to the monster closet. This is where you've hidden all that debt. I've learned that most people who are overloaded with debt can't tell me exactly how much they owe, to whom they owe it, and what the various terms of the debts are. This is because they don't like to think about it. So they put it into their imaginary debt closet hoping for the best but fearing the worst. (Talk about a weapon of mass destruction—this is one that's likely to blow up at any moment!)

But this is the day that all of that changes! Ram that crowbar into the door of the your debt closet and pry it open. Then drag out

162

every one of those ugly debt monsters, line them up in the middle of the floor, and turn on the bright lights.

Pay the minimum monthly amount on all of them except one. This is the one you're going to murder first. Some advisors say to start with the debt you owe the least on. Fine. Others say to start with the one that has the highest interest rate. Great. Frankly, I don't care which one you start with. Simply pick the one you hate the most—the one with the ugliest green hair growing out of its tongue—and kill it!

"Well, how am I supposed to do that, Steve?" you ask.

Simply apply my 3-point steroid pack: Sell, cut, and work like mad. This is job number one. You're going to be fast, furious, and focused. This is when you get rough and tough with no fluff!

The minute that first debt is gone, go after the second one by using the money that's now freed up from the first debt. Do the same with numbers three, four, and so on. Dave Ramsey calls this "snowballing." Suze Orman calls it "rolling down." Clark Howard calls it "laddering." Personally, I just call it getting a financial life!

I've found that most people who do this in a serious way while applying my 3-Point Steroid Pack can get totally out of debt (not counting their homes) within one to four years.

⚿ Key 5
Pre-act So You Won't Be Forced to React

Generally speaking, I'm an optimistic sort of fellow. I don't get too rattled by predictions of gloom and doom. In my experience, the only people who make money by convincing others that the sky is falling are usually the helmet salesmen. With that said, a little balance is in order here, too.

According to at least one expert in the field, 75 percent of all of us will have a major financial setback within any ten-year period. That doesn't include all the lesser emergencies like when the washer and dryer break down (and one of them floods the floor), or when your car's engine dies just after having the transmission repaired. Life is not fair. If everything in your life is going well now—get ready. Something is going to go wrong! The only predicable thing about life is that it's unpredictable.

Am I being needlessly negative? Nope. Only realistic. Wall Street is the perfect example of this. In late 2007 when the Dow tipped to 14,000, pundits everywhere were buying more stock and dreaming of huge long-term returns forever. Nearly a year later, when the Dow was below 8,000, everyone was predicting Armageddon. Many believed the markets were gone forever. Of course, as we've witnessed, both extremes were wrong.

The fact is: Bad things happen to good people. But practically no one is ready when they happen. For instance, if all the stock market gurus who claimed to be able to "outperform the market" were able to do as they claimed, why didn't they sell all of their stock in 2007 when the Dow was over 14,000—and wait for the markets to recover from its subsequent fall into the 7,000s?

As Murphy's Law tells us: If something can go wrong, it will. That's why it's vital for you to have an emergency fund. Without it, when bad things happen, they'll be much worse. Without an emergency fund, you'll be tempted to start misusing your credit cards when there is a crisis, which makes everything tougher in the long run.

My advice? Pre-act—so you aren't forced to react. Do whatever you have to do that's legal and moral to set aside at least a few hundred dollars fast. Get some serious overtime. Get a second job. Clean a few houses. Rake some leaves. Do anything! But get those first few dollars. Then begin building your Murphy fund. My goal is to have an amount that's at least 5 percent of my annual income in my Murphy fund.

Let me share two final tips:

1. Never use this money to buy a new dress or a couple of extra vacation days. This is for emergencies only.
2. Put your Murphy fund in a separate savings account so it doesn't get mixed up and spent with your checking account money.

⚷ Key 6

Do a Personal Financial Freedom Plan (Aka a Budget)

I prefer to call my budget a Personal Financial Freedom Plan because it reminds of its benefits. It's personal, and it will give me financial freedom—if I will only *plan!* In both the live seminar and our *No Debt No Sweat! Boot Camp* small group video curriculum, we teach extensively on this topic. In the process, I share a nine-step approach to doing a successful family budget. For brevity, I've shortened that longer list to six important reminders:

1. Know what your "true income" actually is.

How much money do you bring home each month? This is what we actually have to work with. I've learned that many people really don't know what they earn. When I'm counseling someone, I'll often ask, "So, how much do you earn?" Frequently, the person will look at me and say, "I don't know" or "That WD-40 Form that my boss sent me, or the guy at post office sent, said I made $50,000."

Ding! Ding! Ding! Wrong! That's not what you made. That's what they call your gross income. And the reason they call that your gross income is because that's how you feel when you realize you didn't get all that money! That $50,000 was before they took out tax withholdings, Medicare, union dues, and everything else they could think of. By now, your $50,000 is starting to look more like $40,000. You must know what your true (take-home) income is in order to know what you have to work with.

2. Do your "PFFP" every month—in writing.

As far as I'm concerned, there is no such animal as a budget that's not in writing. If it's not written down—it doesn't exist.

3. Learn to prioritize.

Ask yourself, "If I only had $800 this month—what would I do with it first?" Would it be your giving, your shelter, or your food? Whatever it is, put that at the top of the list. Then what comes next and so on. This way, you'll pay the rent before the cable bill!

4. Don't forget the set-aside items.

Most of us have some things we don't buy every month. Some of us pay for our car insurance every six month or for a vacation once a year. But if you are not setting money aside for those items every month in their categories in your PFFP, you won't have the money when you need it.

5. Learn to distinguish between what's essential and what's optional.

The truth is, the essentials list is pretty short. It includes items like housing, clothing, food, transportation, and giving. After that, most other things are options. Note: Don't be confused by what your friends are doing—most of them are up to their eyeballs in debt!

6. Do your first budget on paper—not the computer.

I love computers, and I don't argue with folks who like Quicken, Turbo-Tax, and similar products. But there's just something about putting it down on paper that makes a budget feel real. You can always convert it into 1's and 0's on your computer later if you wish. On the next page is a Personal Financial Freedom Plan form that you may find helpful as a thought sparkler for your budgeting. Feel free to photocopy and use it if you wish.

Personal Financial Freedom Plan

Family Budget For: _____

For the Month/Year of: _____

EXPENSE	$ AMOUNT	% of INCOME
Giving		
Church		
Mission Efforts		
Ministries We Support		
Other		
Shelter/Housing		
Rent		
Mortgage (1st)		
Mortgage (2nd)		
Homeowner's Insurance		
Property Taxes		
Maintenance & Repairs		
Home Improvement		
Yard Care		
Exterminator		
Furniture		
Other		
Utilities		
Electric		
Gas		
Water		
Sewer		
Garbage Collection		
Computer/Modem		
Telephone (Landline)		
Cell Phone		
Long Distance		
Other		

EXPENSE	$ AMOUNT	% of INCOME
Food		
Groceries		
Necessary Restaurant Visits (i.e., for business)		
Other		
Clothing		
Child #1		
Child #2		
Child #3		
Child #4		
Mother		
Dad		
Other		
Debt Service		
(Hopefully, in time, this section will become shorter and shorter.)		
Car #1		
Car #2		
Bank Credit Card		
Student Loan		
Store Credit Card		
Other		
Transportation		
Gas/Diesel		
Oil Change		
Tires/Repairs/Maintenance		
Car Insurance		
License/Tax/Tag		
Parking		
Toll Road Fees		
Next Car Set-Aside *(No More Car Loans!!!)*		
Other		
Medical		
Health Insurance		

EXPENSE	$ AMOUNT	% of INCOME
Doctor Visit &/or Co-Pay		
Dentist Visit &/or Co-Pay		
Optometrist Visit &/or Co-Pay		
Eyewear/Dentures/etc.		
Drugs &/or Prescriptions		
Therapy		
Other		
Other Insurance		
Life (Dad)		
Life (Wife)		
Life (Children)		
Disability		
Umbrella		
Long-term Care		
Other		
Children		
Allowances		
Child Care		
Babysitters		
Lessons		
Athletic Teams		
Activities/Field Trips		
Lunches		
Birthday Party Gifts		
Future Weddings		
Other		
Gifts and Presents		
for Family and Friends		
Christmas		
Birthday		
Wedding		
Anniversary		
Holidays		
Other		

EXPENSE	$ AMOUNT	% of INCOME
Education		
Homeschool Curriculum		
Private School		
Uniforms		
College		
School Supplies		
Public School Expenses		
Adult Study Courses		
Other		
Entertainment and Goofing Off		
Cable TV		
Recreational Eating Out		
Vacation		
Magazine/Newspapers		
Films/Tapes		
Parties		
Play Money		
Other		
Savings and Investments		
"Murphy Fund"		
"I Don't Need This Job" Fund *(Goal: 3-9 Months Expenses)*		
Investments		
Other		
Miscellaneous		
Dues/Membership Fees		
Toiletries/Personal Care		
Barber/Beauty		
Dry Cleaning & Laundry		
Postage/Mailing/Delivery		
Pet Expenses		
Other		

🔑 Key 7

Be a Big-League Giver

Make giving a priority. Simply put, I believe it's impossible to live a truly joyful life as a stingy person. In *No Debt No Sweat!*, I make a strong case for giving. Rather than going into the details of tithing and debating percentages here, let me share three scriptural points:

1. We should give from our first fruits. This concept is mentioned more than twenty times in the Bible. Proverbs says, *"Honor the LORD with your wealth, with the first fruits of all your crops; then your barns will be filled to overflowing, and your vats will brim over with new wine."* (Proverbs 3:9, 10, NIV) In today's vernacular, this simply means God gets the first and the best. It's wrong to wait until the Sunday offering plate is passed around to look in our wallets to see if there's anything left for God.

2. Giving should be a joyful experience. Paul told the first-century Christians, *"Each one must do just as he has purposed in his heart, not grudgingly or under compulsion, for God loves a cheerful giver."* (2 Corinthians 9:7, NASB) If this is a struggle for you (as it has been for me), try this: Give until it feels good!

3. We should give as we've been given. God is marvelously benevolent. He has rarely told anyone to give something that he hasn't first given that person. The apostle sums it up this way, *"… each one of you is to put aside and save, as he may prosper, so that no collections be made when I come …"* (1 Corinthians 16:2b, NASB) Each of us should make personal and regular inventories of our blessings—then give accordingly. And don't worry. Among the people I've known who have tried, none of them have been able to out-give God!

🔑 Key 8

Insure Yourself and Your Loved Ones

These days, insurance products are promoted everywhere. You can go to independent agents, company salesmen, and even the

Web. The bottom line is, most of us need to look closely at our insurance coverage. Many people either have far too little insurance, too much, or the wrong coverage. Here are some of the types of insurance many of us should consider:

› **Life insurance.** This insurance protects the people who depend on you for income, should you die. Life insurance falls into two general categories: whole life and term life. Both have pros and cons. Term life products tend to be much cheaper than whole life insurance. The whole life sales guys are pros at convincing uneducated buyers that they need their products for "investment" purposes. I recommend that most people get pure and cheap term life insurance. Then they can do their investing elsewhere.

I usually recommend that people buy an amount of term life insurance that is roughly equivalent to at least eight to twelve times their annual income. Homemakers—that includes you! Stay-at-moms need coverage, too. This means Mom and Dad need to sit down and figure what it would cost annually to replicate the homemaking, child care, clerical work, and the other hundred things Mom does—then multiply that amount by eight to twelve times and buy the coverage. Be aware that there are various types of term life policies. Consider things like the length of the term and whether you will be eligible to purchase affordable coverage at the end of the term if you so desire. Of course, as with all other insurance products, understand that all companies are not created equal and products vary widely. Be sure to buy only from highly rated companies. (Before buying, you might want to check their A.M. Best, Finch, S&P, or other rating companies' reports.) Also, never allow one policy to lapse until you have its replacement confirmed. Too many people have done this only to find that, because of age or health issues, they were uninsurable. Lastly, never buy an insurance policy without reading (and understanding) your contract.

172

› **Health insurance.** I can't say it strongly enough: You need health insurance! Even if you're young and healthy, it's dangerous not to have good health coverage these days. Approximately 16 percent of our economy is spent on health care. Even a short uninsured hospital stay can wipe many families out. Three weeks ago, I had an outpatient surgery performed on my throat. So far the bills for that surgery and related medical attention have exceeded $20,000—and they're still coming. Without insurance, my throat would have been cut in another way, too! One way to reduce health insurance costs for some people is to buy high-deductible policies ($1,500 or more) and set up a Health Savings Account to help with the individual's portion of the costs. As I write this, the health insurance debate is raging. Stay tuned as health insurance is likely to morph before our eyes in coming years.

› **Car insurance.** Don't even think about driving a car without adequate insurance. I say "adequate" because there are more and more companies pitching "cheap" car insurance by selling you only enough to meet your state's minimum coverage requirements. As a caring person, you need to ask the question, "What if I only have the minimum, but I cause a wreck that kills or maims people for life. Don't I owe it to them to be reasonably covered to minimize the damage done to their lives?"

›**Homeowner's insurance.** As with all insurance, review you homeowner's policy regularly and maintain adequate coverage. Many policies have automatic step-up features, which try to keep up with rising home repair/replacement costs. This is the coverage that typically protects against liability claims, fire, theft, and, in some cases, other losses. But beware of what your homeowner's policy doesn't cover. While policies differ, most do not cover flood damage. Many don't cover mold or a host of other things. Others don't cover (or have very limited coverage) on things like computers and jewelry. When you get a little mailer from your insurer—read it. They're probably informing you of something else they've decided not to cover!

A Word to Renters

Even if you don't own a home, you probably do need insurance coverage. Look into some good renter's insurance that will protect your stereo from theft—and you from some liability.

›**Disability insurance.** Far more people are disabled than killed. Think about getting a solid disability policy to help maintain your income in the event you're unable to perform your job. Prices vary tremendously on disability policies. You can have some control over pricing by selecting a policy that doesn't start paying until you've been out of work for a substantial period of time or stops paying after a few years.

›**Long-term care insurance.** Personally, I think this is a good product for people to consider, at least by the time they reach their early fifties. Nursing home and assisted living care are tremendously expensive. This is the coverage that has saved many middle-aged adults from having to spend their life savings paying for aging parents. Again, as with all types of insurance, shop 'til you drop. Policies, pricing, coverage, and service vary significantly from company to company.

This is not the final word on insurance. Some of you will want to consider other forms, such as umbrella policies (designed to give extra protection over certain existing insurance coverage maximums), and errors and omissions (especially useful if you're a business professional). Read and study. There are numerous online insurance quoting services. Many (but not all) are helpful and reliable.

A Web site I have found somewhat helpful is Insurance Information Institute's site at **www.iii.org.**

⚷ Key 9

Prepare for Your Future

One important key to getting ahead financially is simple to understand, but oh so hard to do. People who retire without "pension tension" are the ones who have consistently lived on less than they earned and saved a significant amount of the difference.

This means taking advantage of tax-benefited investments like your company's retirement plan, IRA's (individual retirement plans), SEP accounts, and the like. This means understanding that the second part of your life is going to depend, in great part, on how well you manage, save, and invest your money now. The old adage is so true: If you don't manage your money, someone else will. There are at least four principles that wise investors tend to appreciate:

1. Start early.

I can't overstate the importance of this one. Every year I speak to thousands of people desperately behind the curve with their retirement programs. In my seminar, I show a hypothetical example that illustrates the benefit of starting early. I build it around Jack and Judy Jumpstart who married at age twenty and began investing $2,000 annually for eight years—totaling $16,000. Of course, this illustration is merely for comparative purposes, and there are some interest rate and return assumptions inherent in this, so there's no guarantee you will match these returns. But in my illustration, Jack and Judy's $16,000 has grown to more than $1,000,000 by retirement time. I tell of another couple, Herb and Helen Hurry-up—both age fifty. To have the same million dollars at retirement, Herb and Helen will have to save $23,000 annually for seventeen years (that's almost $400,000). Granted, this is just an illustration, no guarantee, but it does graphically show why it's important not to spend your twenties and thirties buying "his and her cars" and taking a lot of cruises.

2. Compounding.

Every great investor understands the concept of compounding. Simply put, compounding allows an investment to grow faster by generating earnings on top of reinvested earnings. In other words, you take the interest, dividends, cap gains, etc., that you earn on an investment and reinvest those earnings for a chance to earn more.

3. Asset allocation.

One of the fundamental principles of investing is not to put all of your investment nest eggs in one basket. I urge people to read and get smart on how to properly divvy up their money. For instance, 2008 was a terrible time for the stock market. On average, it was down about 40 percent for the year. Many people saw their retirement accounts decimated. It was a bad year for Bonnie and me, too, but not that bad. I reviewed the year's closing balances in early 2009. For the year, Bon and I were down less than 20 percent. Not good—but certainly not as bad as the average.

The reason isn't because I'm smart or have insider information. The main reason was because I practiced what I preach. We have our money broadly diversified. We're invested in real estate, cash, stock and bond funds with very small amounts in more than 10,000 companies in more than twenty countries, as well as various other interests. Some studies have shown that more than 90 percent of investment returns are not based on being smarter than everyone else and figuring out sly ways to buy low and sell high. Instead, in many cases, these market returns are related to how an investor allocates his money.

4. If it sounds too good to be true, watch out.

Be wary of the quick, "sure" thing. Investors who are constantly switching investments and trying to "time the market" usually come out on the short end of the stick. Riverboat gamblers don't make good long-term investors. Read the small print: "Past performance is not a guarantee of future returns." In many cases, the hot mutual funds that outperform the market during one period, underperform in the next. There will always be speculators, day traders, and market timers, but sooner or later the bottom usually falls out. What comes after that can be a real bone crusher!

As I conclude this portion, let me state the obvious: There are no guarantees. An investor can do all the right things (or even all the wrong things) and still be surprised (pleasantly or unpleasantly) by the results. These pointers are simply for your consideration. Of course, before you make money decisions, study and get qualified professional help. Consider your own specific circumstances, tolerances, timelines, and goals, and then step cautiously.

⊙━ Key 10

Do the Important Stuff

I believe everyone, whether you are rich or poor, should do the basics:

› **Make a video and do an inventory list of everything in your home.** If you ever have to file an insurance claim because of theft or a fire, you'll be glad to have the proof.

› **Have a will that clearly tells those left behind what your wishes are.** On this point, I'm old-fashioned. Although there are lots of opportunities to purchase will forms online, for most people, I recommend spending a little money and going to a qualified attorney. Depending on your situation and net worth, this may be a relatively inexpensive way to avoid a lot of confusion later.

› **Leave some ideas for what you would like included in your funeral service.** You might list the songs or scriptures you would like read. Maybe you would choose to include some thoughts that could be shared. Of course, be thoughtful. Don't put family members in even greater stress by requesting costly things that will do financial damage. And be sure that at least one or two family members know where your notes are. It's a terrible thing for a widow to run across her deceased husband's notes in a drawer three weeks after his funeral. (I'll have more on this point in Key #11.)

› **Consider signing a living will.** If you're ever medically unable to speak for yourself, having a living will may reduce stress for your loved ones, should they be forced to decide what you would prefer.

🔑 Key 11

Be a Pack Rat: Keep Your Important Papers

There may come a day when you (or someone you love) needs those old tax filings and receipts, your will, the house papers (including repair and maintenance project costs), or your investment information. Far too many of us are sloppy with our affairs. Many people have no idea how to locate their 2003 tax returns, their returned checks for 2004, or last year's IRA statements.

Two of the most important containers Bonnie and I have are the ones where we keep our important papers. They hold no money or precious metals. Instead they hold our valuable records and data. Bonnie and I (and the kids) know exactly where to go to find the papers whenever we need them. Since they are in one spot, everything is together and easy to access.

Also, as cheap and easy as it has become, today it's foolish not to make copies of all of your important papers and data and put those in a different location. Remember, fire, floods, and thefts have claimed millions of original documents in the past.

Bonnie recently scanned the hard copy originals of our important files and downloaded them onto two separate memory stick drives. One of those memory sticks will go into our safe-deposit box at the bank, and we'll put the other in a safe place elsewhere. (Note: Your bank safe-deposit box may not be the best place to put some items. In some cases, experts say, safe-deposit boxes can be "frozen" at an individual's death or in the event of a bank's closing. In normal situations, those boxes will eventually be "unfrozen" and available to their owners, but such a situation could happen at an inconvenient time. That's why I like a third location for important items.)

How Long Should You Keep Your Documents?

Recently, I was reading an article whose author attempted to tell others how long they should keep various documents. For instance, he explained that, in some cases, you need to maintain tax records for three years; in other cases, six or seven years; yet in other cases, forever!

I've heard all sorts of formulas for how many years to keep various documents. You can do as you wish, but as for me and my household, we keep most things forever. Obviously, I don't keep the warranty on a $12 can opener for ten years after I throw it away. But, within reason, I hold onto most things permanently. Sure, it takes some storage space, but I believe the benefits are worth it.

Years ago in a bankruptcy proceeding (not mine; I was one of the creditors who went unpaid), someone misrepresented the fact that I owned a certain piece of real estate. They were claiming that the property had belonged to a business, not to me. Fortunately, I had the records from about twenty years earlier clearly proving me to be the owner. Without those papers, I would still have probably prevailed, but the few thousand dollars I spent in legal fees could easily have reached many times that much!

The next two pages contain a checklist and worksheet you may find helpful. Neither form is all-inclusive, but maybe they will help as you bring some order to your important papers.

Family Member's Name	Age	Social Security Number	Address	Home Phone

Work Phone	Boss' Name	Cell Phone	Medications	Doctor Name & Phone

ITEM	✔	ITEM	✔
Birth Certificates		Insurance Policies	
Baptismal Records		Investments	
Passports		Car Information & Proof of Ownership (Copies at least)	
Wills			
Living Wills		Real Estate Papers, Deeds, Mortgages, Title Insurance, Closing Documents, etc.	
Powers of Attorney			
Doctors and Contact Data		Burial Plot Information And Papers	
Doctors, Prescriptions Meds/Vitamins		Safe-Deposit Box Inventory	
		Educational Records	
Employment Records		Military Records and Service Numbers	
Bank Accounts		Product & Other Warranties and Guarantees	
Social Security Numbers		Inventory/Registry of Major Personal Properties	
Drivers License (Copies: Fronts & Banks)		Net Worth Statement and Credit Scores	
Credit Cards, Numbers, Contacts (Copies: Front & Back)		Federal/State/Local Tax Returns, Records, Receipts, etc.	

Partial Listing of Important Papers and Documents
You Should Keep in a Safe Place:
Quiz yourself and your family for other important
items you may wish to add to this list. Remember to
check it occasionally and keep it current.

🗝 Key 12

Stay Healthy

For most people, their greatest wealth-building asset is their health and ability to work. Humanly speaking, your greatest wealth is your health. It's vital to do everything you can to stay well. Obviously, there are lots of illnesses and injuries beyond our control. But the vast majority of physical maladies can be prevented with a little common sense and self-control.

Being sick is expensive! Illness costs billions of dollars each year in lost productivity. As I mentioned earlier, I'm presently recovering from a vocal cord problem that has kept me sidelined for several months. (I haven't found many audiences who want a speaker who uses sign language.) And at this moment, the message of this particular key is acutely poignant for me. This experience has reminded me that it's not just the direct dollars I miss out on when I'm ill. Sickness costs in a fistful of other ways, including:

› **Out-of-pocket medical costs.**

› **Medical-related costs.** This involves the extra mileage of going to doctors and therapy. It also includes all the medications and stuff you have to buy to deal with the illness.

› **Lost time and income for other family members.** I have no idea how many hours Bonnie has patiently sat in waiting rooms. Her time is valuable, and we lost the benefit of that time through this ordeal.

› **While hard to calculate, the emotional toll is costly, too.** When you're sick physically—you tend to become discouraged. Even though I was capable of writing and doing other things, there were wasted days when I simply didn't have the emotional energy to get up and get going. After my heart surgery about eighteen years ago, I determined to do everything I could to stay healthy as long as possible. In my case, that meant getting on a serious exercise program and a low-fat diet. I've not always performed perfectly—but I have remained disciplined. (I haven't had a steak in almost eighteen years, and I run 5 miles on a StairMaster three days a week.) And I feel great! This good health helps me perform my work better. Trust me, doing a four- or five-hour seminar can be very draining. Plus, I tend to feel better emotionally.

Although it's not mentioned in most financial books, staying well is one of the most financially important things you can do because it blesses on two levels. First, if you're well then you can work, and work means you have an income. Second, as I've already mentioned, staying well reduces your outgo on medical expenses.

🗝 Key 13

Importance of Balance

The devil isn't playing with a full deck. When we stop to think, we realize that God made the world and everything in it—and everything God made is good. So it's fair to ask, "What does Satan have to work with?" Really, he has nothing to work with except the good things God has made. Satan simply takes those good things from God, and twists and perverts them. Then he tries to sell them back to us. Sex in marriage is a party—a very good thing. But outside of marriage, it is fornication—a very bad thing. Ambition is good if it inspires us on to peak performance. But if our ambition causes us to crawl over others to get what we want—that's bad.

Money is the same way. If we use it as God intended, it's a good thing. But if we allow greed to dictate the terms of our life, it becomes a catalyst for sin. In 1 Timothy 6:10, Paul tells his young protégé, *"The love of money is the root of all sorts of evil, and some by longing for it have wandered away from the faith, and pierced themselves with many a pang."* (NASB)

Many years earlier, our old friend Solomon looked over his empire and made two seemingly contradictory statements. In one comment, he equates wealth as a gift from God: *"Moreover, when God gives any man wealth and possessions, and enables him to enjoy them, to accept his lot and be happy in his work—this is a gift of God."* (Ecclesiastes 5:19, NIV)

In the next chapter, he speaks of wealth's darker side, *"God gives a man wealth, possessions and honor, so that he lacks nothing his heart desires, but God does not enable him to enjoy them, and a stranger enjoys them instead. This is meaningless, a grievous evil."* (Ecclesiastes 6:2, NIV)

Maybe instead of contradicting himself, Solomon is simply showing us both sides of the same coin. Maybe it all boils down to living a balanced life. There comes a time when enough is enough. Striving for more stuff doesn't bring more satisfaction. Instead, it simply makes us want more. There's a beautiful passage in Proverbs that sums it up pretty well:

"Give me neither poverty nor riches; Feed me with the food that is my portion, That I not be full and deny You and say, 'Who is the LORD?' Or that I not be in want and steal, And profane the name of my God." (Proverb 30: 8-9, NASB)

Money doesn't bring happiness, but it can make for an easier life. If correctly used, it can lead to joy (not necessarily the same as happiness) as we share what we have with others and see the blessings it brings in their lives. My goal: to be financially fit forever.

A Word to the Sandwich Generation

Dealing with Grown Kids and Caring for Aging Parents

The comments in this final section are squarely built on two scriptures:

1. *"Train up a child in the way he should go: and when he is old, he will not depart from it."* (Proverbs 22:6, KJV)

2. *"Honor your father and your mother, that your days may be prolonged in the land which the LORD your God gives you."* (Exodus 20:12, NASB)

If you're between forty and sixty years old, you're part of the Sandwich Generation. "What's that?" you ask. It's a relatively new phenomenon. These are the modern-day adults who are being squeezed from both sides: Dealing with restless children and aging parents. In previous generations, kids tended to grow up more quickly and leave the nest more permanently. In the past, people didn't live as long. When Social Security began in the 1930s, the average life expectancy was about sixty-seven years. Today, many people are living twenty-five, thirty and thirty-five years into retirement.

All of this is good, but it can make for difficult circumstances for the Sandwich Generation. As I speak to people around the country, I'm meeting more and more middle-aged adults who should be busy saving for their retirement, but are still supporting grown kids (or at least paying college bills) while also trying to care for their parents. If you identify with this, let me share a few ideas you may find helpful in managing your time, money, and the demands placed on you.

› **Don't let the inmates run the asylum!** It's almost always a mistake to become a crutch for our children, but I see good parents doing it all the time. As a matter of fact, Bon and I have had to fight this temptation. Sooner or later, kids should grow up and leave.

I recently counseled an elderly lady who was struggling with huge financial problems. As we sat talking in her living room, the basement door opened and out stepped a forty-something-year-old man. "Who is that?" I wondered. "He's my son," she told me. "He lives downstairs." Then the mother went on with a diatribe of excuses for why this healthy grown man still lived at home depleting her minimal assets and contributing nothing. I was fuming!

Admittedly, that was an extreme case, but it behooves all parents to set boundaries and draw lines. It's important to remember that softness and love are not always the same thing. Assuming normal health and intelligence, the most loving thing a parent can do is raise godly, responsible, self-reliant kids who become contributors rather than societal mooches.

› **Open the lines of communication early with parents.**
Discussing money issues is still taboo with some people from the
Greatest Generation, but it's vital that we do so. The healthiest financial situations are usually homes where the Sandwich Generation
sits down early with the Greatest Generation and asks the hard
questions—all with an attitude of love and deference. This may
take time. There may be old wounds that have to heal first. Some
apologies may be in order. Showing appropriate respect is key here.
Do whatever is appropriate to open the lines of communication.
Then discuss the toughies:

1. How much do you have saved, and where is it?
I can't emphasize enough the importance of this one. Elderly
people tend to be far too trusting. It might be wise for you to personally go with your parents and meet their advisor. Ask the hard
questions—do a true due diligence in their behalf. If the advisor
becomes offended or defensive, consider that a red flag.

2. What insurance coverage do you have?
If your parents have life insurance, learn all about it. If they
don't have good long-term care coverage, consider getting it. Be
sure their homeowners and Medicare supplemental coverage
is paid and proper for their needs. Look for insurance that they
may be paying for needlessly. For instance, if they no longer are
driving—why keep paying for car insurance?

› **Avoid depleting your retirement fund to care for your
parents.** This has to be considered on a case-by-case basis, but in
general, it can cause more problems than it solves. It may seem wise
on the surface, but ultimately it may only shift the cost of your retirement to your children—at which time, if things continue going the
way they are now, will cost even more. If the money is short, look

for ways to share the care of your parents with siblings or relatives. Look for ways to mix and match your gifts as you serve your parents. I'll have more on this shortly.

> **Ask your parents to talk with you before making any major purchases.** Again, elderly citizens are favorite targets for unethical home repair people, financial products salesmen, and the like.

> **Select a designated caregiver.** Ideally, this is one of the kids, but be cautious and thoughtful about how you do this. Select the person with the greatest heart of mercy. Check your ego at the screen door and accept the fact that your parents may prefer one sibling over another for this task. Hopefully, this is the child who lives closest to the parents. Also, if you assign one sibling the task of running point— remember that doesn't relieve the others of their responsibilities. It just means that responsibilities may shift somewhat. For instance, the caregiver may be relieved of rendering any financial help—that will become the responsibility of the other kids. Possibly the other siblings will agree to send the caregiver on a paid, annual vacation. The non-caregivers can mow the caregiver's yard, clean his and her home and run some of the errands.

By all means, understand that fatigue is a real issue here. The caregiver deserves regular days (or weeks) off when the other siblings will fill his/her spot.

> **Prepare emotionally and financially for the last two moves.** In many cases, there will come a time when Mom or Dad need more care than you can give them in their home. Decide early what your family preferences will be. Will one of the kids bring them into their home? Will you look to a long-term care provider? And about that final move, this one will be tough. Frankly, this

suggestion is more for your benefit than your parents'. Sit and visit with your parents. If their health and emotions allow, ask how they would like you to treat their funerals. Do they have favorite songs? Is there someone special they would like to preside? What would they like?

Change is never easy. Often, it is expensive. But with a bit of planning and prayer, the road ahead can be managed. By making the right money decisions along the way, a family can transition from one generation to the next with a lot less stress and regret.

If you have made some money mistakes, remember what I've said before: It's never too late to begin doing the right thing. This adage has both temporal and eternal implications.

7

Be a Hero
How to Become an Inspiring Mentor
(And, How to Find a Mentor)

When you boil it down, there are essentially two types of leadership. The first is *power-driven leadership*. This model survives only in the most primitive, dire situations. When people who are being led are under bondage, they have no loyalty to a greater cause. They don't follow because of aspiration. They submit because of desperation or, in some cases, intimidation. Leaders who prevail through intimidation and ruthlessness don't receive many gold watches. They may be feared, but they are seen as the enemy. No one holds their principles in high regard or cares about their legacy. And it's a safe bet that their followers (children, employees, etc.) will rebel at the first opportunity. One of the supreme examples of this failed leadership paradigm is in Charles Dickens' 1843 classic, *A Christmas Carol*. Do you really think Bob Cratchit showed up for work on Christmas day because he loved working for Ebenezer Scrooge?

> "If your actions inspire others to dream more, learn more, do more and become more, you are a leader."
> – JOHN QUINCY ADAMS

The second model is *inspirationally-motivated leadership*. This is leadership from the heart. Followers under an inspirational leader excel because they are trained and inspired to be excellent performers.

They see the big picture and catch the vision. This type of leadership is the essence of effective mentoring. Whether it's a parent training a child or an office manager instructing a new recruit, studies show that this model works!

Remember, also, that a mentor and his or her protégé do not have to agree on every point or come to the same conclusion on each issue. Just because I look to someone as a mentor doesn't mean that I will agree with all of his or her beliefs and life choices. And, as a mentor, I shouldn't expect my protégé to buy into all of my political, philosophical, or doctrinal conclusions. Mentoring is not mind control. It's the process through which a more mature person helps a less mature person discover the broad life skills needed to make good life choices. A mentor is simply a person who, after walking a few steps further down the path, holds up a torch for the one following behind.

> "Really great people make you feel that you, too, can become great."
> – MARK TWAIN

Case Studies in Real-World Mentoring

You've probably heard the old story of the four-year-old who came downstairs from her bedroom crying.

"What in the world is wrong?" her concerned mother asked.

"It's dark in my room, and I'm scared," was her trembling reply.

"Oh, honey, don't worry," she said. "God will take care of you."

"But," the little girl protested, "I can't see God."

"Don't worry," her mother said. "He's there even though you can't see him."

Still crying, she looked up and asked, "Will you come up and lie down with me?"

"Why," Mom asked, "don't you believe God is there?"

"Yes, but tonight I need someone who has skin."

When I began my research for this chapter, my plan was simply to outline the keys of effective mentoring: how to be one and how to find one. Later, I will do just that.

But for now, a real-world example might be the most effective way to begin our discussion and communicate how and why mentoring is vital to any organization, whether it's in a family, church, or business. It seemed appropriate to put some "skin" on mentoring before delving into its details. So I began researching various institutions that have been built on cultures of effective mentoring.

I settled on three that I believe are fabulous models of effective mentoring. One is **American Airlines,** a good example of corporate mentoring. Another is **Dr. Robert Ossoff** at Vanderbilt Medical Center, an educational mentor. The third is **Pat and Shirley Boone**, who are incredible examples of personal and family mentoring. Since space won't allow me to go into full case studies on all three, I've decided to focus on the Boones. I believe their family and their example of mentoring will be most applicable to most of us. First, however, let me make a few passing comments about American Airlines and Dr. Ossoff.

Taking the High Road

As one of American Airlines' biggest fans, I've watched this company do business for years on hundreds of flights. After the terrorists' attacks on September 11, 2001, the bottom fell out for the airline industry. People were afraid to fly, and airline companies lost billions. Through those rocky days, I watched American Airlines ticket agents and crews keep a stiff upper lip and do what they do best. Just as things began to improve, oil prices skyrocketed. Then what many believed to be a terribly unfair ruling by the Federal Aviation Administration dealt another costly blow to this company in 2008.

Yet through it all, AMR (the parent corporation of American Airlines) has taken the moral high road. Under the leadership of

CEO Gerard Arpey, the company fought staggering headwinds. Not all of the employees agreed with his decisions, but through the years, Arpey has built a culture of openness and honesty, which I believe is the essence of an effective corporate mentor. As an honest broker, he and his team have slain dragons to maintain a solid coalition of customers, shareholders and employees. To my knowledge, American Airlines is the only one of the five big spoke-and-hub companies to steadfastly refuse to consider bankruptcy. To date, the company has continued funding its employee pension plan.

In a personal conversation, one of the company's high-level officials shared with me how the airline's executive suite struggled to take the moral high road, even when they could have saved money by cutting corners. Moral corporate cultures are not the product of random, do-whatever-it-takes business models. Morality in a business is the product of morality in the executive suite. In turn, that moral compass is reflected down the line. This communication and example-based leadership form the essence of effective mentoring.

Sharing Talents

I'd also like to share the story of Dr. Robert Ossoff, who founded the Vanderbilt Voice Center in 1992. Because of his groundbreaking surgical procedures, Robert has saved the voices of countless singers (we're talking platinum record acts), as well as internationally known speakers and politicians. As I mention elsewhere in this book, the past year has been vocally challenging for me. But thanks to Dr. Ossoff's surgical skills I'm on the mend.

What impressed me most about the good doc was his almost obsessive commitment to mentoring other doctors. Through the years, scores of physicians have come to Nashville to be mentored by Dr. Ossoff. According to one of these doctors, Dr. Ossoff has trained approximately half of the leading otolaryngologists in America. I've noticed an unusually high level of skill and bedside manner among his protégés. Despite his surgical prowess, I suspect Dr. Ossoff's greatest legacy will be that of a mentor.

The Story of Two Wonderful Mentors

Since most of us will never run major corporations or train elite surgeons, it seems more appropriate for me to focus on an example of effective personal and family mentoring. Fortunately, I can point to a number of mentors who have blessed my life. My own parents were two godly examples who taught me a lot. There have been several others through the years.

But as I thought about people I've known over the decades who have poured themselves out the most as mentors to others, Pat and Shirley Boone was the couple that consistently came to mind. In an effort of full disclosure, I should tell you that the Boones have been friends of mine for years. As I write this, I've just spent the last two days visiting and talking with this dear couple. So what I may lack in objectivity, I more than make up for in familiarity. My prayer is that in sharing their story, you will see how lives well lived can touch thousands of others for good.

For those of you from a later generation, a little introduction is in order. Pat met Shirley Foley (daughter of country music legend Red Foley) in the early 1950s at David Lipscomb High School in Nashville, Tennessee. In high school, Pat became a rising singing favorite in Nashville; and Shirley became a cheerleader and homecoming queen who lost her mother when she was seventeen. The couple grew to love one another through those experiences.

From his earliest days, Pat's dream was to be a mentor. Like his role models, his goal was to be a schoolteacher and a preacher. A serious student, he went on to earn a sheepskin from Columbia University, graduating magna cum laude. But becoming a teacher and preacher wasn't Pat's destiny. Soon after they began their college careers, Pat and Shirley eloped and started their lives as husband and wife at the

ripe old age of nineteen. It was about that time that Pat was thrust
into the national spotlight as a three-time winner on the *Ted Mack
Amateur Hour* (the equivalent of today's *American Idol*.) In 1954, they
moved to Denton, Texas, where Pat continued his studies to become
a teacher. In addition to his college classes, he was busy preaching on
Sundays and hosting three weekly shows on WBAP in Fort Worth.
By this point, the young couple had proven themselves quite fertile.
The first of four daughters was born during Pat's sophomore year.

A fateful call came in 1955 when Pat was invited to fly to
Chicago to record his first national record. Within weeks, "Two
Hearts Two Kisses" reached the Top 10. As they say, the rest is
history. The next three years saw three more Boone-ettes, during
which time the family moved from Texas to Teaneck, New Jersey,
where Pat promptly enrolled at Columbia University and became
a fixture on Arthur Godfrey's network morning TV show. In 1957,
he became the youngest person ever to host his own weekly prime-
time network television show. And as the disc jockeys say, "the hits
just kept coming." Numerous number one and Top 10 records kept
Pat on the charts for more than two hundred straight weeks—and
on the road most weekends. In the second half of the '50s, Pat's
only real record sales competitor was Elvis.

As we discussed in the conflict resolution chapter, the '50s have
been portrayed as America's Happy Days, but there was a cancer
growing in our country. Much of today's societal decay can be traced
back to the late '50s when teen rebellion was first sanctioned. Our
culture was heading for trouble. Pat realized this. When Elvis had
been asked why he didn't get married and settle down, he responded
with a smirk, "Why buy the cow when I can get the milk from under
the fence for free?"

Although "mentoring" had not yet become a popular buzzword,
Pat saw that teenagers needed guidance. So while still in college, he
wrote *Twixt Twelve and Twenty* to mentor teens who were writing him

by the thousands literally, asking for his advice. Pat's fundamental purpose was to lead, or mentor, by example. He wanted to teach young people the life skills they needed for successful living. Still in his early twenties, Pat spoke with authority on the issues of respect, moral living, loving God, and building healthy relationships. And, boy, were people ready for his book! It was the No. 1 nonfiction bestseller on the *New York Times* list for two straight years. And all proceeds, over a million dollars, went to establish a Christian college in Villanova, Pennsylvania.

But the Times, They Were-a-Changin'

The 1960s was a different time for Pat and Shirley. Having grown up in a show-business family, Shirley resolutely hung onto the hope of a normal life, complete with a picket fence and a husband who taught school and preached on Sundays. But that wasn't to be.

Pat's career continued to grow—and so did the distance between he and Shirley. Pat slipped into the Hollywood party scene with Shirley looking on from the side with a broken heart. Their girls were beginning to reach their teen years, and Shirley felt Pat wasn't doing enough to hold the family together. Pat and Shirley have both written at length about this turbulent time, so I won't repeat it all here. Suffice it to say, the Boone marriage, children, and the family's spiritual focus were all in real trouble. Because of Pat's entertainment entanglements and spiritual drift, he was not the mentor his family needed at this point. Even Shirley began to drift and felt despondent and desperate.

Sometime in late 1968, with things at their worst, Shirley was inspired by another spiritual mentor to seek the power of the Holy Spirit to help her be the wife and mother she longed to be. Later that day on her knees in her bedroom, she did just that ... and experienced His presence. Almost immediately, the change began. Pat was, at first, determined to simply wait and see how long Shirley's shift lasted. But as the months passed, her walk with Jesus proved too contagious to ignore. Pat, too, sought that same power and felt himself change from within. That was more than forty years ago. Since those days, as with any family, the Boones have had their ups and downs. There were plenty of business successes and failures, joyful weddings and terrible illnesses, hit records and embarrassing public moments. But through it all, Shirley and Pat have continued to grow in their faith and their witness before a world that sorely needs spiritual mentors. Their choice to live and work in Hollywood—the epicenter of hedonism—may not have been yours or mine. But they were determined to bloom where they were planted—and strove to hold up the torch in a dark world.

What I Learned from Pat and Shirley

My goal is to one day be able to say with Paul, *"I have fought the good fight, I have finished the race, I have kept the faith. Now there is in store for me the crown of righteousness, which the Lord, the righteous Judge, will award to me on that day—and not only to me, but also to all who have longed for his appearing."* (2 Timothy 4: 7, 8 NIV)

As Pat, Shirley, and I sat and visited in their den, I asked them two questions:

1. What is a mentor?

2. How have you allowed God to use you as mentors?

As we talked, the word "mentor" quickly began to morph. I soon realized that, for this couple, mentoring is synonymous with other concepts, such as setting the right example and being a positive witness to others.

When I asked Pat and Shirley who their mentors had been, they had different answers. Pat could point to his mother and dad. Margaret and Archie Boone passed away nearly ten years ago. But having also been mentors and dear friends of mine, I could appreciate the stories Pat told of how his parents doggedly pointed him and his siblings toward Jesus. Much like my own mother,

Margaret Boone never wasted time when a spanking was in order. She believed in loving discipline and didn't hesitate to yank a misbehaving young Pat out of church for a meeting with a switch. His father, a successful architect and builder, employed Pat and his brother, Nick, in the summers. Looking back, Pat remembers the on-the-job mentoring that took place as his father taught the boys hard work and ethical business practices.

Due to her mother's illnesses and her father's travel, Shirley grew up without as much parental oversight. Much of her mentoring came in her young adulthood, also from Pat's folks, as well as from numerous books and Christian films. Movies like *The Robe* and *King of Kings* served as some of Shirley's early mentors.

The Bible talks about being "tested by fire." In truth, one of the reasons the Boones have been such faithful mentors is because they have spent more than fifty years in the harsh spotlight of public attention. Unlike you and I who live relatively anonymous lives, everything Pat and Shirley did was on display for the world to see. Every flaw and struggle was seen. This left them with no place to hide—and a clear decision to make: Would they simply capitulate to the pressures of Hollywood or make a determined decision to hold up Jesus and be public mentors for his cause? Thankfully, they chose the latter. Here are some takeaways from our conversation on what makes a good mentor:

› **A basic humility.** When he messes up—a good mentor admits it. One of the things Pat and Shirley have always done is admit their mistakes and grow from them. Having grown up in a world where most adults didn't admit their faults, I have always admired (and related to) those few who did. When I'm struggling with a sin, I much prefer the mentor who is willing to say, "Steve, I've been there and done that," to the one who purses his or her lips and pretends to be stunned by my failure.

› **Calloused knees.** It's critical that those you mentor realize that you, too, have a mentor. You approach him in prayer. One of the most poignant moments in the Boone family happened in the 1970s after a difficult disagreement with one of the girls. Everyone had gone to separate corners. For Pat and Shirley, that meant quietly going to their bedroom to pray for God's direction and wisdom. During their prayer, one of their other daughters walked in and saw them on their knees, praying with tears rolling down their cheeks. As news traveled from daughter to daughter, the kids realized how intensely their parents took their obligation as mentors. This act spoke far more eloquently than any words could have.

› **A desire to share what works.** When Pat and Shirley are convinced they have found a solution—you can't shut them up! In the late '60s, when the family determined to make a public stand for Jesus, there was a price to be paid. Suddenly, Pat's career was on the line. I will always admire the gumption this couple showed through this turbulent period. In previous years, Pat had managed to blur his image as the Goody-Two-shoes guy with a Bible under his arm. He was comfortable at parties and became increasingly adept at telling questionable jokes. But, when he recommitted to following Jesus in a meaningful way, he wasn't sure if his career would survive. Ultimately, it didn't matter. All that counted was Jesus. So with the tenacity of a pro wrestler, Pat and Shirley decided to hold up the banner of Jesus everywhere they went. The family sometimes sang Christian music in their shows and at highbrow political functions. Any talk show host who dared invite them on was likely to hear their testimony.

And guess what? Despite real concerns, Pat's career didn't falter. As a matter of fact, God blessed it with a second wind. The *Boone Family Show* quickly became one of the highest grossing acts in the world!

> **Being the real deal.** As I reminisce, I can remember those days back in the '70s. I recall visiting with the Boones one night at a venue where they were scheduled to do two shows. Between the shows, we sat and visited in their dressing room. Outside were hundreds of fans anxiously waiting to see this famous family perform. If this had been the *Steve Diggs Show*, my head would have been as big as the concert hall. But in their dressing room that night there were no "stars" or prima donnas. Instead, I remember visiting with a family who was very comfortable in their own skin. The girls relaxed on the couch watching *The Doris Day Show*, while Pat and Shirley and I talked about spiritual matters. I saw that the "things of this world" were not their paramount interest. Despite all the adulation and hubbub, this family had their feet planted.

> **A fundamental optimism toward life and the future.** Pat will readily admit to making some wrong choices in the '60s. But confessing and correcting those mistakes catapulted him to a brighter future. Committing to Holy Spirit guidance helped him and his whole family grow stronger. As he explained to me, a broken bone can be reset and healed; and the healed bone can actually become stronger than before. This is why Pat and Shirley are the last to cast a stone at another person. Part of their mentoring has been to fallen Christian leaders. I am touched (and challenged) by the empathy they show to such burdened servants of God.

> **Not shying away from taking a stand**. One story that illustrates this goes back a number of years. Pat bumped into Muhammad Ali in an airport. Ali demanded to know why Pat had said, "I hope Ken Norton breaks Ali's jaw." Sure enough, Pat had made the comment, but for a reason very different than Ali suspected. Pat knew that Ali was not living by the principles he had been taught as a young Cassius Clay. Pat says, "I said I hoped Norton would break

his jaw to remind him that he was still Clay." The fighter, who was struggling with the temptations of celebrity, asked Pat how he stayed faithful to Shirley. Pat reminded Ali that the Bible says, *"Therefore, since we are surrounded by such a great cloud of witnesses, let us throw off everything that hinders and the sin that so easily entangles, and let us run with perseverance the race marked out for us."* (Hebrews 12:1, NIV)

A bewildered and unrepentant Muhammad Ali walked away—only to have his jaw broken in the ring a few weeks later by Ken Norton.

› **Setting clear rules early—and sticking with them.** In the case of their four daughters, Shirley and Pat made a startling decision by Hollywood standards. They wouldn't allow their daughters to date until they were sixteen—and then, only after they had met and approved of the boys. Whew, the girls thought their parents had just crawled out of a cave! After all, in a culture where most parents had no rules—and some even allowed coed sleepovers and bought pot for their kids' parties—this seemed like puritanical nonsense. But Pat and Shirley stuck to their guns and, today, their daughters couldn't be more grateful.

› **Strong male leadership at home.** Don't get me started here. I know this isn't politically correct, but I'm convinced that the best homes are the ones where the man acts like the man. I'm not going to take space here going through the mental gymnastics of explaining why this isn't to be construed as a license to be a bully. My point is simple: I believe there would be far fewer radical feminists, confused kids, and broken homes if dads would man-up to their responsibilities and grow spines.

To her credit, Shirley sensed this truth. Although Pat tried hard to be home as much as his work allowed, he was traveling a lot during those days. In his absence, Shirley chose to show him honor and respect by constantly invoking his beliefs and preferences as she raised the girls. Often when Pat was gone, Shirley would suggest that she and the girls "do what Daddy would want us to do in this situation."

Ladies, no matter how strong or weak your husband is in his leadership skills, you can extend his influence (mentoring) by showing him unswerving respect and allegiance. The rewards are worth it.

› **Listening and talking to God.** When things were at their worst, Shirley was at the point where she would have given up. But, instead, she determined to apply God's principles toward a man for whom she felt little love. Shirley began praying, "Lord, love Pat through me." She will tell you that God began to mentor her through this very prayer. Shirley says, "Day by day, God began to open my eyes to Pat's good traits; and simultaneously, his Holy Spirit opened my eyes to my own flaws."

God has continued to mentor Shirley through her prayer life. Our Father has a way of "arranging" things when we're open to his mentoring. A while back, Shirley found herself seated on a plane next to a well-known minister, who was at a low point in his life. He opened up to Shirley, complaining about how his wife didn't appreciate his ministry and frequent travel. "My wife knew I'd be gone all the time with this ministry," he explained.

Shirley, attuned to the prompting of the Spirit, responded with irrefutable wisdom, "Didn't Jesus leave everything ... including being with God ... to minister to his bride?"

› **A high premium on never quitting.** It's hard to mentor another if you don't take your own advice. Shirley and Pat will readily admit that the problems they have faced have left scars. But, as Shirley pointed out, scar tissue is even stronger than the original skin. As I sat with these dear friends in their home, it was profoundly obvious: They are glad they never quit.

I want you to do more than survive. I want you to thrive. Shirley and Pat offered insight on this, too. They explained that hardships build stronger bonds if we let them. Just like Holocaust survivors or people who are in a train crash together, there's an unbreakable bond. Couples who share hard times can forge solid bonds from those difficulties.

> **An ability to heal.** Pat says the two most important healing factors in his and Shirley's marriage have been a sense of humor and a willingness to always forgive. The Bible has the perfect remedy, "Do not to let the sun set on our wrath." Today I can tell you that the challenges only made the Boones stronger. The tapestry of Pat and Shirley's lives is rich with love, warmth, and a beautiful peace that is strong enough to weather whatever lies ahead because their ultimate trust is in the Great Mentor.

So Where Does This Leave Us?

Since I've always subscribed to the old adage that the "proof is in the pudding," it's fair to ask, "So, how has all of this played out for the Boones?"

Today Pat and Shirley are at retirement age, but you wouldn't know it to look at them. Pat could still beat me by fifty pounds on a bench press. Shirley still has the gleam in her eyes that caused Pat's heart to race in the '50s. But the bread crumbs they've left behind are what mean the most to me. I jokingly tell Pat and Shirley that they've got the dirtiest swimming pool in Beverly Hills. Due to their mentoring through the years, more than three hundred people have confessed their sins and have been baptized in the Boone's pool.

Shirley created and serves as president of We Win Ministries. Built on a lifetime of experience, she's using this outreach to empower women—both saved and unsaved—who are in need. She also serves on three boards.

Pat has served on numerous boards at nonprofits and used his celebrity to raise hundreds of millions of dollars for Easter Seals and various Christian charities. Today he serves as chairman of the advisory board at Pepperdine University and is a tireless worker for a host of good causes. (As I was writing this chapter, someone interrupted me with a phone call asking for Pat's office number to invite him to speak at a charitable event.)

The crowning achievement of Pat and Shirley's life of mentoring came recently when they funded the Boone Center for the Family at Pepperdine University in Malibu, California. This Christian-founded school is mandated to educate, strengthen, and encourage wholesome, godly young men and women. The goal of the Center is to improve existing families—but even more fundamentally to teach young people how to build healthy, lasting relationships and establish stable, godly families.

Shirley and Pat are incredible examples of what God can do when a young couple is dedicated to touching the lives of others with a heart for mentoring.

> **The key characteristic** of a mentor is outlined by the apostle Paul in his advice to the Christians in Philippi, *"Finally, brethren, whatever is true, whatever is honorable, whatever is right, whatever is pure, whatever is lovely, whatever is of good repute, if there is any excellence and if anything worthy of praise, dwell on these things."* (Philippians 4:8, NASB)

Nine Keys to Becoming a Mentor

My idea of romance is "kill and eat." When I have a task, I like to grab it by the horns and "get 'er done!" So, let's dispense with the niceties and get down to business with nine pointers on how to be a successful mentor to the people you love and lead.

1. Be there.

Like anything else that's worth doing, mentoring requires investing time and energy. I've learned from some masters—and from some who weren't. As a boy growing up, I looked forward to meeting a certain Bible professor at college. Although I'd never heard the word mentor, I dreamed of developing such a relationship with him. I would soon be disappointed. While he was a good man, I quickly learned that he didn't have time for me. Every time we got together, I felt rushed. Despite his good heart, he was never available to me.

Conversely, Alton Howard, a much busier man, always had time for me. As I've written elsewhere, Alton was a man of God who had scored hugely in the business world. At different points in his life, he'd been in the oil business, the jewelry business, presided over a tremendous real estate empire, began a national chain that included hundreds of stores, and owned a successful publishing company that sold millions of books. Not to drop names, but I can tell you that Alton and Sam Walton were on each other's speed dials.

As a young businessman, I can remember calling Alton with a problem or struggle and hearing him say, "Well, Steve, why don't you just fly down here, and we'll talk about it." I still remember one of my journeys to visit Alton. We spent a long time into the night discussing my business and future plans. Then, finally, I went to bed. The next morning, Alton handed me a sheet of paper with a handwritten action plan for how to achieve my goals. I suppose he had stayed up even later than I—simply to help a young man who needed his counsel. He never made me feel rushed. Sitting in that big family room or snacking in his kitchen, Alton always had time to be there for me.

Being there is important. I made my share of mistakes as a dad, but one of the things I did right with our kids were our midnight fun runs. When they were young, I would sometimes

206

sneak into one of their rooms late at night, wake them up, and say, "Hey, let's do a fun run." In a flash, the pajamas were off and the jeans were on; and we were headed for the donut shop or an all-night diner where we would simply sit and visit. These were special times. Each kid felt special—and so grown up. (After all, we didn't even tell Mom!) I'm sure there are plenty of child therapists out there who would consider this bad parental judgment. To which I would respond, "So what?" Today, we have four wonderful adult kids who consider their mother and me to be their best friends and confidants. To be a mentor, you've got to be there. **It pays big dividends.**

2. Lead with moral authority.

Simply put, to be an effective mentor, you've got to practice what you preach. Kids' hypocrisy meters run overtime. If your walk and your talk don't sync up—you're in trouble. This isn't to say that a mentor has to be perfect. If that were true, there would be none. We all fall short of God's ideal. Many of today's most effective mentors are the same people who have experienced some of the deepest personal valleys. It all has to do with the difference between *tripping* into a sin and becoming *trapped* in one. We all trip up, but mentors don't wallow in the mess.

Often, the most effective mentors are the ones who admit their frailties and faults. This openness on the part of a mentor helps their protégés realize that their own mistakes are retrievable. Knowing that you have made mistakes—yet have overcome them—can be a powerful, enabling message to the people you lead. Your protégé probably already feels like a loser; it helps to see that other flawed people (like you) can succeed.

One of the best illustrations of this is as close as the all-night infomercial world. Have you ever noticed how the most successful (arguably not always the most honest) infomercials tend to use testimonials from average people who look like they aren't unusually smart or educated? It's because people are inspired by those with whom they identify. There is something encouraging and empowering when we see a fellow struggler overcome great personal challenges to achieve a grand goal.

One caveat here: Don't go to extremes with this. Be sure whatever you share with a student, employee, or a child is for their benefit—not yours. Often otherwise effective mentors unburden themselves at the cost of their protégés. If you need to confess a sin, go to a peer or a mentor of your own—not someone too young or immature to appropriately process the information. Be careful not to unload baggage that will damage your long-term effectiveness.

Your goal here isn't to be a buddy or a peer. It's to be a respected leader. Pouring out your guts can be a mistake. If you lose credibility, ultimately you harm the one you're trying to help, because that person may then be unable to "hear" your message. This is why I don't encourage mentors to use their protégés as confessional booths. There is a proper time and place to confess our sins and failures. Usually that's to God. Sometimes, we need to confess to others: *"Therefore, confess your sins to one another, and pray for one another so that you may be healed. The effective prayer of a righteous man can accomplish much."* (James 5:16, NASB)

Notice that James talks about the prayers of "a righteous man." It seems reasonable that "a righteous man" would also be a mature man. Implicit in James' statement is the idea that we should confess our sins to someone who is fortified strongly from within.

Before I leave this point, let me return to an earlier comment. We have a tendency to turn virtue into vice. Sometimes the very people who have the most to share by mentoring others refuse to do so because of their own failures. There is a misconception that one can't mentor another unless he or she has lived a perfect life. This is why lots of parents, who have smoked marijuana themselves, don't discuss drugs with their kids.

Mentor Hall of Fame

Some of history's most imperfect people became great mentors. King David murdered and stole another man's wife, but forged the concept of worship for the Hebrew nation. By many accounts, Franklin D. Roosevelt was a self-serving elitist, but he brought America through the Great Depression and two simultaneous wars with his fireside chats. His calm mentoring reminded a frightened nation that, "The only thing we have to fear, is fear itself." In 1990, Michael Milken was accused of various misdeeds on Wall Street. For many, he came to epitomize the greedy investors of that era. While most believe that Milken was unfairly railroaded by overly zealous government agencies, he did end up serving prison time. After his release, a lesser man might have sought revenge or simply faded away into oblivion. Not Michael Milken. Upon his release, he set out to make his life count. He founded the Melanoma Research Alliance and the Prostate Cancer Foundation. His positive influence on the medical world led to a 2004 cover story in *Fortune* magazine entitled, "The Man Who Changed Medicine." As I've warned elsewhere in this book, don't let Satan's reminders of your past deplete your energy to do good in the future.

3. Stick to an unambiguous set of core values and a clear, consistent "life message."

These are the values that transcend the present and are relevant in all situations. While methods will change from task to task, effective mentors have a consistent, discernable life view founded on a bulwark of basic integrity. And effective mentors take the challenge of communicating these ideals seriously. Many mentors spend a lifetime refining their communication skills to more effectively inspire those they lead. I write at length about this in the next chapter, "Brand: YOU."

4. Be passionate.

World-class mentors hold to their convictions with a near reverence. And they are driven to pass these principles on to others.

5. Choose to do something unique.

Mentors get to write their own ending. Did you know that some top Hollywood directors shoot alternative endings to their films? Then after all the scenes are shot and all the focus groups have had their say, the director sits down in the editing suite, selects the ending he finds most appropriate, and splices it in. A mentor isn't a victim to his circumstances. He determines his circumstances, or short of that, determines his response to the situations of life. By passing on your core principles, you become generationally immortal.

6. Motivate with possibility thinking.

The enthusiasm of great mentors is contagious. They not only see the big picture—they get others to share it with them. Successful mentors have a way of getting past the present and seeing the future for what it can be.

7. Be more than a dreamer.

Good mentors understand the difference between healthy optimism and false optimism. They're kind enough to be truthful and realistic. The apostle Paul encouraged the Ephesians to constantly be *"… speaking the truth in love, we will in all things grow up into Him who is the Head, that is, Christ."* (4:14, NIV)

8. Be careful not to overwhelm the one you are mentoring.

This is easy to do. I've done it far too many times. There have been a number of occasions when someone came to me simply wanting some advice on how to make a few extra dollars to pay off some bills. In some of those cases when I knew the person had a lot of potential, I've suggested that he start his own business. I've heard myself say things like, "Until you're working for yourself, you'll never be paid what you're worth. It's because, in order to stay in business, the company must make a profit. The way they do that is by paying you less than what you earn for them. So, why not do something on your own?"

I might go on to encourage the person to start a yard-care business, a cleaning company, or a computer repair operation. So far, so good. But, that's when I've frequently gone too far and overwhelmed my poor subject. I'm a big dreamer. And besides, after forty years of business experience, I can jump the mental fences pretty fast these days. What might have scared the tar out of me at age twenty seems like child's play today. So I keep talking—when I should shut up. After all, by now I've done what I was asked to do. I've shown the young couple how to make the money they need. I've mentored. It's time for me to stop. But now I'm the one who is enthused, and I keep going, "Then, you could grow the business. Start by gradually building enough clients so you can go full time—and quit your day job." By this point, the young wife is quaking in her shoes thinking, "What if this doesn't work—how will we pay the bills?" But I go on. "Then, when you're doing this full tilt, you can hire someone to service your existing accounts, while you start marketing the business and making calls on potential new clients. Eventually, that will be your full-time work, as your employees fulfill the contracts you arrange. Then, you begin to add new salesmen to sell more accounts …" And on I go.

Warning: This is an inexcusable mistake for a mentor to make. This is like asking someone about the weather—and getting a lecture on global warming! As a mentor, the first thing you should do is figure out what your young advice-seeker really needs—and address that issue. No more and no less.

9. Speak to people's hearts as well as their heads—and look for their "real needs."

As I've said elsewhere in this book, people don't operate on a strictly logical level. We also operate from our hearts. As a mentor, it's your job to be intuitive and aware of the fears and desires of your young protégés, as well as what motivates them. Your real goal should be to gently lead the person to see the hand of God in his or her life. This involves learning to respond to your protégé's perceived needs (the reason they have come to you) and their deeper needs. These are needs they may not yet be mature, or open, enough to even realize; usually these needs are spiritually based.

If people trust you for help with their perceived needs, they will listen to your advice on more important issues they may be unaware of having. Who knows? Maybe this is a God-given opportunity—an intersection of the temporal and the eternal. Why not go beyond your immediate task of advising someone how to pay off delinquent bills, ask the boss for a raise, or stop fighting with a spouse? Why not explore and even challenge the person's core values: Why is he behind on his bills? What will she do with her raise? What is causing the stress in their marriage? How is their walk with the Savior?

One day, Jesus was faced with just such a situation. He met a woman at the well whose perceived need was to draw water and get on with her daily chores. But Jesus, looking into her heart, saw her deeper needs. He decided to mentor her spirit. As you read the story below, pay special attention to the portion I've put in italics. Notice how the woman begins to change the subject when Jesus zeroes into the heart of her struggle. She tries to dodge the real issue by attempting to sidetrack Jesus into a doctrinal discourse. But he stays on message. Notice how Jesus kindly, but firmly, proceeds to make his point:

"When a Samaritan woman came to draw water, Jesus said … 'Will you give me a drink?'

The Samaritan woman said to him, 'You are a Jew, and I am a Samaritan woman. How can you ask me for a drink?'

Jesus answered her, 'If you knew the gift of God and who it is that asks you for a drink, you would have asked him and he would have given you living water … Everyone who drinks this water will be thirsty again, but whoever drinks the water I give him will never thirst. Indeed, the water I give him will become in him a spring of water welling up to eternal life.'

The woman said to him, 'Sir, give me this water so that I won't get thirsty and have to keep coming here to draw water.'

He told her, 'Go, call your husband and come back.'

'I have no husband,' she replied.

Jesus said to her, 'You are right when you say you have no husband. The fact is, you have had five husbands, and the man you now have is not your husband.'

'Sir,' the woman said, 'I can see that you are a prophet. Our fathers worshiped on this mountain, but you Jews claim that the place where we must worship is in Jerusalem.'

Jesus declared, 'Believe me, woman, a time is coming when you will worship the Father neither on this mountain nor in Jerusalem … Yet a time is coming and has now come when the true worshipers will worship the Father in spirit and truth, for they are the kind of worshipers the Father seeks. God is spirit, and his worshipers must worship in spirit and in truth.'

The woman said, 'I know that Messiah' (called Christ) 'is coming. When he comes, he will explain everything to us.'

Then Jesus declared, 'I who speak to you am he.' (John 4:7–26, selected portions, NIV)

If You Need a Mentor, Admit It

As Shirley Boone will tell you, just because you are a mentor doesn't necessarily mean that you don't also *need* a mentor. One of the most touching moments during our recent visit occurred when Pat told me about how Shirley had asked him to be her mentor. To fully appreciate this, recall that Shirley was a beautiful, popular girl—but her family life was not ideal. Due to her mother's illness and her father's travels, she didn't experience the Ozzie and Harriet lifestyle. By high school, she was a boarding student at David Lipscomb. She always dreamed of a home and someone whose arms were big enough to hug her through the darkest moments.

Some years ago, she reached out to Pat in a most unique way. She gave him a photograph of herself as a little girl. On the back of the picture she had written the words, "Take care of this little girl—she needs you." Shirley's willingness to be totally vulnerable and open served as a mandate to Pat. He cherishes that picture and its challenge. That little inscription serves as Pat's call to duty in his love and service to Shirley.

How *Not* to Find a Mentor

If you realize that you need a mentor—congratulations. Most people stumble through life never aware of this most basic human need. And even among the minority who do, most never make a concerted effort to achieve that goal. So, if you fall into the camp that realizes your need for a mentor, and you're motivated enough to search one out, beware of two pitfalls. To paraphrase an old song, it's typical to look for mentors in all the wrong places. Some of the people we tend to go to for advice include friends, co-workers, classmates, and bowling buddies.

One of history's greatest examples of seeking the wrong mentors is recorded in 1 Kings 12. Rehoboam had just become king over all of Israel and was at the zenith of his power. His new subjects appealed to his decency, asking him to relieve them from their lives of slavery. This was Rehoboam's once-in-a-lifetime opportunity to build a bond of love and respect with his people. But he blew the opportunity by going to the wrong mentors.

"Then King Rehoboam consulted the elders who had served his father Solomon during his lifetime. 'How would you advise me to answer these people?' he asked. They replied, 'If today you will be a servant to these people and serve them and give them a favorable answer, they will always be your servants.' But Rehoboam rejected the advice the elders gave him and consulted the young men who had grown up with him and were serving him. He asked them, 'What is your advice? How should we answer these people who say to me, 'Lighten the yoke your father put on us'? The young men who had grown up with him replied, 'Tell these people ... My little finger is thicker than my father's waist. My father laid on you a heavy yoke; I will make it even heavier. My father scourged you with whips; I will scourge you with scorpions." (Selected portions, NIV)

Sure enough, Rehoboam took the advice of his homies—and guess what? The people rebelled, and ten of the twelve tribes left to begin a new kingdom.

Two Red Flags

As the story above points out, rarely will you get the best advice from a peer. Why? There are two reasons. First, they're probably as dumb as you are. And, second, even if they know the answer, they may be too competitive to tell you the truth!

This is why it's wise not to have only one mentor in your life. Try to find several. This is more important than ever, because today's more mature citizens are not from your granddad's generation. Many otherwise stellar mentors are, themselves, in high stress, high turnover jobs. Often the best potential mentors move (or are moved) every few years. Simply put, a single mentor system is dangerous because your mentor may be transferred tomorrow. And, even if that is not an issue, many of today's senior workers are so busy trying to stay afloat themselves they hardly have the time or energy to spend teaching you how to swim. So, as you read the next section of this chapter, think in terms of multiple mentors, even when I use the singular.

Six Mentor-Finder Pointers

So, how do you find a mentor? Let me share a few pointers:

1. Look for someone with a diploma hanging on his wall, like this:

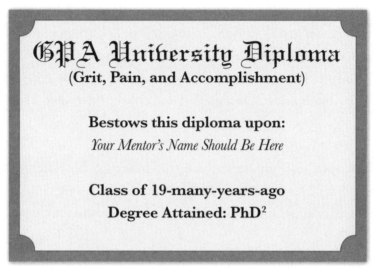

In a phrase: look for someone who has a degree in "Real Life 101."

2. Be bodacious.

Start at the top—and then work down. You have nothing to lose. Here's a hint: Frequently the best mentors are low-key people from whom you will literally have to pry the information. It's not that they don't want to help you; it's just that good mentors tend to be modest people who often see their greatness as "nothing more than what anyone else would do." I wonder how many baby boomers only learned of their father's WWII heroics by going through a footlocker of mementoes after the funeral.

3. Make a potential mentors list.

These would be people you feel could perform as your personal mentors, such as:

> **Family members who have accomplished great things.** Some kids (even when they're forty) have never noticed the greatness of their own parents. Too often we travel around the globe searching for an emerald when we have diamonds in our own backyards.

> **Church leaders.** One of the reasons Christians go into full-time ministry is because they have a genuine love and concern for others. Many of these good people are willing and capable mentors.

> **Schoolteachers.** After all, by definition, a teacher has something to teach. Some of the best mentors are people devoted to teaching others.

> **People who have achieved success in your field of interest**. These may be private or public people. I know this is a tough thing for a timid person to do, but why not reach out to public figures? Scour trade journal articles for people you would like to emulate. Do Google searches. Read their stories. Then swallow hard, and send a letter, or an e-mail, or place a call. Ask if you could arrange a "courtesy call" to become better acquainted. Usually that short visit will tell you whether the "spark" exists that could grow into a mentoring relationship.

> **Clients.** Some of my best advice as a young business owner came from older clients. I still remember Tom Ritter. When I was twenty-something, he seemed like an ancient sage. After all, he was in his mid-fifties and lived in a mansion across the street from the governor! He liked me, and I liked him. I always tried to serve his business needs, and he was kind enough to openly discuss business strategies that, in turn, helped me run a better company.

4. Develop an action plan for making the contact.

> **Learn about the person.** Do your homework. It's a sign of disrespect to ask for a meeting and not be prepared. In the 1990s, I had a weekly radio show called *Coast to Coast Gold with Steve Diggs*. It was a three-hour oldies show. Each week we ran the music from the

217

'50s and '60s. Along with the tunes, each show featured an interview guest. It was fun hosting Brian Wilson of the Beach Boys, Martha Reeves, Bobby Vinton, and a record-rack full of the other stars from the early rock 'n' roll era. I soon learned that the interviews were always best when I did my homework. So before each interview, I spent time learning about the star. One of my greatest compliments came one day during an interview with a star in his Los Angeles office. He stopped in the middle of the interview and seemed stunned that I knew so much about his four-decade career.

This can pay big dividends when you meet your mentor. You're likely to get much more attention and advice if the person realizes that this is important enough to you to have become familiar with him or her *before* your meeting.

› **Plan your introduction.** Is there a mutual friend who would be willing to introduce you? Will you be together at a church function, a seminar, or a ball game? Frankly, if I suspect I may bump into someone whom I'd like to get to know better, I plan what I'm going to say in advance. Sure, that means I have done a lot of needless advance planning for meetings that never happened, but I've never regretted being prepared when the moment presented itself.

If you must fly solo (and you're forced to introduce yourself)—great! After all, who knows you better than you know yourself?

› **Make a written request.** Avoid blindsiding a person, especially if you don't already know him. Think about sending an e-mail. Or, even better, send a handwritten note on good quality paper. It's well worth running over to an office supply store and paying the scandalous price of about $10 for about that number of sheets. If it helps you make a good first impression, it'll be some of the best money you'll ever spend.

› **Consider bringing along a "gesture gift."** This is something the person will appreciate because of the thought (rather than the dollars) you put into it. For instance, if your would-be mentor likes a certain author or topic, bring a copy of a book by that author or on that subject—and write a personal note inside the front cover.

› **Make a phone call.** If you feel comfortable (and don't think it will offend your prospective mentor), pick up the phone. But, just as with the handwritten note, do this only when you've organized your thoughts and prepared yourself fully. Think about writing out a script of exactly what you want to say. Below is a sample that you might find helpful:

"Hello Mr./Ms. _____. My name is _____. We don't know one another, but the good news is—I'm not calling to sell you anything. However, I would appreciate about three minutes of your time, if that's convenient. I am a young man/woman who has admired your (work, skills, or talents) in the area of (his/her field of expertise) for a long time, and I have finally gotten the courage to call and ask you for a very special favor. Would you be willing to share a little bit of your time, maybe twenty or thirty minutes, with me? I would like to ask some questions and learn from your experience. The fact is I need a mentor. It would honor me to take you to breakfast or lunch—or meet with you wherever and whenever is most convenient."

If doing out-of-the-ordinary things scare you, join the rest of the world. Everyone is afraid. That's what will keep most of you from trying this. But if you'll kick your fears in the teeth, grow a spine, and take charge of your life—you just might find yourself talking to a new mentor.

And so what if he says no? You haven't lost anything. Besides, at least you'll never have to wonder, "What would have happened if I had tried?"

› **Show proper deference.** Remember, the person you're approaching is already where you would like to be either professionally, spiritually, academically, or in some other way. He has done a lot of hard work and study to achieve what he has achieved. You are not his peer! This is no time to be flip. While a respectful sense of humor is great, being a smart aleck is a mistake. Be careful.

› **Plan ahead.** Decide what you want to ask *before* your meeting. Prepare specific questions, such as:

- "How did you overcome your fear of not being able to meet payroll?"
- "How did you find the courage to speak to an older member of your congregation about a sin in his or her life?"
- "How do you stay motivated?"
- "Is it wise for me to invest in this piece of equipment, or would it be better to rent the same item?"
- "How did you balance your business commitments and your family life when your children were small?"
- "What is the single most important piece of advice you can offer on how to succeed in this effort?"
- "How would you handle a situation where the people you lead are misunderstanding your motives?"

As you prepare for your meeting, consider writing your questions out on paper. This is important for several reasons. First, if you aren't prepared your mentor won't take you seriously, and you'll be less likely to get his best advice. Second, this helps you stay on message. Third, it reduces post-interview regrets.

There's nothing worse than getting that once-in-a-blue-moon opportunity—and blowing it! When you walk away and realize the time was wasted on small talk, and you never got into the real issues that had caused you to ask for the meeting in the first place—that's a real bummer!

6. Do more listening than talking.

One thing true of most successful people is that they like to share information. They like to teach, provided they feel the student really wants to learn. Otherwise, in many cases, you'll feel their scorn. Most successful people don't tolerate foolish people well. Avoid talking about yourself until you're invited to do so. Then, be prepared with interesting, truthful, brief answers. Leave as much time as possible for your mentor to mentor you.

Also, bring a notepad (the one with your questions on it will work just fine) and take notes. This will show your mentor how valuable his comments are to you. And you won't forget what he has shared with you when the blur of the meeting is over.

Savoring the Bread Crumbs

As a general rule, I find that the best mentors are those who had the best mentors. If you were blessed to have a great mentor or two in your early life, you have a duty. Jesus was never bashful about challenging his followers to use their talents. Over and over, Jesus reminds us that our talents are not just for our enjoyment.

"From everyone who has been given much, much will be demanded; and from the one who has been entrusted with much, much more will be asked." (Luke 12:48b, NIV)

Determine to pass that blessing forward. On the other hand, if you've never had a great mentor, determine to become a great one yourself. Use the energy that comes from your sense of loss to develop a dogged determination to break the cycle.

Whichever you become—a mentor, a protégé or both—make it your determination to leave the woodpile a bit higher when you leave this planet.

Develop "Brand YOU"
How to Share Your Life Story

With a title like this, I owe you an explanation. Frankly, this may prove to be the most difficult chapter of the book for me to write. Sometimes when you're passionate to share an important truth, like I am here, it's easy to get frustrated, but I desperately hope to communicate my heart. I hope you will have an epiphany (or a "boing moment") as you read this. The bold side of me hopes that you will gather takeaways from these

> "It is better to fail in originality than to succeed in imitation."
> –HERMAN MELVILLE

next few pages that will help refocus the thrust of your relationships. But I know that while some of you will "get it," the rest of you will probably put this book down wondering, "How did that thing ever get published?"

That's okay. Let's get started.

Missing My Mother's Story

My mother died in February 2004. There was never a doubt in my mind that she loved me with all her power. She was a great wife, mother, and dedicated Christian. But there had always been a sadness in my heart, because she and I never really talked about a lot of stuff. At some level, it was as though I never knew her.

But that was how many people from her era grew up. As children, they were so busy trying to get by that they didn't have time for a lot of emotion. Mother was born in the early 1900s. As one of eight children raised on a dirt farm in Kentucky, she grew up hard. Her family loved each other, but there wasn't a lot of time for frivolity. Then the Depression hit. Next, it was World War II. Mom had to cope with the real world from an early age. And she did so with excellence! Always a great student, she was a schoolteacher by the time she was seventeen.

> "Today you are You, that is truer than true. There is no one alive who is Youer than You."
> – DR. SEUSS

Those are all facts I've known most of my life. Still, I never felt like I really knew my mother's life story. She would share bits and pieces, but then the wall came up. She would only go so far. Many times, especially since her death, my mind has drifted into restless thoughts causing me to wonder, "What did she really believe, and how did she feel about things?"

This past Christmas, Bonnie gave me a special gift. It was in a large white envelope. "What," I wondered, "is this?"

Opening it, I slowly pulled out a stack of papers that Bon had found while organizing some of my mother's old files. It was my mother's handwritten autobiography!

As soon as the other gifts were opened, I slipped away to get reacquainted with my mother. As I tore through the stack of papers, her life story unfolded page by page. Things I'd never understood came into focus. I met the mother I'd never fully known, but had desperately longed to understand.

As she recounted the story of how she grew up, I began to understand how she had become the woman she was. She wrote about the things in her childhood that brought her joy and sadness. She told about the war years and how, after graduating ahead of her class, she started her life "adventure." (Remember, this was before respectable young ladies educated themselves or dared to travel alone.) She recalled her decision as a young single woman to move to a "secret" city in Tennessee during the war. Her plan was to move to Oak Ridge (the top-secret construction site of the atom bombs that would end the war) and become a teacher. She recorded her adventures and how she met the love of her life, Herbert Diggs.

She wrote much more. But that's enough to help you understand my point. While I was blessed to read every line Mom had put on paper, wouldn't it have been better to hear it directly from her years ago? Her principles, convictions, and commitment to Christ blessed me, but had she simply spoken the words and opened her soul more while we were still together, that would have been an even greater blessing.

The Bottom Line

Like my mother, we all have a message or "life story" that deserves to be communicated. As a matter of fact, most of us have hundreds of minilife messages to share along the way. These are the things we have learned. They are the commitments we have made. These stories include our core convictions and why we think they're important. And if they are important, doesn't it behoove us to learn the skills necessary to communicate them to those we care about? This is what I mean by our "life story."

Think of your story as a big box of life experiences that you give to the ones who follow after you. In turn, they will use the contents of your box to enrich and deepen their own lives. They will eventually pass on their life stories, with fragments of yours woven into theirs. The people you share your life story with are your "target market." (I'll discuss that term later.) Also, understand that you will probably have various target markets, such as your family, your closest circle of friends, those you mentor, folks you teach at church, and people you manage at work. As you will see in our next chapter, the overriding purpose for sharing your story is to help others see how uniquely God designs you to glorify him and others.

Tools for Telling Your Story

In this chapter, I want to show you how to effectively present your "life story." Doing so requires the development of three skills:

1. The ability to communicate

2. An understanding of advertising theory

3. A dash of salesmanship

Since advertising theory embodies all three, I'm going to use ad theory as both the metaphor and the methodology to teach the skills required to effectively present your life story. Advertising theory is all about communication and salesmanship. My favorite definition of advertising is "the truth well told." To effectively communicate your life story, you'll need to know some advertising basics.

First is *positioning*. I want to teach you how to position (or brand) yourself. In other words, if you were a product sitting on a store shelf next to a dozen similar products, what would you do to catch the attention of passing shoppers? If you were one of six banks at a busy intersection, how would you get a new community resident to open an account with you instead of one of the other five banks? If you were a brand of toothpaste, what would you do to be the one that ends up on the bathroom counter getting squeezed? How would you break through the "clutter" and get noticed in a memorable, compelling way that captures the buyer's attention and sells you instead of one of the other competing brands?

Remember, if you have a message that's worthwhile, it needs to penetrate, stimulate, and motivate your audience. Today there's a lot of competition for people's attention. Whether your audience is a prospective customer, people in your church, or one of your kids, without effective personal positioning (or branding) your life story will get lost in the "clutter."

Branding:
From the Professional World to Our Personal Lives

I'm going to ask your indulgence. Before I give you the time, first I want to build the clock. To do that, let's continue our lesson in Advertising 101. Be patient, and this will all begin to make sense as we go along. What I want to share are some of the skills I was forced to learn (and, in some cases, originate) on the fly during my days in the business world.

As I've discussed elsewhere in this book, I ran a marketing communications firm (aka advertising agency) for more than 25 years in Nashville. We grew to be a force in our field, winning shelves full of awards and some major national citations. As the years passed, we were blessed to work with increasingly sophisticated clients. In most cases, I began discussions with all of our clients the same way. I started by describing the basics of an advertising campaign. Not because they didn't already understand, but because I wanted us to all be on the same page. There were always three concepts I wanted my clients to understand before we launched an advertising campaign. This way we all spoke the same language and shared common goals and expectations.

Gradually something occurred to me: These are the same three elements that people should understand and apply to their personal lives. Because whether you like it or not, your success will be measured by your public's (i.e. family, co-workers, people you teach, etc.) decision to accept your ideas and beliefs (your life story) over competitive ideas from other sources.

To accomplish this, you must understand that what you communicate has a lot to do with packaging and presentation. Is that fair? Probably not, but it's how the game gets played. So rather than sitting on the bench debating the rules, it's best to learn them and become proficient at applying them. Hundreds of books have been written on advertising, and thousands of courses have been taught on effective advertising technique. For a few years, I taught college-level advertising practice and theory. I still chuckle at the idea of *me* teaching college. I was never the academic sort. Many of my own college days were focused on everything but classes. (I still remember waiting to buy my books until the night before the exam, then being extremely careful not to "crack" their spines so I could return them for a refund the next day.)

I noticed that many textbooks and teachers were confusingly, and needlessly, complex. Some were too theoretical. Others were just plain boring. It seemed as though none of these professors used five words when ten would do just as well. So as you might imagine, my college teaching career was marked by a decidedly lowbrow, "just the facts, ma'am" approach. I wanted the students to "get it." I saw no need to complicate a crowbar.

With this as my background, I wrote a book in the early 1990s on advertising called *Putting Your Best Foot Forward*. My desire was to de-complicate advertising so any small business owner could understand how to market his or her company. It was remarkably well received. People liked it because it was easy to understand and got to the point. It tickled me when the in-house marketing department at a nationally known, publically traded company ordered and reordered my book to train their sophisticated marketing team.

When I discussed advertising in my book, with a client, or to a group of college students, I always tried to keep it clear and understandable. So let's hit a few of the basics of how good advertising works. Then I want jump right into some personal applications that will increase your ability to succeed by using these concepts to share your life story (or, as the pros would say, brand yourself).

The Three Parts of a Successful Advertising Campaign

Have you ever noticed how many things come in threes? Many sermons have three points. The average sales pitch has three phases—the setup, the presentation, and the close. Even the most basic building block of matter, the atom, has three primary parts. So, it shouldn't surprise you that a successful advertising campaign has three parts, too. Each are as vital as the legs on a three-legged stool. If any one of these elements is ignored or improperly addressed, the entire campaign suffers.

These three essential ingredients don't change. It doesn't matter whether you're selling a product or a service, or whether you sell to the general public or just to other businesses. In fact, it doesn't even matter what your budget is. Whether you're Coca-Cola or the mom-and-pop lunch counter that sells Coke with its sandwiches, the same methodology applies. When I ran an advertising agency, I always knew that our success or failure was determined primarily by how well we understood and addressed these three basic building blocks. Let's briefly scan these three components.

🔑 Key 1

Plan Your Positioning

When developing an ad campaign, positioning should be the first consideration. I define positioning as the perception (or mental picture) an advertiser presents to his or her target audience.

How are you perceived? What does the public think of when it hears your name? What mental pictures are conjured up by the thought of your product or service? Positioning involves giving your product or service an image that appeals to a particular segment of the market. This became a popular buzzword in the 1970s, when instead of simply promoting a product's features, positioning-conscious advertisers became interested in how their product or service stacked up against the competition in the consumer's mind.

For many companies, the first two building blocks of their positioning efforts are what I used to refer to as their "look and hook." This encompasses the logo design (the *look*) that is the visual identity of the company and a singular tagline (the *hook*) that sums up its benefit in a few words.

Later in this chapter, under the "Take the B.O. Approach" section, I will discuss this idea more fully. But suffice it to say, an effective look and hook will have a major impact on an advertiser's success in the market.

You may recall some of the most famous ad hook lines of the earlier positioning era:

- **American Express:** "Don't Leave Home Without It"
- **U.S. Army:** "Be All That You Can Be"
- **7-Up:** "The Uncola"
- **Volkswagen:** "Think Small"
- **Prudential Insurance:** "The Rock"
- **Nike:** "Just Do It"

Positioning boils down to an attempt on the advertiser's part to do something that will legitimately gain his or her product a place (or position) in the consumer's mind. If you successfully gain that number one position in the mind of your audience—you win. You'll become the biggest, most successful firm in the category. Think about it for a minute. If I asked you to name our first president, you'd say "George Washington." But what if I asked you to name our nineteenth president? Would you know it was Rutherford B.

> *As organizations grow* and the needs of their customers evolve, so must their positioning. Years ago, General Electric used the hook line: "We bring good things to life." Today with far more emphasis on their technology than their lightbulbs, General Electric's tagline is "Imagination at Work."

Hayes? What about President number 28? Or 34? Not so easy, is it? You see, when a firm (or a person) holds the number one position in their public's mind, it has a big advantage. For instance, the name Kleenex is synonymous with facial tissue for many people, and Coke is frequently used to refer to any soft drink.

Don't get the idea that, to be effective, positioning must always establish the product in the number one spot. Many companies have been extremely effective with their positioning without ever becoming the top dog in their respective category. For instance, Southwest Airlines isn't the biggest, but in recent years they've been more profitable than the much larger United Airlines. Snapple is constantly outsold by Pepsi, but it has a long, impressive, and profitable track record.

One interesting positioning story began in 1959—a time when a lot of advertisers did self-congratulatory promotions. Each one claimed to be the biggest and the best. In those days, Hertz was the unquestioned leader in the rental car business. If you're a baby boomer, you may recall their television commercials where a driver floated out of the sky into a convertible as the jingle sang "Let Hertz put you in the driver's seat." And airport rental counters during that time were loaded with Hertz customers.

Whether anybody knew it or not, there was a #2 car rental company named Avis. They'd been around for years. The trouble was that Avis had experienced several disappointing years. But finally about 1959, the company decided not to take it any more. Gathering their resources and using some good marketing, Avis created an all-new position, developing an ad campaign that drew a lot of attention. The company made advertising history by admitting that it was not the biggest, the boldest, or the most bombastic. Instead, it downplayed its status. Avis positioned itself as an aggressive company intent on satisfying customers and launched the new slogan "We're #2, but we try harder."

In a world of similar services, Avis positioned its brand in a way that was memorable, truthful, positive, and persuasive. As the public began to notice the ads, customers began to respond. America's love affair for the underdog evidenced itself with significantly increased activity at the Avis counters. Over the years, the company has continued to grow. Much of the success Avis enjoys today can be traced back to a gutsy positioning decision in the '50s to simply tell the truth in an unforgettable, compelling way.

In the '90s, the word "positioning" was used less and less. Gradually, I noticed ad people (including some of my own employees) using the word "branding." I think they thought it was something new. But it was really just a fresher way of communicating the same idea. The bottom line is: Every product needs to find its own identity, unique voice, position, or if you prefer, brand. Today many ad people talk about "building a brand."

Whatever you call it, it boils down to the simple truth that effective marketing takes good positioning, or branding. A little later in this chapter, I will draw a parallel between how marketers position (or brand) a product and how you need to position (or brand) yourself.

A tip of the hat to Tom Peters may be in order here, as he was arguably the first person to use the phrase, "brand you" in his 1997 book *Fast Company*. Since then, this two-word phrase has become part of the lexicon. But note that when I use the phrase, it appears as **Brand: YOU.** I cap all the letters in "you" because I want to emphasize how critical it is for each one of us to be totally ourselves when it comes to branding (or positioning) our life story. We do no one any favors by trying to copy others in this all-important effort. But before we go further on the branding/positioning concept, let me touch on the other two parts of an effective advertising campaign as they will play a integral role of my final analogy.

⚷ Key 2

Know Your Target Market

To be at its best, an advertising campaign be should directed to a clearly defined group of people, which becomes the *target market*.

When asked who they want to reach with their advertising, the tendency of amateur advertisers is to say, "Everyone!" That may have the ring of great ambition about it, but it's a foolish goal. In the strictest sense, it's also impossible. Even if money was no object (and, believe me, it always is) and you spent trillions of dollars buying every form of advertising available, there'd still be a few mountain hermits who wouldn't get the word!

But on a more realistic level, it's important for advertisers to clearly define whom they want their message to reach. This reduces wasted time and money. If you manufacture a specialized product that scans shipping orders for mail-order companies, for instance, it would be a terrible waste to spend millions of dollars buying television spots on major network shows. Instead, wisdom would dictate a more surgical approach: possibly ads in trade journals that reach mail-order businesses, or a Web site or direct mail to those companies.

Your product's target market may be large or small. It may be broad or narrow. You may want to reach all the adults in your service area, or simply married moms of toddlers who live in the north end of town and have an income of $80,000-plus. Typically, some of the criteria that would be considered in a target market might include sex, age, income, religious preferences, geographical location, educational level, job status, political concerns of customers, as well as their fundamental need for the product or service.

⚷ Key 3
Select a Media Mode

An advertising campaign's *media mode* includes the various vehicles used to present a positioned product to its defined target market. Some of the most widely used vehicles include print (newspapers and magazines), broadcast (radio and television), Internet ads, outdoor (billboards and bus benches), collateral (brochures, mailers, and store displays) and transit (bus and subway signage). If you limit yourself to these traditional ways of reaching your audience, however, you may miss some golden opportunities.

An example of the effective use of a non-traditional media mode occurred some years ago when we were promoting a candy manufacturer who had just opened a new store in a large downtown area. Radio and television were prohibitively expensive. Still, we wanted our target market (upscale consumers who worked in that area of the city) to visit the store. So we hired a friendly-looking college kid, dressed him in a tux with tails and a top hat, and put him on the sidewalk nearby. He greeted passersby and handed them coupons for free pieces of candy. Since they were coupons (instead of the actual candy), the people had to come into the store to redeem them. While they were there, they became familiar with the store, and many of them made an initial purchase. **Mission accomplished.**

Today advertisers use many non-conventional media modes. One that comes to mind is the product placements we see on television shows. Next time you watch a show and see a recognizable food product sitting on the dining room table or a familiar store in the background, you can bet some shrewd advertiser may have paid dearly for that product placement.

Now, for the Practical Application

The purpose of this book is to share skills that will enhance your effectiveness in whatever realm your life takes you. One of the most important things an effective person can develop is his own position or brand. "Whoa—what do you mean by that, Steve? Are you trying to 'sell' me like a tube of Crest?" Well, yes and no.

I'm not trying to reduce you to some impulse purchase that will be consumed and thrown out. But I am suggesting that you can greatly enhance the success and effectiveness of your interpersonal relationships if you learn (and apply) a few tricks of the advertising trade. Why not present yourself in a memorable, credible, enduring way that will encourage others to hear your life story, not only with their ears, but also with their hearts? In the process, people will take you more seriously. For instance, why not always precede your visits with a thoughtful handwritten note telling the other person what you hope to accomplish during your time together? Or why not bring along a small gift?

Does this all somehow sound demeaning—or trite?

Some people react negatively to the notion that they should be "packaged" and presented like a new brand of toilet tissue. I understand that feeling. Sometimes the notion of "branding" Steve Diggs turns me off, too.

But I think this resistance is borne of misunderstanding. After all, we may reason, anything that's worth its salt doesn't need to be marketed, and we often associate modern advertising techniques with deception and subterfuge.

Sure, we've all seen lots of products advertised with big claims that failed to deliver on those promises. You can dress it up with a wardrobe of euphemisms, but anyway you cut it, to promise more than you deliver is dishonest advertising. No matter how beautiful the gold ring in its snout—it's still a pig. And, if you're a moral person, you want no part of that sort of thing.

But it doesn't have to be that way. I believe good advertising is also truthful. Granted, a lot of what's out there isn't very truthful. Far too often a mediocre product is polished and dressed up to look like much more than it is. That's wrong! More and more consumers are realizing that "whatever the ad's headline giveth, the small print at the bottom taketh away."

What I'm promoting here is responsible product presentation. The best (and only acceptable) form of advertising is when you take a great product and simply dress it up enough to help the public see its true value.

You might compare all of this to creating a resume. No one questions the need a job seeker has for a good, polished, all-inclusive resume—right? But there is a right way and a wrong way to do one. When you sit down to prepare a resume the question is: Will it be built on lies or accomplishments? It's the same with your personal branding efforts. We're not discussing a package of hype, exaggerations, and lies. We're discussing how to honestly and legitimately present your life's story.

You're the Product—Put Your Best Foot Forward

Ultimately it's a very personal issue that each of us must grapple with: whether what we are, what we stand for, and the messages we want to communicate to others are valid. If you are the real deal, you owe it to your audience (whether it's a child, a spouse, a client, an employee, or a church member) to brand (position and present) yourself in a way that they will "hear" with their ears and their hearts.

How to Develop "Brand YOU"

As we've discussed, to effectively position (or brand) any product before its audience, it must first build a solid image for itself. This image must be built on an awareness of both its own strengths and weaknesses, as well as those of its competitors.

Here are some tips from the advertising world that will help you more effectively brand (or position) yourself:

1. Be truthful.

An advertiser who misstates the benefits or essence of his product irreparably mispositions it. The public may believe the claim and respond once—but never again. The Avis story is a good example of a company that succeeded by simply telling the truth and admitting it was number two. Honest advertisers know not to exaggerate or hype the facts. If you're the newest company in your field, don't position yourself as an old, established, traditional organization. Instead, consider taking a "lean, mean, and hungry" position in the marketplace. If you aren't the biggest contender in your industry, don't try to convince people you are. Instead, present your company as a small, hands-on, highly responsive firm with lower overhead.

WalMart, for instance, has always positioned itself as the place to go for good, name-brand merchandise at discount prices. This strategy has proven tremendously successful, because it's consistent with the truth. It would be a disaster for WalMart to reposition itself as an upscale, ultra-exclusive retailer. Saks Fifth Avenue, on the other hand, has found success with just such a position. Conversely, it would be a mistake for Saks to try to position itself as a high-volume discounter.

This all applies as you develop your brand or position. Don't present yourself as something you aren't. God has given you special strengths and unique abilities. Learn to accentuate them. Just like a young company, if you're a young businessperson, don't try to fool the old-timers by pretending to be a veteran. Some of my most rewarding early business successes came when I disarmed old vets in the business world by admitting that I was young and needed their help and advice. With this admission, I could promise that what I lacked in experience I would more than make up for with my hard work and enthusiasm. The point is to learn to present **Brand: YOU** in memorable ways that people will respond to favorably.

2. Understand the difference between ministering and marketing.

Closely related to the importance of truthfulness is understanding the difference between ministering and simply being a good marketer. I believe God calls all of us to be ministers. It doesn't matter whether you sell insurance or are a homemaker, or whether you're a student or a teacher. You will never be at your personal best until you are motivated by a desire to minister (serve and help others). No, I'm not against marketing yourself. I built a career on it. But if we allow marketing to become an end—rather than the means to an end—we will never fill the holes in our own hearts, or in the hearts of others.

Through the years as I ran the agency, we worked with a number of Christian publishing firms. In the course of that process, I noticed something interesting. Some of the firms really believed in what they were doing. Sure, they marketed their books but, at their core, they were driven by a desire to help people live better Christian lives. Some of the other companies, however, seemed far more interested in marketing and improving their bottom lines. I often saw these publishers make terrible compromises. Some aligned themselves with ungodly organizations for financial gain. Some signed book contracts with popular authors who could sell a lot of books but whose teachings were spurious.

> **I want to challenge you to begin a lifelong quest to be the real deal. Focus on being a minister rather than just a marketer.**

3. Don't be afraid of being different.

The basic criterion of good positioning is that it should differentiate you from other people with different messages. To borrow from the business world, good advertisers make it easy for disinterested people to see and identify them. Like a good advertiser, promote your unique advantage—that element that distinguishes you from the crowd. Strive to be as different from the competitors as possible. This will give your audience (whether you're advertising a product to millions of people or simply trying to sell a prospective customer an insurance policy) something to hang their hats on when they hear or see your name.

4. Be clear and know your audience.

Many advertising dollars are wasted each year on cute, clever ads that no one understands. Even if an advertiser leaves them laughing, humming, and tapping their feet, he's lost the battle if the audience doesn't remember the name and benefit of the product. Some of the ads that win the most awards are also some of the least effective when it comes to communicating a clear, selling message.

This is why it's so important in advertising and in your own personal branding efforts to know your audience. Truth is not relative. But the way you present your message (position) must vary with your audience.

In 1 Corinthians 9, Paul says, *"To the weak I became weak, that I might win the weak; I have become all things to all men, so that I may by all means save some. I do all things for the sake of the gospel, so that I may become a fellow partaker of it."* (v. 22, 23, NASV)

If you're speaking to people in a small, rural area, don't try to dazzle them with your big city flair and bravado. If your audience isn't well-educated, don't try to impress them with all the big words you know. Speak to people where they are. Be sincere. Don't be too slick. Be yourself.

5. Take the B.O. approach.

One of the interesting things I learned in the advertising business was that a business owner could be his own worst enemy when it came to advertising his product. As the owner, he knew too much. He knew how granddad started the company with a $6 loan from his preacher. He knew all the products and their features. He knew the staff by name and how long each had worked with the company. He remembered the 100-hour weeks he'd spent building the business. Although it sounds counterintuitive, this knowledge made him the wrong person to define the company's position. It's the same reason surgeons don't operate on their own kids—they are too close to the situation. The result of advertiser-produced ads is that they tend to be too focused on the advertiser—and not focused enough on the benefits desired by the public.

> **My point here is simple:** If an advertiser's positioning is going to succeed, it must relate to the customers' needs—not his or her own.

The same holds for you as you develop your own personal brand or position. If you plan to succeed, you will have to take what I like to call the "B.O. Approach." Simply put, you will have to be Benefit Oriented. Everything you do must be aimed at helping someone else get what he or she wants or needs. When others realize that you bring benefit into their lives (i.e. share life-changing principles, save them pain, make their work easier, or help them look good before their bosses), they will love **Brand: YOU**!

6. Be memorable.

Every successful advertiser knows one thing: If the public doesn't remember the advertiser's name and claim—he won't achieve his aim. An advertiser must be remembered to stand a chance of succeeding. The same is true for **Brand: YOU**. You must be remembered. But being memorable isn't always easy. For advertisers, it means using all their available tools: a consistent logo, and a familiar look and hook in all of their ads. This consistency helps an advertiser break through the clutter and get into the audience's mind.

To effectively position **Brand: YOU**, you must do more than the minimum. For instance, in my early business years, I was also a real-estate salesman. As the new kid on the block, it was tough to get known. I didn't have any family contacts to draw on. I wasn't a member of the "right" clubs. Plus, I'm a lousy golfer. So I had to come up with a gimmick, something that branded me in my public's mind. As any agent knows, listing lots of homes to sell is the lifeblood of the business. Without good listings, it's hard for a realty salesperson to survive. So I busied myself getting listings. One of the best sources for listings is calling on the "for sale by owner" ads. But I was constantly frustrated when I knocked on the door of a "for sale by owner," only to see a stack of business cards from every other real estate person in town already sitting on the coffee table. I realized that I had to reposition myself in a distinctive, memorable, likable way. **Brand: STEVE** needed a gimmick.

My solution: In the morning I'd go to the florist and buy several beautiful, single, long-stemmed roses in boxes. Then, as I stopped at homes to introduce myself, I gave each lady a rose. Wow—it worked! The ladies liked it, and husbands who didn't pay any attention to the other guys' business cards were willing to meet with me in the evenings to find out who was giving roses to their wives!

7. Be consistent.

Frequently this is where an otherwise successful advertising program falls apart. Good advertising is consistent. Think about it. The great campaigns all have a consistent theme, look, and sound. Do you remember the tune State Farm Insurance has used for years in their jingle to remind you that, "Like a good neighbor, State Farm is there?" Or how about the little green reptile that keeps showing up in the Geico ads? In the same way, **Brand: YOU** needs to be consistent. Be sure that your presentation, your message, and your essence are consistent from one situation to another. This breeds familiarity. And, remember, people respond best to those they know and those with whom they feel comfortable.

8. Be gutsy.

One of the biggest temptations advertisers have is to cut bait and run when they're hit with a little criticism. Many potentially great ad campaigns have died early deaths because someone got cold feet and pulled the plug too early. Advertising is no place for the faint of heart. There are no guarantees—things can go wrong and failures do occur. One thing is for sure, though—no program will work if it isn't given a chance.

There's a direct application here for **Brand: YOU.** When you've determined a logical, truthful course of action, don't be easily dissuaded. There will always be critics and folks who anticipate your failure. But when you set your hand to the plow, be resolute. After all, to be respected, **Brand: YOU** must be decisive and confident.

9. Learn advertising speak.

Successful advertising is clear and on message. It gets to the point. Newspaper space is sold by the line, and TV commercials are sold by the second. Once the message is perfected, it's repeated over and over and over again. To effectively develop **Brand: YOU,** the same is necessary. You must prepare in advance. This means you should "can" your basic message. "Ohhh," I can hear you groaning, "I don't want to have a canned presentation. I want to be spontaneous."

I've got a simple response to that: hogwash! Only the most inexperienced and lazy people reject the idea of "canning" their messages and presentations. Remember, there is always only one best way to do anything. And for the successful person, when he finds that best way to present his message, he simply repeats it over and over again.

A "canned" presentation is the most professional, thoughtful way to share and communicate. But remember, too, if it sounds "canned"—it isn't. An important part of "canning" (or preparing) your message is making it sound fresh and alive every time you share it. There are presentations that I have given more than three hundred times. My greatest challenge isn't remembering what to say; it's always reaching deeply inside of myself before I step before an audience and being fully engaged, enthusiastic, fresh, and sincere.

10. Reach and frequency.

In the advertising world, media buyers often use the phrase "reach and frequency" to describe a media plan. Simply put, this refers to how much of your defined target market you will reach, and how many times you will reach it over a given period of time. For instance, if your market is adults between 24- and 44-years-old who live in the Denver area, that represents 100 percent of your target market.

Obviously, in a perfect world, you would like to reach all of those people. But if your budget is such that you can afford only to reach all 100 percent one time each week, your ad dollars will be wasted. Studies show that for advertising to be effective, it must reach the same audience multiple times. So, a wiser way to invest your limited dollars might be to reach only 25 percent of your target market with four messages each week. The same principle applies as we present our life story. You can't afford to be everything to everyone. It took me years to learn this principle. I had a hard time understanding why everyone wasn't passionate about the same ministries that I was.

In the 1980s, when so many of us were protesting at the abortion clinics, I couldn't understand why all the people at church weren't out there with us. Today, I see things a bit differently. While others shared our beliefs, they had not all been called to that particular ministry.

Your life story is your life story. You are answerable to no one but God. Avoid dancing to the music of others or trying to fit someone else's picture of perfection. Avoid reaching so broadly that you're frequently unable to go the distance. Decide what's important to you and communicate it as often as appropriate to your target market.

243

Two Types of Life Stories

Elevator and Stairway

Over the years I have heard various people apply the elevator and stairway analogy in the business world. However, for our purposes, I want to apply this same analogy to our personal lives.

As you determine how you will present your life story, remember that audiences and circumstances will change. It's fine for a preacher to spend thirty or forty-five minutes delivering a convicting sermon at his church on Sunday morning. But it would be a disaster for that same minister to speak thirty minutes to the high school football team at their pregame prayer when he's been asked to, "Spend five minutes encouraging the boys." Sure it's important, but is it appropriate for the situation? Will he be "heard?" Probably more will more be lost than gained.

I encourage you to develop two ways to present your life story:

1. Your Stairway Story

2. Your Elevator Story

Your Stairway Story

I call this your Stairway Story because, depending on the height of a building, climbing the stairs can take quite a long period of time. This is the full, unabridged version of your life story that you share only when time and circumstance permit. You will tell your Stairway Story to the people with whom you are closest and for whom you care the most.

Parents should have a carefully prepared stairway version of their life stories to share with each of their children. The right moment will come. It's your responsibility to seize it. I believe this is the point of Deuteronomy 6:6–8.

"These words, which I am commanding you today, shall be on your heart. You shall teach them diligently to your sons and shall talk of them when you sit in your house and when you walk by the way and when you lie down and when you

rise up. You shall bind them as a sign on your hand and they shall be as frontals on your forehead." (NASV)

I suggest creating a Stairway Story to share with each of your children. This is an important point to grasp. Even within a single target market (i.e., your own children), there will frequently be subgroups, each needing a version of your life story tailored specifically to them. To miss this point is to miss your goal of effective communication. Remember, communication happens only when both parties leave with a common understanding of the data. Again, scripture acknowledges this very point:

"Train up a child in **the way he should go,** *even when he is old he will not depart from it."* (Proverbs 22:6, emphasis mine, NASB)

You'll note I emphasized the words, "the way he should go." Wiser people than I have explained that there is a nugget in this passage that some of us overlook. Many believe that "the way he should go" phrase actually speaks to the responsibility of a parent to understand the different needs of each child. It's our biblical mandate to make allowances for those differences. Bonnie and I, having raised four *very* different kiddos, can attest to this truth firsthand. If you're a parent of multiple children, you, too, have seen this. They may all have come out of the same hangar, but boy, do their trajectories differ!

Whoever your audience is, when they hear your stairway story, they should go away clearly understanding your core beliefs—and why you believe them. This is witnessing at its best. To be clear, witnessing is not so much the stuff of Sunday morning church, as it is the opportunities we take during the teachable moments. These are the times I have spent with one of our kids on a long car trip talking about God's plan for his or her life. These are the times when I sit down on a plane, ready to write an article, but have a talkative seatmate who has just gone through a divorce and sees no purpose in living. These conversations happen in lonely hospital rooms after all the other visitors have left, and you sit with a twenty-six-year old mom who's just been diagnosed with cervical cancer. These conversations occur between a starry-eyed couple *before* they pick the ring and a date. These are the conversations that matter. At moments like this, **Brand: YOU** had better have its game face on.

Your Elevator Story

Then there are those moments when time is of the essence. You have five minutes, not a second more, to inspire the team. You need to speak a word of encouragement into the ear of a young widow whose husband has just come off the military transport plane in a box. You're asked by a TV commentator, "So, what's important to you in this election?"

I call this my elevator story. It's the condensed version of my stairway story. And, as any ad man knows, this is the toughest one of the two. It's always easier to do a thirty-second commercial than it is to squeeze everything into a ten-second version.

To strain our advertising analogy a tad further, your elevator story is like the ad campaign we discussed earlier. The temptation for many business owners is to tell the public way too much. After all, they have an important company story and want everyone to know it. Trouble is, in a world where the average consumer is exposed to more than 1,500 advertising messages daily (consider the number of television/radio ads you hear, billboards you pass, Internet ads, etc.), most people screen out most of that advertising. They are simply too overloaded to pay attention. And the advertiser's message is never really "heard" because it doesn't focus on the target market's needs.

This is why billboards are frequently so cluttered with superfluous information. What I mean is this: A billboard, like your elevator story, isn't designed to tell the company's whole story. It simply needs to get the consumer's attention with one tantalizing concept. Good billboard advertising is exclamatory—not explanatory. Try this little test. Next time you're driving, look at the billboards along the road. You'll see a trend. Most of the boards put up by big companies who use good ad agencies include very few words. Frequently it's nothing more than a great photo with three or four words and a logo. After all, that's about all you can absorb in the few seconds it takes to drive past the sign. Then notice the billboards put up by small companies that don't have the benefit of good advertising advice. Those are the boards that will have the company name, logo, slogan, three phone numbers, address, years in business, and a picture of the owner's dog!

Many of life's greatest opportunities come and go in a flash. Frankly, I think it's inexcusable not to be prepared for these golden moments. One of Jesus' closest friends said it best:

"But in your hearts set apart Christ as Lord. Always be prepared to give an answer to everyone who asks you to give the reason for the hope that you have. But do this with gentleness and respect, keeping a clear conscience, so that those who speak maliciously against your good behavior in Christ may be ashamed of their slander." (1 Peter 3:15, 16, NIV)

> **Here's the question:** Do you have a clear, convicting answer for your core belief system that you can share in the time it takes to travel a few floors on an elevator?

A Warning to the Wise

If nothing else, the advertising world is fickle. It's a world of trends. What's hot today is tomorrow's cold, chopped liver! One of the newer trends of offbeat, outrageous advertising is called "oddvertising," according to Alex Bogusky.

In an article in *American Way Magazine*, Bogusky, an advertising professional with the firm of Crispin, Porter & Bogusky, calls it "compelling, startling, and troubling, all at the same time." This era dates back to the late '90s when the dot-coms were at their zenith. One of the most extreme examples was when an advertiser ran an ad of gerbils being shot from a cannon! Today's advertising is getting more and more offensive and desensitized. What used to be taboo is becoming the norm.

Good advertising should be clever and fresh. But appealing to people's most prurient desires is wrong. As you develop your life story, avoid the temptation to do outrageous things simply to get attention. Remember, part of the effectiveness of your life story is *how* you tell it.

A Final Secret: The GBE

Before we wrap this up, let me share one last concept that will make your life story more effective. Understand the benefit of the GBE, or the **Goose Bump Effect.**

At the agency, we used to regularly ask the question of an ad campaign, "Does it have the GBE?"

Good advertising goes from head to heart. It should give you goose bumps!

Granted, to be legitimate, a product must have a logical (head) benefit. There should be a clear, quantifiable reason to buy it. But in truth, most people are hardwired to operate from their hearts. Frankly, I don't think that's a bad thing. Anything worth its salt is a combination of head and heart.

A marriage that is built on only one or the other will not be happy. Maybe the couple is responsible, pays all their bills on time, and is polite to one another—but without some hot, fun sex—their relationship is going to be pretty boring. On the other hand, the couple who can't keep their hands off each other before they're married, but fight over everything from the kids to the color of the carpet, have an out-of-balance relationship.

With that said, understand that your life story (**Brand: YOU**) will never be fully heard until you communicate it in a way that touches your target market's heart.

•Learn to use words that people understand.

•Offer more than facts.

•Build word pictures.

•Be gut honest.

•Get in their shoes.

•Don't talk at them; share with them.

I'm always dazzled when I read the Gospels. (I just finished Luke; now I'm in John.) Everything about Jesus spoke to the GBE. In heaven, he had it all. The angels praised him. His father adored him. So, why not come to earth as a king? Why not arrive with an entourage? Why not have the biggest convoy of chariots on the globe?

Maybe it was because he chose to touch peoples' hearts instead. That's why the lady with the hemorrhage dared to approach him. That's why children ran to him. That's why the disenfranchised of society yelled, "Jesus, heal me!" Maybe he knew that the only way to really "connect" was to give us all goose bumps and allow himself to be pulverized by cowards, beaten by arrogant religious leaders, laughed at by a criminal, and murdered in the most despicable way man could conceive.

It gives me goose bumps. How about you?

Develop the Greatest Life Skill
Learning to Trust God

At the moment, I'm not sure how this chapter will end. You'll learn why in a few minutes. But I will start with one undeniable fact and follow it with three confessions that I need to get off my chest.

FACT: If it hasn't already happened, sooner or later, some really bad stuff is going to happen in your life. At that point, you will either crumble, or you will grow stronger. If you prevail, it will not be because of external sources. Instead your survival will be dependent on internal resources. These are the inner resources that only God can give. Jesus promised the woman at the well, *"If you knew the generosity of God and who I am, you would be asking me for a drink, and I*

> (Those who fear the Lord) ... "do not fear bad news; they confidently trust the Lord to care for them,"
> – PS. 112:7 (NEW LIVING TRANSLATION)

would give you fresh, living water ... Anyone who drinks the water I give will never thirst—not ever. The water I give will be an artesian spring within, gushing fountains of endless life." (John 4:10, 14, The Message)

Now for those three painful confessions:

1. As recently as twenty-four hours ago, I had not planned to write this chapter. But that was before I visited Ann Ricker at the hospital. I had thought I was going there to minister to her; however, God had another plan. But I'm getting ahead of myself—more about Ann later.

2. This will be the most audacious chapter in the book because I'm going to attempt to teach you something that I still have not learned fully. I am a pilgrim, a novice. I'm struggling to reach safe harbor for myself as I write this. God is revealing and confirming truths to me, even as I form these thoughts. I feel totally unworthy to write this chapter but totally committed to giving it my best shot. If God will grant me the ability to communicate through his eyes, rather than my own, then I will succeed in this effort. (I suppose that since you're now reading this, it is a testimony that God helped me get it on paper.)

> "I have held many things in my hands, and I have lost them all; but whatever I have placed in God's hands, that I still possess."
> – *MARTIN LUTHER*

3. It may not be in vogue in today's "make *me* feel good" Christian culture, but I still believe that when we ignore God's voice, he has a way of getting our attention. For the past three-and-a-half months, I believe the Lord has had me in the woodshed. Through my life, when I have ignored God's nudging long enough, he has never hesitated to take me to his woodshed. As I write this, I'm in a personal, almost bipolar, battle. One moment I feel relaxed and almost giddy to see how God is going to resolve the struggle I'm presently battling. The next moment my faith dissolves like sand under my feet on the beach, and I'm scared to death.

While I don't fully understand yet, I suspect God is dealing with me in this manner for one of two reasons. Maybe this is a positive thing: God is trying to help me become stronger. He's using this situation to shake me out of my comfort zone and stretch my spiritual legs a bit.

Possibly I've become too complacent. Maybe I've failed to focus on what is truly important. Sure, I'm still going to church and running all over the country speaking to Christian people. But maybe it's become more about me than God. Maybe there are some lessons God has been trying to teach that I have been ignoring. James told the early Christians that such trials can help us mature spiritually.

"Consider it pure joy, my brothers, whenever you face trials of many kinds, because you know that the testing of your faith develops perseverance. Perseverance must finish its work so that you may be mature and complete, not lacking anything. If any of you lacks wisdom, he should ask God, who gives generously to all without finding fault, and it will be given to him. But when he asks, he must believe and not doubt, because he who doubts is like a wave of the sea, blown and tossed by the wind." (James 1:2-6, NIV)

But, on the other hand, maybe the situation is more dire. Could it be that I have actually been outside of God's will? Could I be in need of, even deserving of, his discipline? If so, God must love me a lot! In these last months, the truth of Hebrews 12 has been very evident in my life. *"My son, do not make light of the Lord's discipline, and do not lose heart when he rebukes you, because the Lord disciplines those he loves, and he punishes everyone he accepts as a son."* (vv. 5, 6, NASB)

Either way, I think God is speaking, and I had better start listening.

The Story Behind This Story

As you know, I am a professional speaker. I teach important life skills from a Christian worldview. I'm also a minister. In those capacities, I speak two or three hundred times each year. I love the travel. I love to teach and inspire others to be peak performers. I love visiting new places and meeting people. (I figure by the time I get to heaven I'll know half of the people there!) So you can understand that anything that impedes my ability to speak is a real concern.

It happened in the fall of the year. I had just concluded a two-day seminar near Russellville, Arkansas the night before. The next day,

I became concerned when I noticed that my voice was unusually weak.

"It's just tired," I told myself. Besides, it had to get better, because that evening I was due to speak to another group—for two-and-a-half hours! But that evening, things were not better. As a matter of fact, ten minutes into the seminar, I had to stop. Again, I thought, "A few days of rest, and I'll be fine."

That didn't happen. So a week later, Bon and I went to the Vanderbilt Voice Clinic. This world-renowned voice center is where many of Nashville's top music stars go when they're in trouble.

"Dr. Robert Ossoff and his staff had helped me before, surely they could do it again," I reasoned.

Not this time. When the doctor pulled the scope out of my throat, he looked worried. "Steve," he said, "you have a bleeding vocal cord."

Wow! That wasn't what I wanted to hear.

"Hopefully," he tried to reassure me, "this will clear up with two weeks of voice rest and steroids."

That was more than three months ago. Since that day, I've been on months of total voice rest (spelled, no t-a-l-k-i-n-g at all), taken three rounds of steroids, and endured more than ten vocal scopes. But my problem has grown worse.

Presently things are in a bit of a tailspin. We've already had to cancel/reschedule a fistful of speaking engagements, flights, and hotel stays. The lost income has hurt. Being nonproductive has been painful. The world I grew up in communicated the subtle message that my value was based on what I did. Although I've spent most of my adult life trying to erase those old tapes, I still battle the religious legalism and stress-driven lifestyle they caused.

As you already know, I am a "Type A+" personality. That means I'm a fixer. I'm in the habit of handling stuff for myself—by myself! That's what we fixers do best. When something is broken, I figure a way to put it back together. If something gets in my way, I kick down the door! So as you can imagine, not being able to fix things for these past three months has been tough.

As an aside, I will tell you that through the years Bon has learned that I'm not the best "sounding board." Too often, when she has come to me with a problem, she's gotten irritated when I jumped up and started "fixing it."

She has complained more than once, "Steve, I don't want you to fix it. I just want you to listen!"

Of course, my response is, "Then don't bring the problem to me if you don't want me to fix it. That's what I do. If you want someone to listen and end in a group hug, talk to your girlfriends!"

While she has always been my hero, I have thanked God for Bonnie a million times during these last fifteen weeks. For these months, she has made an impossible situation livable. With a master's touch, she has handled delicate negotiations that I would normally have trusted to no one but myself.

We fixers also like to talk. It's therapeutic. Talking helps us process our thoughts. It helps us fix things. So you can imagine how frustrating it is not to be able to answer the phone or carry on a conversation. These days communication is done through lipreading, with hand claps (one for yes, two for no), or in writing! I have literally drained more than one new pen dry of its ink—and don't get me started on how many e-mails I've written.

Hundreds of times I've prayed for God to get me through this. At times I've sensed his hand at work. Sometimes it's been only a fleeting glimpse. But as the weeks have become months, I'm sensing his presence more and more. God has gotten my attention. He is making me conscious of things I've been too busy to see before— things I've taken for granted or rationalized away far too easily in the past. My consistent prayer has been for healing, but only when (or if) it is to God's glory. That's been hard to pray, but I really do want God's will to be done here. If there is a greater truth I'm missing, I want God to show it to me. But in all candor, there is a side of me that shutters at what that could mean.

Maybe God won't allow me to speak again. What a thought! In the blink of a spiritual eye, my emotions go from zero to sixty with that one. In a sliver of a second, my spiritual voice says, "Great, God will open a new door of opportunity!"

Then, before the dust of that thought settles, the panicked questions start. "But how will I pay the bills?" "What else would ever be so much fun?" "What if there is no God with a rational plan?" (Yes, in my effort here for full disclosure, I'll admit that that thought has crossed my mind.)

My Forced Sabbatical

Nearly four months ago, when the doctor put me on what we hoped would be two weeks of silence, he said, "You may find this to be a very profound experience." I took that to mean that in the silence, I might "hear" some things I'd been missing in the cacophony of my 100-mph life. But that was fifteen weeks ago. This is now.

As more time passed, I became increasingly frustrated. With an angry heart, several weeks ago I sarcastically began referring to this period as a "forced sabbatical."

How dare anyone (including God) interfere with *my plans*—after all, I'm doing spiritually important stuff with my life! But as I've said before, Jesus' own ministry was a ministry of interruptions. Jesus was always available to God's change of plans. Whether it was Zacchaeus, the height-challenged tax collector who interrupted his trip to Jerusalem, or the crowds that insisted on his attention when he was trying to get some well-deserved rest, Jesus was always available to God's "Plan B."

During these months, various Christians have come up to me and said, "I can't wait to hear you tell us what God has taught you through this experience."

Those were hard comments for me to deal with. The truth is, I wasn't "hearing" much from God.

Was he talking, and was I missing it?

Had he broken off communication—maybe too disgusted with me to waste anymore of his time?

Had he forgotten me?

Had he given up on me?

Yes, there were those momentary glimpses when I thought I heard God, but for the most part, it's been pretty quiet.

Fortunately, there have been some of those "God glimpses." These were moments when God showed me a perfect passage from the scriptures at a critical moment. (By the way, if you haven't read Psalms 25 recently, check it out. That single Psalm has held my head above water on a number of recent occasions.) Regularly, the phone would ring, and it would be Terry Rush or another friend with a holy word of encouragement for Bonnie to pass on to me. I'll never forget the night my elders prayed over me and anointed me with oil, or the evening when Mike and Sharon Yates came to our home with a group of friends to pray.

Incidentally, the very next day, Satan hit hard. It seemed the walls were closing in. I got so angry at Bonnie and frustrated at the whole deal that I slammed my notepad on the floor—and would have been cussing if I could.

Even in that moment of my own sin, God was there in the form of Bonnie. Rather than stomping off, she held on tight and said, "Steve, last night our prayers assaulted the stronghold of Satan. Doesn't it make sense that he's trying even harder to destroy you today?"

In truth, I felt a duty to chronicle some of the things I was learning through this experience. And they have been eye-opening.

› **I've learned that, despite my incessant need to "fix" things, I really have no power, save what God allows me.** It's an illusion to think that this world really needs Steve Diggs. God will do his will—with or without me.

› **I've learned that there is a real blessing in forced silence.** For one thing, I sin less. It's much harder to gossip, speak cruelly, tell a lie, or brag about myself. This situation has also kept me out of some trouble.

Last night, Bon and I went to a party at some friends' home. About the time we were leaving, Bonnie made a comment that made me angry. I was indignant. She had embarrassed me in front of my friends! (In truth, it was an innocent, unimportant point, but for a few minutes it seemed huge to me.) If my voice had been working, I know exactly what I would have done. The minute we got into the car, I would have put my mouth in gear before getting my brain out of neutral. I would have let Bon know that I was ticked off. Then she would have become hurt, or defensive, or angry—and the whole evening would have been shot. (Who knows, I might even have had a chance to camp out on the family room sofa all night long!)

But without the ability to speak, I didn't say a word. All the way home, I processed what had just happened. I realized it was really nothing. Besides, how many times has Bonnie turned the other cheek with me? What would Jesus want me to do in this situation? The answer: forgive, forget, and grow up. I did. We ended the evening snuggling together in bed.

› **I've learned that it's okay with God for me to be scared**. I'm only human. Mark 15 shows how very human Jesus was. On the night of his betrayal, he pled with God not to allow them to kill him. But here's where we sometimes differ with the Jesus-style: Jesus ended his prayer by inviting God to have his will be done.

> **I've learned that the more I focus on others through this period, the better I feel.** How dare I make such a big deal out of this? At this very moment, we have a number of friends without jobs. I have two other dear friends who have gotten life-threatening news about their cancer. And then there's that baby with brain cancer. How dare I be so wrapped up in me!

> **Conversely, I'm learning that the more I try to "fix" things, the less happy I am.** Stress causes regress. It's pointless to worry about our investments and finances. I can't do anything of substance to impact them at this point. I'm trying to learn that peace comes by simply "waiting on the Lord."

> **Through this entire experience, I have thanked God over and over for the gift of a good wife.** Bonnie is the most incredible person I know. She has weathered this with me as my best friend, pal, and cheerleader. She always finds the good. When something bad happens, the first words out of her mouth are frequently, "Well the blessing in this is …" She keeps my heart smiling. She is the closest thing I've seen to God on this earth.

Without this experience, I would never have seen these truths so clearly.

A Healing Visit

As I just mentioned, one lesson I'm relearning through this experience is that I'm happiest and most at peace when I get out of me and start doing something for someone else. Lately I've been making more hospital visits.

As I mentioned at the beginning of this chapter, yesterday I went to visit my friend Ann Ricker. Ann and her husband, Steve, are two of the most precious Christians I know. A few weeks ago, Ann was diagnosed with cancer. They weren't sure what type or how extensive it was. But from the start Ann was upbeat. She seemed strangely at peace with the whole affair. I secretly envied her.

Her diagnosis led to surgery. The doctors were concerned the disease had invaded her lymph node system. Earlier when I had visited and prayed with her, Ann had asked, "Please pray that they'll find fewer than three cancerous lymph nodes. The doctor says that will indicate that it is less serious."

Immediately Bon and I had began to pray that there would be zero malignant lymph nodes.

Yesterday when I went back to visit Ann, she was in good spirits. Inside, I was anxious to know what the pathology report had shown. Finally I got up the courage, and scribbled a note, and handed it to her, "What did they find in your lymph nodes?"

Ann smiled and said, "There was only one with cancer!"

I was happy for her. But in truth, I was also unhappy. Why did she have to have any malignant lymph nodes? Why? This means more months of treatment and years of uncertainty. Why didn't God just heal her completely?

Of course, I didn't put voice to my thoughts. (Again, probably a blessing of not being able to speak.) But over the next few minutes, I realized the true purpose of my visit. There, in room 321 at Stonecrest Medical Center, Ann began to minister to the minister.

Let me share with you some of the takeaways I left Ann's hospital room with. Some of these are things Ann said. Some are thoughts that God has shared with me as I've pondered our time together.

1. She said, "Why is it that when troubles come we say, 'why me?' It occurred to me that I needed to re-think some things. What if, conversely, I turned my typical way of thinking around and began asking the same 'why me?' question every time God blesses me? I'd never stop saying, 'why me?'" (Wow, that one mowed my toes off at the ankles!)

2. After our visit, for some reason Romans 9 seemed especially poignant, *"But who are you, O man, to talk back to God? Shall what is formed say to him who formed it, 'Why did you make me like this?' Does not the potter have the right to make out of the same lump of clay some pottery for noble purposes and some for common use?"* (v. 20-21, NIV)

This is where Paul reminds Christians who is *really* in charge. The fact is: God is the potter; I am his clay. As the potter, God has the sovereign right to do as he wills. Sometimes I get this backward. That's easy to do in our self-actualized, self-indulged, self-centered culture. But it is a truth as old as the ages that will remain true long after we have sucked our last breaths. The point remains: This is not my life. I didn't make me. God made me. I am his clay. If he wants to heal—praise his name! If he chooses not to heal—praise his name! Proverbs 19:21 tells us, *"Many are the plans in a man's heart, but it is the Lord's purpose that prevails."*

The scripture brings a beautiful balance to all of this. The Psalmist says, *"Delight yourself in the Lord and he will give you the desires of your heart. Commit your way to the Lord; trust in him and he will do this: He will make your righteousness shine like the dawn, the justice of your cause like the noonday sun. Be still before the Lord and wait patiently for him …"* (3:4ff)

3. There were tears in Ann's eyes as she shared another gem, "Steve, I've learned not to ever limit God. He can do anything he wants." Her point was simple. She doesn't know how all of this will play out, but God does. And that makes it okay. Here was this courageous woman, facing a far greater medical issue than mine, yet she was the one blessing me!

The Ebenezers of Life

Driving home, I began to remember some of the Ebenezers in my life. The word "Ebenezer" literally means "stone of help." It refers to a story in 1 Samuel 7 where God miraculously saves the

Israelites from the Philistine warlords. After God's salvation of his people, Samuel built a stone altar, or an Ebenezer. It was a permanent reminder of God's power.

> **For me,** Ebenezers are the answered prayers I can look back at which remind me that there is a living, loving, involved God. This is a God who has no limit—and no shortage of power.

Forgetfulness can be a tool of Satan. If he can get us to forget the past victories and answered prayers, and look only at the momentary storm waters lapping at our feet, we'll panic. But if we remember all the times God has stilled the waters and set us on dry ground, our present crisis won't be nearly as frightening.

I want to share three Ebenezers that have helped me hold on in the shakiest of times. I do this with full realization that some of you will not like, or agree with, what I have to say here. That's okay; I can handle it. You see, I've made a deal with God that trumps any concern I have for your sense of propriety. My deal with God is that I will share these stories whenever I have the opportunity. These are miracle stories. I won't apologize and won't try to explain them.

I will say this: I do not know how God makes his decisions. I do not understand why one person receives a miracle healing and another godly person dies in pain. I don't know if it has anything to do with a person's theology or previous lifestyle. All I know is this: if I don't tell these stories, something in the core of my being senses that God will not be pleased with me. So here goes.

Ebenezer

The Growth on Megan's Spine

Bonnie and I are blessed with four children. Megan, our oldest, had a beautiful godly peace about her from her youngest days. She gave her heart to Jesus, and I baptized her at age eight. She never looked back. Megan was generally healthy, but she did have a little bit of scoliosis (spinal curvature). So when she fourteen, her doctor scheduled X-rays to be sure the condition wasn't progressing.

On the morning of her X-rays, Bonnie said, "Why don't you sleep in, and I'll take Megan to the hospital for the X-ray." I dutifully rolled over in bed and dozed off. Sometime later I awoke and realized that Bon and Megan were still gone. I called Bonnie on her cell and learned that they were still at the hospital. Long story short: Multiple X-rays showed a two- or three-inch growth attached to Megan's spine!

That began one of the worst days of our lives. I remember it was a Wednesday. At the Antioch church, we have two mid-week gatherings every Wednesday evening. I had already gone to the earlier service and gotten home when the call came from Megan's doctor. He told me that the medical experts were concerned. All the X-rays from all the angles showed the same growth. Megan needed immediate attention. The doctor had already scheduled her surgery for the next morning. The obvious concerns: At best this would be tricky surgery, with doctors hoping not to damage to her spine. At worst, a growth of this sort could be cancer. I was scared.

Standing stunned in my home office after the phone call, all I knew to do was call the church. Thankfully, my friend and our minister Walt Leaver happened to answer the phone. When I heard Walt's voice, it all came out. After the call, Walt walked throughout the Antioch church building, one class at a time, telling people about Megan's situation. Church-wide, people began praying for Megan.

Early the next morning when we arrived at the hospital, Christians were already there waiting for us. We held hands and prayed. Megan was taken back to begin the ordeal. About an hour had passed when the doctor walked out with a handful of X-ray films. We were directed to one of the viewing rooms with light boards on the walls. One by one, the doctor put the films into the grips, flipped on the backlights, and pointed at the images of Megan's spine. "These are the shots from this morning," she said. "I don't have an explanation for what I'm about to say, but there's nothing there!"

Sure enough, the X-rays looked just like the ones from the day before, but there was no longer a growth on my daughter's spine! That was nearly fifteen years ago. Today Megan is healthy. She serves as a children's minister and is planning to get married this spring. What happened to Megan's spine during that difficult night? I'll let you draw your own conclusion.

Ebenezer 2

The Airplane Ride Home That Almost Didn't Happen

On June 25, 1999, about forty kids from our church had just concluded a missions trip in Mexico. They were worn out and ready to come home when they boarded two jets in San Diego heading for Nashville. As it turned out, two of our own kids were on that trip and on the same plane, flight 2090.

It was 2:40 p.m. as the jet pushed back from the gate, and the kids were excited and ready for a fun flight home. Our daughter, Megan, was seated near the rear of the plane reading a devotional book. Her brother, Joshua, sat a few seats ahead. As the jet sped down the runway building speed for takeoff, everyone was relaxed, expecting—well, nothing. But just as the big airliner lifted from the ground at the end of the runway, the unthinkable happened—every pilot's worst nightmare. Just when the plane needed the most thrust, it lost an engine! As the smell of smoke filled the cabin, Megan looked for her brother and the closest exit. Some of the adults became agitated. But the kids began to pray asking for God to hold the MD-82 in the air.

Nearly two thousand miles away in Nashville, I saw the news on CNN. What I would have given to change places with those kids! The pilot, a veteran with thousands of hours under his belt, braced for the worst, but determined to do his best to keep the plane in the air. Finally the big jet gained enough altitude to remain temporarily airborne. Doing everything he could with the remaining engine, the pilot steered out over the Pacific in a desperate effort to dump fuel. (As those of you familiar with flying will know, a fully fueled airplane is too heavy to land again safely.) With most of the fuel dumped, he then turned the nose of the silver bird toward Miramar Air Force Base and was given emergency landing clearance. When the crippled plane finally pulled to a stop, the shaken passengers deboarded and were allowed to wait in one of the military buildings.

It was a touching sight when this seasoned pilot walked back to where our several dozen kids sat collecting themselves and told their leaders with a sober voice, something to the effect, "I knew you guys were in the back praying that we would get down safely. God was listening. Your prayers kept this plane in the air. You have him to thank."

Ebenezer 3

The Day God Touched My Heart

As I've mentioned, in 1992, at age thirty-nine, I had heart bypass surgery. We'd known for years that I had heart disease; finally it was time to do the surgery. After those five bypasses, I changed my lifestyle. I started regular, vigorous exercise. I relaxed more and worked less. Doctors put me on a bunch of pills and vitamins. I radically changed my diet and lost a lot of weight. At this writing, it's been most of twenty years—and I still haven't eaten a steak!

There was one major hiccup, however. In late 2000, I wasn't feeling good. So on November 7, we went into the hospital to do an invasive test. After the test, the medical folks were concerned. Things hadn't gone very well. That afternoon, my cardiologist sat down with Bon and me and began his conversation with the words, "This isn't going to be a very pleasant meeting." He then proceeded to explain that my five bypasses were doing fine, but I had developed small artery disease. He further explained that that meant the hundreds of little arteries that wrap and feed the exterior of my heart were clogging up and breaking down. He went on to say that because of their quantity and smallness, bypassing them was not an option.

"So, what does this mean?" I asked.

"It means that collectively, those little arteries are killing you. You probably only have a year or two left," was his reply. We were told to come back the following week, on November 14 to follow up. (Translation: to make plans to slow life down.)

Whew! That had been a tough meeting. I recall Bon walking with me into the corridor in a dazed stupor. Then we simply fell into one another's arms. The next week was a hard one.

You can always tell who your best friends are. They're the people you go to when things are at their worst. I recall getting with my dear friends Rubel Shelly, Mike Root, and Don Finto. Their prayers always get through. My elders were all over the case, too. They met with me to pray and anoint me with oil. Via the Internet, word got to people all over America. I learned that there were people literally praying a 24-hour vigil for me!

On November 14, we went back to the medical center prepared for another difficult meeting. But braced with a week's perspective and thousands of prayer warriors, Bon and I had begun to sense a fresh inner strength—a sustaining power and peace that defied explanation. We were somewhat prepared for more bad news. God, however, had other plans for that meeting. The doctor began by explaining that he and the cardiac team at this nationally renowned heart hospital had spent the week viewing and reviewing my studies.

Then he said something like, "I have no explanation for what I'm about to tell you, but every time we've looked at your videos from last week they seem to have changed. It's as though your heart is getting better and better—creating new arteries. You're still a sick

266

pup, but that one- to two-year diagnosis is off the table. I'm guessing you may have another ten or more years. And then, we might be able to look at a heart transplant."

"Stunned," you ask? Yeah! What do you do when that happens? We praised God—over and over again. Suddenly life seemed so much more precious! I remember going to the grocery store and buying green bananas. I took them to some of my prayer warriors, and announced glowingly, "God has healed me! I can buy green bananas again!"

Of course, I understood that my condition was still there. And since this is a progressive disease, I knew it would get worse over time, and I likely wouldn't feel well for some of those remaining years. Well, I can tell you this: It has now been more than ten years since that day. I've had two major follow-up studies at the hospital. On both occasions, they told us my condition was stable and actually appeared to have improved! I feel great.

As I mentioned in another chapter, I work out rigorously several times every week—five miles on a StairMaster in thirty-four minutes. (I'll admit to a little bit of cheating. I tend to rest some of my weight on the armrests.) I regularly work fifty- to seventy-hour weeks. I travel all the time, frequently pulling more than a hundred pounds of gear through the airports. And, most of all, I'm happy!

Do I have to say it again? Okay, here goes: I believe that God still works miracles!

What Lies Ahead?

Frankly, I don't know. Throughout this experience of losing my voice, I've been in the capable hands of Dr. Robert Ossoff. Nearly two decades ago, he founded the Vanderbilt Voice Clinic, and today it is world famous. Dr. Ossoff and his team have pioneered vocal techniques that bring many of the world's most famous singers, performers, and political leaders to his office. Here in Nashville, lots of people depend on their vocal cords to make a living. Many of those people are still singing today because of Dr. Ossoff.

I've talked a pretty good game so far in this chapter, but right now my knees are wobbly. As I write this, it's been several months since my vocal cord ruptured. We've had a lot of ups and downs. There were days when we thought the ordeal was almost over only to find that the hemorrhage had grown worse. There was the time about six weeks ago when Dr. Ossoff was discouraged and predicted a 60–70 percent chance that I would require major vocal cord surgery. Then, a few weeks later with things improving, he guessed the chance of surgery was reduced to about 50 percent. There were those giddy three weeks when the improvement was so pronounced that the doc allowed me to resume my schedule. I made three speaking trips during those weeks, only to find that the problem had grown worse.

Then on December 11, Dr. Ossoff told us that if the bleeding stopped by the next week, he might try a less invasive laser procedure in the hope that I could be back to work in a couple of weeks. That was encouraging. Thank God, a week later the bleeding had stopped. Dr. Ossoff, however, encouraged me to consider the other option. He felt that long-term results might be better if we pursued the major surgical approach rather than the laser. He explained that the surgery would hopefully fix the problem permanently. But there were no guarantees, and it would require two to three months to heal instead of a couple of weeks.

As I write this last insert, it's New Year's Day 2009. My surgery was performed ten days ago. By all reports, it went smashingly. Dr. Ossoff was able to perform the "micro-flap" procedure he pioneered, with the goal of reducing scarring and rendering a healed vocal cord to its original fidelity.

For now, I remain on total voice silence. Next week we return to Vanderbilt to see how I'm progressing. Lord willing, I will be able to begin work again by the first of March. I am so grateful to have had Dr. Ossoff as my physician. But the truth is Dr. Ossoff is not the "Great Physician." Through fearful health problems and frightening life events, we've held onto God's hand this far. We believe he will provide.

But the question I'm asking myself is, "Steve, what if Dr. Ossoff hadn't been there? What if your vocal cord problem had gotten even worse? Then, would you find it so easy to be thankful and trusting?"

The truth is, I don't know. But I would like to think that, if that were that situation, I would be more at peace today than I would have a few months ago. I believe God has opened my eyes to some keys that, if applied, will help me trust him more the next time a crisis arises.

Trust Builders

Trusting God cannot be reduced to a to-do list. That is not my goal here. Growing to trust God in both the good and bad times is a process. It isn't like mixing Kool-Aid with water. It takes time and personal discipline. And I believe it requires a willingness to allow the Holy Spirit to permeate every crevice of the heart.

Very little of lasting importance in my life has happened in an instant. Usually growth has come slowly. Sometimes I haven't even realized it was happening until I turned and looked back at where I'd been. But, at the risk of sounding trivial, I would like to share a few "Trust Builders." These are specific ideas that you may find helpful in your personal journey.

1. Make an Ebenezer list.

List the times God has answered your specific prayers. Then when fears and doubts creep in, review that list. Frankly, I had rarely codified the prayers God answered in my life in list form until recently.

269

But now I do. I keep it with me. And when the darkness and fear closes in, I can pull out my Ebenezer list and remember how many times God has picked me up in his big, safe arms and carried me through the storms.

2. Get into the Word.

Here's a personal confession that's hard for me to make: I don't usually spend enough time with my Bible. I'm not proud of that, but it's the truth. During these last months, I've found myself going back to the well of the Word over and over. It has been my strength. It has spoken to me. It has held me up. It has been "living water" to my parched soul. I hope, as life gets back to "normal," that I don't forget my need to remain in the scriptures.

3. Avoid the "noise."

This one requires intentionality. In his little book, *The Screwtape Letters*, C.S. Lewis reminds us that one of the devil's most effective ways of getting Christians off track is not necessarily by dangling a glaring, sinful enticement before them. Frequently the best way to get a Christian off course is by diverting his attention to what Lewis sarcastically called "the real world." There's only so much time in a day (86,400 seconds the last time I checked). We can do only so much with that time. If we clutter too much of it with the busyness of life, time for God will be crowded out. Each of us needs to find time to get away from what the culture would tell us is the "real world" (i.e., work, entertainment, running errands, etc.) and baptize ourselves in "real world" moments with God.

This is more than just Bible reading. It involves the time we spend meditating on why God has put us here and what he wants us to do while we are here. For many, fasting helps. Although I do it far too rarely, there is something about fasting that cleanses the mind and body. It frees the soul to be in a deeper communion with God. And, as Paul put it, it's vital that we "pray without ceasing." This means we need to be in constant contact with God.

Sometimes we formalize our prayers so much that they become plastic and phony. Why not converse with God throughout the day? Talk to him while you're driving your car or riding on an elevator. Sure, it's right and good to get away to quiet places and spend long periods of time in focused prayer to God. But what's wrong with whispering dozens of little prayers as the day progresses? One person has called these "prayer flares." I like that term.

4. Get out of yourself.

The Christian walk is very counterintuitive. It doesn't fit into the template of the outside world. Most people believe that happiness is determined by how much stuff they acquire. But serious Christians know that the opposite is true. Real joy is in direct proportion to how much of themselves they give away to others. As I mentioned earlier in this chapter, I'm learning that I reduce my pain the most when I reach out to help others who are in pain.

While I'm convinced that depression is real and often needs to be medicated, I suspect that a lot of depression would improve if we chose to simply spend less time worrying about our own problems and invested more time mending the hurts of others. Some of the happiest people I know are those who have taken less for themselves and given more to others.

5. Don't sweat the small stuff.

I'm embarrassed as I reflect back on how much of my life has been spent worrying about stuff that will one day burn up. The car I drive and the house I live in are fine, but one day they'll be gone. What will matter are things like the e-mails I write to the kids; the people whose tires I change along the road; and the times Bonnie and I make love in the night.

6. Make yourself available.

My goal is to fully engage the biblical concept: *"Here I am Lord, send me."* I want to have the love that prompts me to start each day with the prayer, "God open my eyes to the goals and needs you have for me today. Show me how to best minister to someone else."

7. Speak less, listen more.

One thing this experience has shown me is how useless (and often harmful) my words have been. Despite the frustrating nature of it, these last months have forced me to really listen to Bonnie in ways I never have before. I already loved her. But today I love her more—in part, because I'm learning to listen to her.

8. Live in the present.

All we have is the present. Yesterday is gone; tomorrow may or may not ever come. Right now I have the present. Interesting name, "the present," because it is the present (gift) that God gives. Peace with God has a lot to do with learning to live in the present God that gives us.

Jesus was simple and to the point: *"But seek first his kingdom and his righteousness, and all these things will be given to you as well. Therefore do not worry about tomorrow, for tomorrow will worry about itself. Each day has enough trouble of its own."* (Matthew 6:33,34, NIV)

10. Understand that God understands.

God knows just how human we are. Even the strongest of us have feet of clay. We all struggle with faith. God knows that. Do you remember the apostle Peter? Boy, did that guy waffle on matters of faith! Think back to the night he decided to walk on the water. It all happened after a day when Peter had witnessed Jesus' miracle of parlaying five pieces of bread and two fish into a buffet that fed five thousand hungry people, complete with leftovers.

That evening Peter and the boys were boating across the six- or eight-mile span of the Sea of Galilee. Somewhere between three and six o'clock in the morning, they were astonished to see Jesus passing their little fishing boat walking on the water without the benefit of any flotation device.

Wow! You can imagine the stunned amazement when they rubbed their eyes and grasped the magnitude of what they were witnessing!

Peter, never one to think before he spoke, said *"Lord, if it's you ... tell me to come to you on the water.'*

Jesus' responded, 'Come.'

Then Peter got down out of the boat, walked on the water, and came toward Jesus. But when he saw the wind, he was afraid and, beginning to sink, cried out, 'Lord, save me!' Immediately Jesus reached out his hand and caught him. 'You of little faith,' he said, 'why did you doubt?'" (Matthew 14:28-31, NIV)

Why do I retell such a familiar story? Because what Peter grew to be didn't come without further "faith stumbles." It was Peter whose faith evaporated on the eve of the crucifixion when he denied even knowing Jesus.

It was Peter who was confronted by Jesus a few days after the resurrection. Exasperated by his "hot and cold" faith walk, Jesus looked deep into Peter's soul and told him what lay ahead. Jesus told Peter that despite his weak-kneed faith, the day would come when his faith would be strong. As a matter of fact, Jesus told him that his faith would eventually become so strong it would lead to his own martyrdom. Peter would one day willingly allow himself to be handcuffed and led to his death for the sake of faith in Jesus.

"'I tell you the truth, when you were younger you dressed yourself and went where you wanted; but when you are old you will stretch out your hands, and someone else will dress you and lead you where you do not want to go.' Jesus said this to indicate the kind of death by which Peter would glorify God. Then he said to him, 'Follow me!'" (John 21:18-19, NIV)

273

In fact, Peter became one of the boldest, most stringent promoters of the Christian faith. While the exact details are debated, we know that Peter died a martyr's death about AD 64. His death was probably at the hands of Nero, the Roman emperor, who publicly proclaimed himself to be the chief enemy of God. Peter and his wife, Concordia, may have been murdered together.

It is said that, just before her murder, Peter held Concordia's hand and spoke to her, "Remember our dear Lord." Then, feeling unworthy to die as his Christ had, Peter requested to be crucified upside down.

Faith: The Precursor of Perfect Peace

With faith as weak as mine, I take courage in Peter's struggle for faith. I think there's a message in Peter's story. Maybe God is able to tolerate my weaknesses and "faith-lapses" as long as my trajectory is headed in the right direction. Faith is a process. My goal is to grow toward God.

Man has been wrong before. For centuries of human history, the collective wisdom said that the sun revolved around the earth. People who dared question this accepted norm were branded and ridiculed by society. But today no one denies that the opposite is true. We all know that the earth revolves around the sun. Spiritually speaking, I tend to forget this principle.

As Max Lucado has written, "It's not about me." I have to stop listening to the world's noise that says happiness comes when self is center. Getting what I want only makes me want more. God's purpose for my life is to bring him glory. God is not my bellhop; he does not revolve around me. If I am ever to develop lasting faith and balance, I must understand my purpose: to revolve around God.

When we start to trust God, we will stop trying to grab the brass ring of happiness. But the amazing thing is: The more we willingly give up, the more we will gain.

Maybe this is why an old man, who had enjoyed the best and the worst life had to offer, was able to relax in a Roman prison as he neared the end of his life and pen these words to a struggling church: *"Be anxious for nothing, but in everything by prayer and supplication with thanksgiving let your requests be made known to God. And the peace of God, which surpasses all comprehension, will guard your hearts and your minds in Christ Jesus."* (apostle Paul in Philippians 4:6-7, NASB)

Visit Steve At:

www.SteveDiggs.com

www.NDNS.com
(No Debt No Sweat! Financial Ministries & Seminar)

www.RetooledAndRefueled.com

or